RIOT, REBELLION AND POPULAR POLITICS
IN EARLY MODERN ENGLAND

Social History in Perspective

General Editor: Jeremy Black

Social History in Perspective is a series of in-depth studies of the many topics in social, cultural and religious history.

PUBLISHED

Please note that a sister series, *British History in Perspective*,is available, covering key topics in British political history

**Social History in Perspective
Series Standing Order
ISBN 0–333–71694–9 hardcover
ISBN 0–333–69336–1 paperback**
(outside North America only)

You can receive future titles in this series as they are published by placing a standing order. Please contact your bookseller or, in case of difficulty, write to us at the address below with your name and address, the title of the series and the ISBN quoted above.
Customer Services Department, Palgrave Ltd
Houndmills, Basingstoke, Hampshire RG21 6XS, England

Riot, Rebellion and Popular Politics in Early Modern England

Andy Wood

First published 2002 by
PALGRAVE
Houndmills, Basingstoke, Hampshire RG21 6XS and
175 Fifth Avenue, New York, N. Y. 10010
Companies and representatives throughout the world

PALGRAVE is the new global academic imprint of
St. Martin's Press LLC Scholarly and Reference Division and
Palgrave Publishers Ltd (formerly Macmillan Press Ltd).

ISBN 978-0-333-63761-6 hardcover
ISBN 978-0-333-63762-3 paperback

A catalogue record for this book is available
from the British Library.

Library of Congress Cataloging-in-Publication Data
Wood, Andy.
  Riot, rebellion and popular politics in Early Modern England / Andy Wood.
    p. cm.—(Social history in perspective)
Includes bibliographical references and index.
ISBN 0-333-63761-5 (cloth)
  1. Political violence—Great Britain—History. 2. Riots—Great
Britain—History. 3. Revolutions—Great Britain—History. 4. Great
Britain—Politics and government—1485- I. Title. II. Series.

HN400.V5 W66 2001
306'.0941—dc21   2001133049

CONTENTS

v

ABBREVIATIONS

BL, TT	British Library, Thomason Tracts
HMC	Historical Manuscripts Commission
HJ	*Historical Journal*
JBS	*Journal of British Studies*
P&P	*Past and Present*
PRO	Public Record Office
RO	Record Office
TRHS	*Transactions of the Royal Historical Society*

ACKNOWLEDGEMENTS

This book has been a long time growing. Its development has been influenced by debates with John Arnold, Lance Dawson, Dennis Glover, Laura Gowing, Paul Griffiths, Steve Hindle, Pat Hudson, Ronald Hutton, Mark Knights, Simon Middleton, John Morrill, Dave Peacock, Dave Rollison, Jim Sharpe, Garthine Walker, John Walter and, most of all, Keith Wrightson. Financial support from the British Academy helped me to conduct much of the research upon which this book is based. I am grateful to Vanessa Graham, who first asked me to write a book for Palgrave, and to Terka Bagley for her patience as this book entered its final stages of preparation. The constructive comments of an anonymous reader for Palgrave improved the final product. I owe special thanks to all those students at the University of Liverpool and the University of East Anglia who have taken my courses in social history and in early modern history. The memory of their sceptical and sometimes irritated faces has returned to haunt me while writing this book, and their refusal to accept my vague generalisations has hopefully improved it. There were times when I felt that this book would never be finished. Illness in the latter half of 2000 nearly prevented me from completing the book; but the support and friendship of Edward Acton, John Arnold, Lucy Simpson and Jenni Tanimoto made it possible to bring the work to a conclusion. Every social historian should take part in the occasional commotion. So, most of all, thanks to Lucy Simpson for leading me in riot, revelry and sundry misdemeanours. We have been arguing about politics and ideas for many years; in 1995–6 she rehabilitated Shakespeare as a source of social history for me; and now she has given me a child. This one is for her: *salud, companera*.

ANDY WOOD

PREFACE

Not so long ago, the boundary between the political history and the social history of early modern England was clear and respected. Political historians of the sixteenth and seventeenth centuries tended to concentrate upon issues in 'high' politics: relations between Crown, Parliament, Privy Council, the episcopacy and leading ministers; administrative and organisational change in government; dynastic, religious and political faction amongst national elites. Conventional political history characteristically preferred a descriptive to an analytical style, emphasised short-term 'high' political causation and operated within assumed spatial and social limits. Spatially, national and county government was privileged above that of the village; socially, 'the political nation' or 'the political community' was assumed to consist only, or primarily, of elites: most importantly, the gentry and nobility.

The interpretative logic and analytical emphasis of the 'new' social history of early modern England that developed in the 1970s and 1980s formed a sharp contrast to the narrative empiricism of much political history. Social historians lifted conceptual language and theoretical frameworks from anthropology and social theory and eschewed short-term high-political chronology in favour of the study of long-term structural dynamics within English society. Moreover, whereas traditional political history viewed the early modern period from the lofty heights of elite institutions, social historians preferred a more gritty, local perspective. Parish government, gender and power relations, popular culture, religion and alternative beliefs, customary law and popular legal attitudes, landholding patterns, economic change, alehouse gossip, social authority and plebeian resistance were all interpreted by social historians as manifest within intensely local contexts. And yet all of these social history themes (and more) have in recent years been seen as sources of popular politics.

Social and political historians of early modern England have often had more in common than either group has recognised. The effective analysis of civil war allegiances, for instance, has broken boundaries between political and social history. Recognising the need for such an integrated approach, in the last ten years in particular, many political historians have sought to ground their research within a deep social context. More recently, and more ambitiously, social historians have begun to assess early modern power relations, authority and resistance in terms of their 'political' content. The consequence has been to broaden and to redefine the meaning of politics within early modern society.

This book represents the first synthesis of that new historiography. It also builds upon earlier historical writing in order to demonstrate how early modern politics was defined by its social context. Fundamentally, the book seeks to assess change and continuity in popular political culture and practice between (roughly) the beginning of the Reformation and the accession of George I. In order to develop comparisons, or to highlight sharp change or long continuity, the narrative occasionally reaches back to the beginning of the sixteenth century, and forwards into the mid-eighteenth century. It pursues some constant themes in the history of early modern popular politics. These include the nature of early modern social relations (traditionally conceived of in terms of the relationship between 'ruler' and 'ruled'); elite perceptions and legal definitions of popular politics; the relationship between social change, state formation and popular politics; the significance of political media, especially speech, print and literacy; the economic sources of social conflict; the changing nature of popular religion; urban and rural distinctions; changing regional patterns in riot, rebellion and popular politics; the ritual, symbolic and linguistic forms of popular politics; and the changing tone of popular political language. Most importantly, it assesses the changing forms of public, collective action in early modern England, especially: the food riot; the enclosure riot; the decline of large-scale rebellion; the significance of threat and demonstration; the organisation of collective protest.

Throughout, the book seeks to locate the history of crowd politics within a deeper understanding of early modern popular political culture and tactics. We chart certain persistent continuities in the history of that culture: the enduring emphasis upon law, custom and patriarchal order; the determining importance of gender roles; the ritualised forms sometimes adopted in crowd protest; the differing local and regional flavours of popular politics. We also assess underlying changes in popular politics and crowd organisation: shifts in the geography of riot and rebellion; the gradual diminution in large-scale disorder; the impact of the growth of literacy and of print propaganda; the development of a moderate protestantism at the heart of popular political culture; the withdrawal of village elites (often identified before the civil wars as 'the better sort of people') from the leadership of rebellion and crowd protest. We shall see how these discontinuities connected to the changing structure of the early modern state. Consequently another enduring theme in this book concerns the creative friction between popular politics and the state. Critical to that relationship were the shifting loyalties of village rulers: the 'better sort of people'. We are therefore interested not only in rebels, rioters and popular resistance, but also in popular participation within state structures. For this reason the book should, in part, be read as an essay in the history of state formation.

Social historians have often been attracted to the study of riot and crowd protest because they have seen the rioting crowd as representative of a larger set of lower-class ideas and practices that might otherwise remain hidden to historical inquiry. The study of riot, rebellion and popular politics therefore carries with it important implications for historians' understanding of social relations in early modern England. There was a powerful politics to this relationship, concerned as it was with speech and silence, access to political space and resources, and popular agency. In order to understand how labourer, farmer and lord understood one another in early modern society, we must study all the elements within that social equation. Ironically, our study of popular politics ends up revealing quite a lot about the gentry and nobility. Especially in Chapter 1, we look at the complexities and contradictions of elite attitudes to popular politics and their relationship to legal definitions of riot, rebellion, treason and sedition. In attempting to suppress popular political speech and organisation, the state generated records which social historians have been able to use in exploration of popular politics. Deploying some of that material, we shall see how popular politics often balanced deferential appeals to the gentry for protective paternalism with an aggressive, occasionally vicious, language of class. Throughout the book, we shall therefore chart the shifting contours of plebeian political language.

Contemporary plebeian descriptions of order and disorder did not simply reflect the distribution of wealth and social power. Despite growing material differences between richer and poorer villagers, rural popular politics often assumed an opposition between a conceptually united 'commons' and an external enemy, which might take the form of the gentry, the fiscal state, plundering armies, or imagined hordes of papists or destructive Church reformers. And yet at other times, popular politics was divided between the 'better sort of people' and the 'vulgar'. Through a series of case studies, we track the changing political uses of social classification. Of special importance in this regard are the uses made of the following keywords of popular political discourse: the commons; the poor; the neighbours; the middling sort; the rich; the traitors; the people. We shall see how these charged social categories provided common linguistic building blocks for an otherwise heterogeneous popular political language. We are also interested in the rhetoric and symbolism of popular politics, especially in how conflict, community and political identity were understood and communicated. For this reason special attention is given to the external constraints within which popular politics operated, especially the legal limits placed upon open political speech and organisation. The growth of literacy over the period as a whole and the explosion of print propaganda during the 1640s and after 1678 are therefore situated within an appreciation of the importance of rumour and news to pre-civil war popular politics.

This emphasis upon language does not obscure a concern with the material sources of popular politics in early modern England. Some of the most heated confrontations that we will encounter concerned rights to land, resources, space and food. Yet the content of popular political language was not reducible to a simple economic equation. Rather, popular perceptions of political and social conflict enjoyed a turbulent and imaginative life of their own. Plebeians often defined conflict in desperate, violent language. High food prices were sometimes understood as the result of a 'plot' amongst the 'rich men' to 'starve the poor'. Similarly, the enclosure of common land, or changes to liturgy or the parish church, could be interpreted in terms of the destruction of the 'common people'. Such exaggerated language highlighted both the importance of material resources to popular politics and the organising role of fear and anxiety in popular political culture.

This book has been influenced by a variety of theoretical approaches to popular politics. I hope that what emerges is an interpretative pluralism which combines the best insights of political anthropology, classical Marxism and Gramsci's interpretation of the state and political culture with an appreciation of the constitutive nature of language in social and political conflict. With retrospect, I realise that two preoccupations recur throughout this book: the relationship between language, identity and economics; and an assessment of the relative failings and insights of Marxist historiography. It is this concern with concepts that identifies this book as a work of social history. This approach is most apparent in the Introduction. Chapters 2 and 4 form a broad chronological assessment, via a set of case-studies, of the changing forms of popular politics in early modern England. In these chapters in particular, we see a political culture in motion.

Chapter 1 deals with contemporary elite interpretations and legal categorisations of popular politics. It looks at how early modern elites understood popular politics, and at some of the contradictions within those views; at how legal definitions of riot, rebellion, treason and sedition influenced popular politics; and it investigates the diversity of early modern state structures, and contrasts that diversity with the simplicities of authoritarian political thought. Chapter 2 interrogates some fundamental shifts in Tudor popular politics through a re-examination of the insurrections of 1536–7, 1549 and 1569. In particular, it highlights the potential violence of early modern social relations; the limited nature of popular insurrection; the importance of ideas of order and custom in popular protest; the role played by religious ideas in the articulation of popular ideologies; and the reasons for the decline of large-scale rebellion in Elizabethan and early Stuart England. Chapter 3 looks at the shifting geography and social basis of small-scale crowd protest against the enclosure of common land; the logic of food rioting; plebeian ideas of community; the function of gender roles in the organisation of popular protest and social criticism; and the structuring role of ritual.

Chapter 4, the largest chapter in the book, is pre-eminently concerned with the character and consequences of the English Revolution. In particular, it scrutinises the relationship between the radical movements of the 1640s and pre-existent forms of popular politics. Early sections look at sources of political and religious conflict in pre-civil war England, paying special attention to the forms of popular politics in towns and cities, to the importance of print propaganda in the outbreak of the English civil war, to the problematic nature of puritanism, and to the relationship between popular religion and popular culture. Three succeeding sections develop an interpretation of rural popular politics in the English Revolution, looking at rural riot in the 1640s, the anti-war clubmen movements, and the Digger movement of 1649–50. The next section interprets the politics of the Leveller movement within its urban environment. Taken together, these four sections relate the forms of popular radicalism and conservatism in the English Revolution to longer processes of social and political change. They also assess similarities and differences in popular politics in rural and urban England. The penultimate section returns to urban popular politics, looking at the role played by print propaganda in religious and political conflict in later Stuart England. The final section addresses the exclusion of the majority of the population from the dominant Whig order of the early eighteenth century.

This book is not designed to provide a complete account of every political movement, rebellion, or riot that occurred in England between the 1520s and the 1720s. Nor does the book survey every aspect of popular politics over the course of that period. Inevitably, there are important omissions. Not enough is said about the Monmouth Rebellion of 1685; or about popular mobilisation during the Glorious Revolution; the ferment of popular politics in the 1690s is scandalously neglected, as is popular politics in the English Republic. The origins of popular hostility to popery are insufficiently analysed; pre-civil war hostility to the Caroline court is only alluded to; the protestant rebellions of 1554 against Mary I are nowhere discussed; English national identities are seen as important in the seventeenth century, but I am dismissive of 'British' identities as a factor in early modern popular politics. Readers will find other omissions, but should bear in mind that this book is not intended as a full survey of its vast topic. Rather, it represents an *argument* about the nature of popular politics in early modern England, and a *polemic* about the relationship between social and political history.

The book has been written from a social history perspective which is open to conceptual insights from beyond the narrowly defined historical discipline, and which has a special interest in the local, the plebeian, and the marginal. As such, at the same time as addressing the period and issues at hand, it attempts to introduce the reader to the logic of social historical explanation. In many parts of the book, I have attempted to sum up important historical debates, and to provide clear accounts of the case studies around which my argument has been organised. In this respect, the book should be seen as an introductory 'textbook', including much material which is already well known to professional historians (especially in Chapters 2 and 4). But the book is also designed both to illuminate the long-term history of popular politics in early modern England, and to present readers with a clear argument that they can choose to accept or reject. As will become apparent, I assume throughout that the study of the historical past involves a dialectic, argumentative, creative process. Although the work therefore aims to introduce a body of historical research to the reader, it makes no pretence either to offer complete coverage, or to represent a bland, neutral survey of recent historiographical developments. On the contrary, if the book provokes its readers and stimulates in them a desire to argue with its conclusions, it will have succeeded.

INTRODUCTION

INTERPRETING POPULAR POLITICS IN EARLY MODERN ENGLAND

I Jack Cade's Vulgar Politics

Theatre-going Elizabethan Londoners might not have found the dramatic representation of class conflict quite as alien as we imagine. Well-read members of theatre audiences might have recognised some of William Shakespeare's borrowings from the printed *Chronicles* edited under the name of William Holinshed.[1] Purporting to cover the whole history of the British Isles, the *Chronicles* were laced with lurid accounts of popular rebellion, sedition and riot. The *Chronicles'* emphasis upon the levelling nature of popular politics might easily have persuaded an uncritical reader that the peasants were always revolting. Albeit for different reasons, the poorer groundlings who paid for standing room within Elizabethan theatres might also have been familiar with the language of rebellion. In Shakespeare's *Henry VI Part II*, written around 1590, the character of Jack Cade was defined by his vindictive and bloodthirsty social critique. This depiction differed sharply from what is known of the real-life Jack Cade, who had led a rebellion in 1450 in which notions of legality and order had been prominent.[2] In contrast, the sanguine fantasies of Shakespeare's Cade, who seeks to slaughter the gentry, seemed closer to some of the seditious talk in English alehouses during the last decade of Elizabeth's reign.[3]

Historians have been able to gain access to such speech, or at least to its reportage (as we shall see in later chapters, the distinction is an important one), because lower-class social criticism could be construed

1

as illegal, and so find its way before the codifying hand of the legal authorities. Fragments of that speech remain locked within surviving legal records, and have been used by social historians as evidence of dissident plebeian attitudes.[4] Such documents also bear upon elite political culture, illuminating not only gentle and noble fears of the commons, but also implying something of their proximity to popular politics. The rulers of Tudor and Stuart England liked to imagine that a cultural chasm separated them from the 'vulgar'. And yet the records of their government remain laced with concern about popular speech and politics. In particular, the records of the Privy Council demonstrate a routine interest in popular political opinion. The leading rulers of the land could quite easily be distracted from considerations of diplomacy or warfare to worry over reports of seditious speech in rural alehouses. Elite and popular worlds, then, were not so far apart as the gentry liked to believe. And so we might imagine how an Elizabethan magistrate, watching Shakespeare's *Henry VI Part II*, could have found much that was disturbingly familiar in Jack Cade's ranting social critique.

Shakespeare, of course, was no historian. The Jack Cade of *Henry VI Part II* was but a contorted simulacrum of the Cade of 1450, given artificial colour by promiscuous borrowings from other English rebellions, especially those of 1381 and 1549. As such, Shakespeare's Jack Cade represented the twisted personification of medieval and early Tudor popular protest. And yet Shakespeare's Cade had touches of authenticity about him. He and his fictitious followers were moved by many of the same concerns as the people whose actions and opinions form the subject of this book. Like early modern lower-class critics of the legal system, Shakespeare's Cade tells Lord Say:

> Thou hast appointed justices of the peace, to call poor men before them about matters they were not able to answer...and because they could not read, thou hast hang'd them.

Like Kett's rebels, those of Shakespeare's invention felt that their rulers held them in contempt for their labour: 'The nobility think scorn to go in leather aprons'. Slipping into proverbial culture, Cade's rebels perceived of work as a moral category: 'there's no better sign of a brave mind than a hard hand.'[5] Rebellion, as we shall see in Chapter 2, could be a means by which plebeians could open a dialogue with their rulers. Such discussions were always full of danger. So we should not be surprised to find that, like some of the rebels of 1536–7, Shakespeare's

Jack Cade was suspicious of trusting the gentry. Offered negotiations by the Crown, some of his followers cry out 'God save the King'; but Cade warns 'Will you needs be hang'd with pardons about your necks?'[6]

So, there are conceptual similarities between Shakespeare's Cade and the real-life politics he personified. But that politics could not be given full voice in its dramatic representation. Like the grain rioters whose vocabulary we will explore in Chapter 3, Jack Cade dwelt heavily upon the symbolism of food. But whereas early modern food rioters were concerned to ensure the restitution of moral order to the market, Cade's concerns had to be presented as more communistic:

> There shall be in England seven half-penny loaves sold for a penny: the three-hoop'd pot shall have ten hoops; and I will make it a felony to drink small beer. All the realm shall be in common.[7]

The Jack Cade of *Henry VI Part II* is a pompous clown whose absurdity is highlighted by the knowing comments passed upon him by his equally plebeian captains. Laying claim to royal descent, Cade announces that 'My father was a Mortimer!'. 'He was an honest man, and a good bricklayer', insinuates Dick the Butcher in turn. 'My mother was a Plantagenet', says Cade; 'I knew her well; she was a midwife', murmurs Dick. But Cade, while pompous and murderous, is not without wit. Sir Humphrey Stafford, the leader of a force of gentlemen sent against the rebels, addresses Cade's base status: 'thy father was a plasterer/And thou thyself a shearman, art thou not?' Cade responds in echo of John Ball's speech of 1381: 'And Adam was a gardener'. Importantly, Shakespeare assumes that rural society produced clear social conflict: Stafford offers battle, warning 'those which fly before the battle ends/May, even in their wives' and children's sight/Be hang'd up for example at their doors'. In answer, Cade combines his bluntest statement of social hostility with imitation of the prophecies attributed by Holinshed's *Chronicles* to Robert Kett's rebels in 1549:

> You that love the commons, follow me
> Now show yourselves men; 'tis for liberty
> We will not leave one lord, one gentleman
> Spare none but such as go in clouted shoon.[8]

Cade's theatrical outbursts echoed the language of popular rebellion in early modern England. In open confrontations with authority, plebeians were sometimes emboldened to imagine a different ordering to society.

or to threaten their rulers with death. In the closed confines of the ale-house, they appear to have done so more often. But Shakespeare's Cade was at best only a partial personification of popular politics. He was at his most voluble when speaking about the slaughter of the gentry. He had less to say about the dominant tradition within early modern popular politics: that patriarchal ideology which stressed order and legality, and which we consider in Chapter 3, Section IV. Yet for a fleeting moment in *Henry VI Part II*, popular politics becomes something more than a bloody Jacquerie. At the close of his rebellion, berating the commons for their failure to stick to him, Cade says that 'I thought you would never have given out these arms till you had recover'd your ancient freedom'.[9] But the legitimising logic of popular politics – apparent here in the appeal to lost rights – is not Shakespeare's subject. Although sometimes challenged by the spirit of carnival, orderly notions of law, custom and household authority retained their hold over popular politics throughout our period. Even when the commons were in arms against the Crown, they repre-sented their demands in written, legalistic documents. Shakespeare's Cade speaks to the carnivalesque spirit of rebellion. But the orderly strain within popular politics finds no voice in the play.

The published chronicles of British history with which Shakespeare worked tended to distort a genuine popular hostility to lawyers and priests into an archaic anti-clericalism. Shakespeare perpetuated and extended this standard account. 'Let's kill all the lawyers', one of Cade's followers suggests in *Henry VI Part II*; to which Cade responds with an extended discussion of how the written word is a weapon of the rich. Encountering a priest, Cade finds it 'monstrous' that he can write, and so the priest is led away to be hanged 'with his pen and ink-horn about his neck'. On taking London (and this time slipping into the history of the 1381 rebellion), Shakespeare's Cade orders the destruction of the Savoy palace and the burning of 'all the records of the realm'. For Shakespeare's Cade, the abolition of literacy was to ensure the levelling of other distinc-tions: 'all things shall be in common'. Yet, contrarily, Shakespeare was a careful enough reader of Holinshed's *Chronicles* to see that the rebels of 1450 had issued a written 'supplication', which they set before the King.[10]

Modern Shakespearean critics remain divided over their interpret-ation of *Henry VI Part II*. For Tillyard, *Henry VI Part II* was nothing more than an uncomplicated statement of hierarchy, and a warning against rebellion. Shakespeare is presented as having fully internalised the dominant values of his age. The vulgar commons, represented by his Jack Cade, are presented as incapable of a rational politics. Driven by their base, animal instincts, they require the bridle of the civilised and rational gentry. Lower-class rebellion can have no coherent politics, leading as it does to a simple anarchy.[11] To other critics, Shakespeare is himself something of a rebel.[12] In this interpretation, Shakespeare's *Henry VI Part II* provides a platform for the articulation of an authentic, plebeian politics. The disavowal of that politics in Cade's humiliation and death is understood as merely formulaic, providing a means by which an otherwise subversive text might escape unscathed from censorship. This literary debate is unlikely ever to be resolved, turning as it does upon the difficult question of authorial intent. And indeed, for our purposes, interested as we are in the forms and language of popular politics rather than in the social attitudes of William Shakespeare, it is far from central.

Our contextualisation of Shakespeare's play raises some issues that will develop into important themes over the course of this book. We have already indicated that popular politics was officially defined as violent, chaotic and tumultuous, and have suggested that contemporary sources such as Holinshed's *Chronicles* or Shakespeare's drama can scarcely be expected to provide objective evidence of popular political attitudes and organisation. Instead, we have implied that, in their search for evidence of popular politics, social historians have preferred to exploit legal archives or the records of governmental inquiries into seditious speech and rebellion. Of course, such records are not free of bias either; like dramatic and literary evidence, the archives of the judicial repression of popular politics are also laden with elite anxieties. Here, again, we touch upon some recurrent themes in this book: the difficulties in discerning the 'authentic' political voice of early modern labouring people; the dangerous, creative relationship between elite anxieties and popular politics; and the tendency for popular political forms to creep into seemingly hostile texts. We have suggested that, despite its ostentatious bias, Shakespeare's *Henry VI Part II* reproduces some identifiable styles of early modern popular political speech and some defining concerns of popular political culture. That we are able to make such sweeping judgements is thanks to the attention given in recent social history writing to early modern popular politics.

II Defining Concepts: Popular Politics

Social historians of early modern England used to avoid politics. During the 1970s and early 1980s, a new generation of historians extended the classic concerns of social history into the sixteenth and seventeenth centuries. New histories of (for example) crime, urbanisation, disease, literacy, population growth, social change and household formation combined to establish a powerful new tradition of social historical explanation within the early modern period.[13] Yet just as this 'new' social history was emerging, early modern historiography became dominated by a confrontation between Marxist and 'revisionist' historians of the English Revolution.[14] This dispute had profound implications for how early modern historians subsequently understood the relationship between state, society, religion, economics and politics. For Marxists, the English civil wars of the 1640s had represented a class conflict between the nobility and a heterogeneous middle class, the resolution of which in the interests of the latter laid the basis for the future triumph of capitalism. Revisionist historians, in contrast, emphasised the lack of correspondence between social class and civil war allegiance; the absence of revolutionary ideas in pre-civil war England; and the accidental nature of the slide into war. In particular, revisionists tended to emphasise short-term, high-political factors and had little time for social and economic explanation. Whereas Marxist historiography assessed early modern society in terms of social conflict, revisionists were more likely to highlight the apparently hierarchical, paternalistic character of pre-civil war England. Many of the organising questions of the 'new' social history were central to the debate over the causes and character of the English Revolution. Equipped with specialist knowledge of issues such as the social impact of puritanism, the nature of social change, the distribution of literacy and its implications for popular culture, and relations between 'ruler' and 'ruled', social historians should have been able to intervene forcibly into this historiographical warfare. Yet most social historians remained distant from the debate over the English Revolution. The resolution of that debate in favour of the 'revisionists' led, therefore, to the artificial separation of the social and the political history of early modern England.

Over the course of the 1980s, with important exceptions, early Stuart political history became preoccupied with high-political issues, distanced from social context and defined by short-term assumptions about historical causation.[15] Revisionist historiography often operated from a narrow, limited definition of politics shared with mid-twentieth-century liberal political science. Since politics was perceived to be generated from the machinery of government, primary attention was given to formal political institutions, especially those operating within the political centre, and to leaders and elites. In the early modern English context, this necessitated a heavy emphasis upon courts, parliaments, the Privy Council, the lord lieutenancy, monarchs, favourites, leading ministers and advisors.[16]

In contrast to revisionist perspectives upon causation, the 'new' social history of early modern England presented social and cultural change as driven by the long-term dynamic of population growth. From this perspective, political events seemed superficial in comparison with the deep processes of demographic and economic change that were reworking the structure of English society. Population pressure, combined with urbanisation and the commercialisation of agriculture, was understood to have generated recurrent social conflict. While such conflict remained localised, it was frequently intense and protracted, and often resulted in collective protest, riot and demonstration. Importantly, that evidence of conflict tended to undermine 'revisionist' assumptions that English society was hierarchical, deferential and based upon 'traditional' distinctions of status and rank.[17] In particular, social historians observed confrontations between and within communities, and between opposed social groups, over access to food, land, fuel, settlement, local-political rights and entitlement. Thanks to the arbitrary separation of political and social history, such 'village revolts' were scarcely integrated into the study of politics. In contrast, although social historians were attracted to the study of local-political conflicts, they often found it difficult to conceptualise their underlying politics and settled instead for thick, empirical description. This conceptual blindness could produce some peculiar interpretative formulations. In his detailed work on rural riots, Roger Manning concluded that despite all the inventive, articulate stubbornness of early modern rioters:

> their motives are devoid of political consciousness and their writings or utterances do not employ a political vocabulary... anti-enclosure riots may be regarded as displaying primitive or pre-political behaviour because they failed to develop into some more modern form of protest or participation in the political nation.[18]

This formulation assumed that 'political' affairs are conducted only within established institutions, that the localism of early modern riots guaranteed their 'pre-political' character, and that conflicts over resources possessed no inherent politics. Such assumptions were to be challenged by early modern historians in the 1990s.

Recent historiographical developments have undermined the artificial separation of political and social history. A close interest in social history has helped to define the new 'post-revisionist' school of early Stuart political history.[19] Post-revisionists' awareness of the social depth of early modern politics has provided added weight to their claim that conflict over constitutional matters and over religious and foreign policy involved a larger proportion of the early Stuart population than 'revisionist' historians had hitherto recognised. This empirical finding had conceptual implications, leading some historians to question the validity of clear distinctions between 'elite' and 'popular' politics. Within Tudor history, a similar historiographical movement is under way. Historians of sixteenth-century religion have reached into the depths of popular political culture in order to explain the peculiarities of the English Reformation. Similarly, the Tudor polity is now understood to have possessed deep roots within English society.[20] This rethinking of the relationship between society, religion and politics in Tudor England owes much to Patrick Collinson, who has called for 'a new political history, which is social history with the politics put back in, or an account of political processes which is also social'.[21] Towards the other end of early modernity, the politics of Augustan England have also been reconceptualised. Since Tim Harris published his path-breaking study of London crowds in the age of Charles II, the historiography of later Stuart politics has been dominated by the attempt to connect elite and popular political activity.[22] This concern has recently been expressed in a growing preoccupation with the apparent formation of a 'public sphere' of open political organisation and debate within later seventeenth-century towns. Within eighteenth-century historiography, the powerful legacy left by the Marxist historians George Rude and Edward Thompson, especially their concern with crowd organisation and popular ideology, has meant that political historians have found it hard to miss the vitality and intensity of popular politics.[23]

The interest recently taken in popular involvement in early modern politics has led some historians to question distinctions between 'elite' and 'popular' politics. In particular, David Underdown has identified large areas of common ground between elite and plebeian politics.[24] Dismissing the old view that 'for most of the people, most of the time, political matters scarcely existed',[25] he finds powerful evidence of the interest taken by seventeenth-century plebeians in every level of political activity, whether concerning the parish, town, county, court, parliament or foreign affairs. In this, Underdown both summarises and extends recent post-revisionist research into early Stuart politics. Much of this work has plumbed what Collinson called the 'social depths' of politics, albeit with a largely institutional focus, and has shown that while popular political consciousness was indeed deep, it was certainly not homogeneous. Moreover, the fact that in the late 1620s and again in the early 1640s both labourers and peers of the realm were to be found arguing over the same political issues, and sometimes in strikingly similar language, has further increased scepticism as to the validity of polarities between 'elite' and 'popular' politics. For post-Restoration political historians, whose subject is increasingly defined by the role of the urban populace within religious and party conflict, that polarity seems almost redundant.[26]

In place of a polarity, Underdown prefers to think about political culture 'in terms of a spectrum'. He identifies a 'common politics' in seventeenth-century England, within which popular and elite 'sub-cultures' interacted. While certain ideas transcended social division – patriarchal ideas about gender roles, for instance – others were rather more socially specific. Hence, although Underdown appreciates the importance of custom to debates over parliamentary authority, he sees the language of custom as enjoying a greater force within plebeian culture. Thus, 'the lower orders did have their own ways of looking at politics, and a somewhat different vocabulary'. Ultimately, Underdown's formulation remains contradictory; and yet he has highlighted a conceptual fault-line which other historians have simply avoided.[27] Evidence for a creative flow of political forms and ideas up and down the social hierarchy of early modern England can easily be found. Unfortunately, so can evidence of the persistence of iron social polarities within contemporary perceptions of the polity and social order. We shall see in Chapter 1 how the dominant forms of elite social theory remained profoundly authoritarian and hierarchical. Similarly, we shall see throughout this book how early modern plebeians often identified economic and religious change with the 'oppressions' of 'rich men' and 'gentlemen'. The central questions therefore remain as follows: if the early modern political nation was as broad as Underdown suggests, why did conventional hierarchical theory, with its ostentatious contempt for the 'irrationality' of the *plebs*, continue to exercise such a hold over elite culture? How do we reconcile evidence of outright social conflict with the growing authority of the state within local society? If the term 'popular politics' implies an inappropriately simplistic view of the socio-politics of early modern England, why did both contemporary gentry and labourers continue to conceive of their world in terms of polarities?

These trends within political history have developed alongside a powerful reassessment of politics by early modern social historians. Recent social history has emphasised both the social depth and conceptual breadth of politics. Fundamentally, politics has come to be understood in social terms: as manifest within the organisation and contestation of disparities of power. Given that early modern notions of authority were pervasive, interlocking gender, age and social inequalities within patriarchal ideology, this redefinition of the political has therefore encompassed a wide range of relationships. Relations between young and old, men and women, employer and employed, master and servant, lord and tenant, landed and landless, literate and illiterate, priest and parishioner, and rich and poor have all come to be understood as 'political'. The spatial location of politics has also been broadened to include the household, the village, the town and the 'Country'. Since social historians have often lifted concepts, keywords, methodologies and ways of thinking from other disciplines, we should not be surprised to find that their recent reconceptualisation of politics finds its precedents elsewhere in the humanities.

Early modern social historians' sense of the political has been heavily influenced by anthropology. Both social historians and political anthropologists have refused to accept that politics is the exclusive property of governors and elites. Instead, politics has been understood to reach deep into society, economy and culture and thereby to become implicated in production, reproduction, exploitation, oppression and resistance. In studying politics, many anthropologists have concentrated upon the social distribution of power and resources. Recent social history writing has followed a similar interpretative path. The relationship thereby posited in political anthropology between power and politics is a difficult one, and has been weakly conceptualised in early modern social history. We critically examine social historians' understanding of power and politics below; but it is important to note that both in anthropology and in recent social history, power is seen as pervasive. Thus, McGlynn and Tuden, in their overview of political anthropology, suggest that 'Power is immanent in human affairs; by definition, human beings are political animals ... power is intrinsic to all social relations where asymmetry is present'.[28] For the anthropologist, 'political behaviour emerges whenever there are groups in opposition. Wherever there are scarce resources there will be a struggle over control of the allocation of these defined resources.' Although anthropologists portray politics as a fundamental characteristic of all unequal societies, politics is known to possess a history: '...the intensity of political action fluctuates over time'. Perhaps most important to the anthropological perspective has been the willingness to understand politics as inherent to everyday life. Heavily influenced by political anthropology, the development theorist Adrian Leftwich produces a similarly broad definition of politics:

> Politics consists of all the activities of co-operation and conflict, within and between societies, whereby the human species goes about obtaining, using, producing and distributing resources in the course of the production and reproduction of its social and biological life. These activities are not isolated from other features of social life. They everywhere influence, and are influenced by, the distribution of power and decision-making, the systems of social organisation, culture and ideology in a society, as well as its relations with the natural environment and other societies. Politics is therefore a defining characteristic of *all* human groups, and always has been.[29]

For Leftwich, while politics is intertwined with social organisation, its fundamental role lies in its distribution of scant resources: food, land, fuel, employment, housing, and so on. In that respect, politics is understood to form the terrain of social conflict.

Just as anthropologists have preferred to study small communities – classically, the rural village – in order to develop a 'thick description', or total account, of everyday life and politics, so social historians have frequently been attracted to 'microhistories' of individual places, social groups, or events. In both cases, the aim has been to illuminate fundamental structures of power through a deeply contextualised case-study.[30] Both for the early modern social historian and for the anthropologist, the focus upon the small community is more than merely methodological. Throughout this book, we shall see how early modern labouring people constituted their political identities within strong senses of locality. As inhabitants of a particular place, early modern plebeians frequently laid claim to legally meaningful local customs, such as the right to pasture; the liberty to glean for shards of corn after the harvest had been taken in; the entitlement to dig for coal or search for firewood on common land. Perhaps seeming humble, quotidian, non-political matters to us, such customary rights were often the subject of fierce conflict in early modern England. Similarly, anthropologists of twentieth-century rural society have shown how claims to communal resources were (and sometimes remain) contested within and between communities.[31] For social historians and anthropologists alike, therefore, the local has a politics of its own.

The cumulative effect of the recent social history of politics has been to displace politics from its traditional location within governing elites and institutions. If anthropology has undermined the perceived monopoly enjoyed by the political and administrative centre over politics, perhaps the most forceful critique of conventional political science has come from feminist scholarship. Because of the flowering of gender studies during the 1990s, the feminist agenda has had a unique influence over the development of early modern social history. In particular, feminists have questioned the distinction between 'public' and 'private'. This distinction 'has been an essential feature of liberal political discourse since its inception' and until very recently has been an important element of the conceptual baggage of western historiography. Thanks to the inheritance of Aristotle and Locke, traditional political science conceived of politics as occurring between rational, enlightened, independent citizens within an open, public sphere. The private, domestic sphere was thereby placed outside the political realm. In contrast, feminists have argued that 'privacy is not something natural, pre-political, or extra-political, but [is rather]...politically constructed'. Defining certain concerns as 'private', feminists have argued, helps to place them beyond contestation; yet, 'the meaning and application of these concepts are the locus of severe political struggle'.[32]

The interconnectedness of gender roles with ideal notions of public and private certainly influenced the rhetoric of early modern popular politics. We shall see throughout this book how lower-class women in early modern England justified their assertive public actions (in enclosure riots, for instance) on the grounds that they were defending their private, domestic economies. In the same way, plebeian men vindicated their political actions by citing their public responsibility to provide for their households. In Chapter 3, Section IV we shall investigate the logic which underlay riotous action against assertive women within plebeian communities, in which such women were mocked as 'Skimmingtons'. These mocking rituals were intended to enforce a normative distinction between the domestic (female) sphere and the public (male) sphere. Once again, there was a politics here: in this case concerning the reassertion of male power.

The new social history of politics in early modern England has therefore been centrally concerned with power. This is seen as an ever-present force, inherent to all aspects of life. In his recent essay on the politics of the parish, Keith Wrightson has identified five key areas within which that micro-politics operated. These comprise the politics of household relations and patriarchy; of community, or (to use the contemporary term) 'neighbourhood'; of local custom and notions of order; religious conflict and state formation; and contests over the expression and form of power relations.[33] Like Leftwich, Wrightson sees the politics of the parish as built upon access to resources. But his account represents much more than a restatement of materialism. Wrightson's concern with social power has been mirrored in other recent social historical writing. Whereas the implications of earlier social history research for the study of politics had been largely implicit, in recent years a much more ambitious agenda has predominated.[34] The politics of daily life, gender, social relations, language, local institutions and popular culture are now subject to much closer scrutiny than had been the case. In so doing, the category of the political has been both expanded and blurred.

We shall conclude this section with a critical assessment of this new social history of early modern politics. First, we will indicate some of the most important subject matter covered by this historical writing. Secondly, we will look at how recent social historians have understood power relations and the polity in early modern society. Thirdly, we will probe two critical weaknesses in those historians' treatment of politics: the tendency for the micro-study of moments of resistance to produce an overly static view of power relations; and the problematic consequences of confusing 'power' with 'politics'. Lastly, we will arrive at our own working definition of politics. We shall argue that, while social historians are probably correct in seeing *power* as diffuse within early modern society, *politics* should be given a more precise and contingent meaning. Rather than seeing politics and power as synonymous, we will argue that politics occurs with any attempt to extend, reassert or challenge the distribution of power. Thus, politics is dynamic, deriving from fluidity, change, interaction and conflict. This broad, conflictual view of politics has the advantage of discerning politics within agency, and hence enabling us to see politics as present within a wide variety of situations, while avoiding the term losing its analytical edge.

The theoretical impulses that have driven the recent extension of the social history agenda have been diverse. Combining the insistence of second-wave feminism that the personal is political with a more understated inheritance from literary theory, gender historians have interrogated the meanings of women's subordination. Rather than being seen as a pre-determined fact of a static patriarchal order, that subordination is now understood to have been formed within a dynamic relationship with men's power, and therefore to have been fluid, contingent and contested.[35] Studies of political rumour, libellous writing and seditious speech have plumbed the depths of lower-class engagement in formal politics, exploring how the control of speech and writing formed an arena within which power could be renewed or contested.[36] Where subordinates were able to communicate and debate news, popular politics was fostered. Hence parish, civic and national elites were often anxious about the control of information, generating a culture of secrecy around institutional politics.[37] The struggle to create popular politics in some part therefore represented a struggle over the public sphere. That struggle was also manifest in struggles over the meanings of words: especially the legitimising language of community, custom and rights.[38] Special significance has therefore been accorded to the development of exclusive parish vestries that regulated access to communal resources and poor relief. Such institutions provided an institutional focus for parochial ruling groups: the 'better sort' or 'substantial inhabitants' as they were sometimes known in the late sixteenth and early seventeenth century, or the 'middling sort of people', as they were to be named during the English Revolution.[39] The existence of such an ambivalent social terminology, alluding as it does to a lack of economic and cultural homogeneity amongst what patriarchal theorists called the *plebs*, has added to scepticism concerning the validity of distinctions between 'elite' and 'popular' cultures.[40] It is important that the spatial focus of most of this recent historiography has been upon much smaller units than the nation-state. Resisting Roger Manning's location of politics in the political centre, social historians of politics have instead been interested in streets, fields, villages, manors, parishes, towns, neighbourhoods, and those vaguely defined 'countries' which defied institutional expression but which nonetheless constituted the most important loci of lower-class culture.[41]

In recent years, this new social history of politics has therefore introduced a colourful crowd of interlopers into the hitherto closed halls of political history. Rather than constituting the raw material for databases of demographic change, or reduced into tabularised discussions of landholding, the shades of Tudor yeomen and labourers are now to be found harassing Thomas Cromwell or bargaining with Protector Somerset. As social historians have levered the *plebs* back into the active roles denied to them by contemporary authoritarian social theorists, so they have forced a reappraisal of politics. The old-established concerns of political history – court faction, administration, clientage, diplomacy, theology and personal ambition – must now rub shoulders with a grubbier, more informal politics of alehouse gossip, age relations, sexual identities, representations, reputations and local memories.

One consequence of this historiographical movement, as we have seen, has been to expand the meaning of politics. That redefinition has been inferential rather than explicit. In their intervention, social historians have produced a wider, more open sense of politics. But they have been so willing to find politics *everywhere* that the term is now in danger of losing its explanatory force. No sharp definition of politics has yet emerged from its new social historians; rather, the content of politics has to be sensed from their empirical research, rather than deduced from any abstract statement. In part, this forms an element within the more general 'shift from scientific to literary paradigms' observed by Joan Scott.[42] In part, it has resulted from the interest in micro-histories of individual moments of contestation, resistance and representation, and in the fascination with the local. Some of the results of that methodology have been outstanding.[43] But while that approach has succeeded in elucidating the structural inequalities of power present within early modern society, in the end it presents a new set of frozen case-studies, in which power seems ever-present, and yet ultimately irresistible. We may, following Michel Foucault, agree that power is ever-present, and so find it lodged within the ordering of early modern households, parish churches and civic rituals, as much as within the edicts of monarchs and councillors. But the danger with such a formulation is that Foucault was less interested in analysing resistance to power than he was in observing its ubiquity.[44] The Foucouldian perspective has helped historians to understand the interconnected nature of institutional and cultural authority and the intimate, insidious nature of authority. But his work is less useful in explaining the open, collective and sustained projection of political agency with which this book is primarily concerned. What has been lost from much recent social history is the sense of large-scale dynamics which the best of the older social histories possessed, and the interest in the clash of political principles, ideologies and abstractions appreciated by the most lively of earlier political historians.

This problem has arisen from a slippage within recent social history between 'politics' and 'power'. This conceptual looseness is most readily apparent in the editors' introduction to the volume within which Wrightson's essay on the politics of the parish appeared.[45] In their complex discussion of authority and resistance, power is presented as omnipresent within early modern society, and as made socially apparent in 'authority'. Authority is 'taken to be the power or right to define and regulate the legitimate behaviour of others'. Authority is also everywhere – its 'ubiquity...in early modern society is well known' – while simultaneously negotiated and contested. Thus, the exercise of authority 'was a political expression because its principal purpose was to perpetuate existing ideologies and structures of power by which rule was preserved'. This involved a contest over the public sphere: 'In order to maintain power, governors had to retain control of...structures [of power] and make public their ideas of acceptable behaviour.' The discussion highlights many of the strengths of the new social history of politics: its impatience with restrictive definitions; its hostility to conceptual closure; the hot enthusiasm for theoretical promiscuity. But it also highlights the difficulty of rendering 'politics' as synonymous with 'power'.

For if politics, like power, is to be found *everywhere*, the term loses its analytical sharpness. I prefer to adopt a more limited and contingent definition of politics. In this book, politics will be understood to occur where power is reasserted, extended or challenged. Politics is therefore the product of deliberate, human agency and is pre-eminently about conflict and change. In this analysis, politics does not occur where the distribution of power remains static and unchallenged. Neither does politics rest only within governmental institutions. The early modern household, for example, constructed as it was upon gender and age hierarchies, was one obvious location of power. As such, it had the *potential* to become a site of politics; but only in those circumstances in which power was in flux – advancing, retreating and reasserting itself. Where servants, apprentices, children or wives challenged the power of the head of the household, politics occurred. But the formal restatement of a static patriarchal authority in eating arrangements, room layouts or speech, while it was self-evidently about the expression of power, need not always generate politics.

The same is equally true of the royal court, or of civic government. Where, for instance, the power of city oligarchs was simply reiterated in civic ritual, or where the monarchical authority was restated in ceremony and display, there need not have been a politics.[46] But like the household arrangements that defined domestic authority, because court or civic ritual represented power, rituals *could* form arenas for politics. Thus, for instance, civic rituals and processions might veil seething political conflict. The use of ritual could be more aggressive. Charles I's antagonism to the riotous life of the poor suburbs of London was vividly expressed in his court masques of the 1630s, where the suburbs were represented by degenerate, hobbling figures, following the gloriously golden representation of the City of London.[47] But to confuse the static presence of power, however magnificent, with its active extension or contestation is to muddle power with politics.

III Social Relations and Cultural Hegemony

In this section, we look at how historians have conceptualised the exercise of elite authority over popular culture and everyday life in early modern England. It is important to appreciate that the early modern state enjoyed only limited coercive powers. This martial weakness, ironically, hinted at the relative success of ruling ideas within Tudor, Stuart and early Georgian England. In the vast majority of situations, early modern English elites depended upon the broad acceptance of their authority amongst those whom they sought to dominate. Of special importance in this respect were widely shared notions of law, custom and patriarchal order. The significance of such legitimising ideas in binding together an otherwise diffuse polity is a defining theme of this book, and one to which we shall constantly return. In particular, this section looks at how historians have adapted the notion of 'cultural hegemony', or cultural domination, in order to understand the subtle means by which the lower classes of early modern England became reconciled to authority. This concept of cultural hegemony presumes not only that social power operates to its greatest effect through the domination of culture, but also that it thereby produces the terms of its own subversion. We also look at how, in order to press claims upon their rulers, subordinates exploited the very concepts that had been designed to win their loyalties: the same notions of law, custom and household order that integrated the early modern polity were also deployed by plebeians in popular politics. This section is therefore concerned not only with cultural forms of domination, but also with how the politics of resistance affected the practice of social relations in early modern England. We commence the section with an exploration of how the emergence of a popular politics was enabled by subordinates' establishment of spaces within which dissent and resistance could be articulated.

As we shall see in Chapter 1, early modern legal definitions of riot, sedition and rebellion defined popular politics as tumultuous, and thereby sought to deny it a public voice. The struggle for a popular politics was therefore also a struggle over the public sphere. Whether plebeians intervened in political life upon the village green or in the open courtyard facing Westminster Hall, their capacity to control space represented a political achievement. In many cases, that control was fleeting and localised. Our concern with the micro-politics of the street, village or town should not obscure the success of early modern governors in preventing the formation of any national political challenge from the lower orders. Control over public space was critical to the efficacy of popular politics, for it could enable the articulation of ideas and the sustenance of political traditions. The enduring collective political agency enjoyed by the Free Miners of the Forest of Dean (Gloucestershire), for example, was partly based upon their access to a legitimising focus for their political culture. This was their Mine Law Court, within which their own vision for the ordering of mining and forest law within their 'country' could be articulated, and their hostility to gentry enclosers and mineowners could be restated.[48]

In rejecting the assumption that politics is properly expressed only in open, formal debate, we should not, therefore, lose sight of the significance of free speech and organisation to the articulation of popular politics. Early modern popular politics was not dependent upon a public sphere – indeed in some cases, it consciously avoided publicity – but it often gained a greater strength where it could gain access to the open terrain of political argument and organisation. This truism was recognised by rulers in the early modern period. As we shall see in Chapter 1, the legislation that defined sedition, riot and rebellion was inspired by governors' ambitious attempts to dominate the public sphere. Once again, there is a very obvious politics here, defined by Wrightson as the 'politics of subordination and of meaning'.[49]

The comparative history of the politics of speech and silence provided by the anthropologist James C. Scott helps us to explore the dangers and potentialities of early modern popular politics. Scott has argued that the distribution and expression of social power in differing rural societies has often shared a 'family resemblance'. In the slave states of the antebellum United States, the feudal system of Tokugawa Japan, or the manorialised villages of medieval Europe:

> slaves and serfs ordinarily dare not contest the terms of their subordination openly. Behind the scenes, though, they are likely to create and defend a social space in which offstage dissent to the official transcript of power relations may be voiced.

To Scott, this 'offstage dissent' could constitute an 'entire discourse', built upon symbols and metaphors of its own. Couched in song, proverbs, jokes, and even present in gestures and winks, that discourse was often opaque to rulers. The existence of this semi-autonomous realm provided subordinates with cultural resources upon which they could draw, both to cope with the daily humiliations and oppressions of class society, and to develop strategies by which social power could be resisted. Although 'many, perhaps most, hidden transcripts remain... hidden from public view and never "enacted"', both 'everyday forms of resistance' by peasants, labourers or slaves, and 'the occasional insurrection', were fostered within the 'sequestered social sites at which... resistance can be nurtured and given meaning'.[50]

Scott's model is not fully transferable into Tudor, Stuart and early Georgian England. Early modern English society was not the frozen caste society for which Scott's ideal type was designed. Instead, it was characterised by structural and cultural diversity: in its rapid social mobility, increasing population, expanding literacy, industry and urbanisation, it has seemed to its social historians to be closer to nineteenth-century modernity than to the imagined stasis of feudalism. Yet we shall see in the next chapter how early modern governors were often tempted into the hegemonic claim that their social world was indeed a static, ordered, hierarchical whole. Where early modern labourers, artisans or smallholders made public claims of their own (for instance, against the enclosure of common land; in denunciation of the 'oppressions' of a particular lord; or in complaints over the high price of food) their rulers often resorted to a standard authoritarianism, in which even the most limited and tactful statement of plebeian discontent could be twisted into the beginnings of a popular tumult.

Elite perceptions of stasis and hierarchy were sometimes more important to plebeian politics than the material realities of flux and change; for it was necessary for practitioners of popular politics to respond creatively to such elite anxieties. Authoritarian social theory (which we study in Chapter 1) had therefore to be anticipated by early modern plebeians. Popular responses to their governor's haughty pretences fell broadly into three forms: confrontation; manipulation; and threat. In the first case, subordinates provoked authority by making bold claims to 'rights' denied them in authoritarian social theory, or (in a less theorised, and still more confrontational manner) by mocking their rulers' authority in a levelling language which was often harsh, obscene or vengeful. In the second, they made appeals to reciprocity and elite patronage in order to criticise those gentry who had strayed from its strictures, or to highlight the limited nature of popular grievances. Finally, subordinates sometimes hinted to their rulers that failure to attend to their grievances would lead to unspecified, anonymous disorder. Social relations therefore operated within the difficult interplay of petition, negotiation, threat and patronage. The complex theatre of social relations, with all its ambiguous ironies and dangerous contradictions, has proved notoriously difficult for historians to categorise. Just as the evidence of riot, revolt, sedition and tumult give the lie to the notion that early modern social relations were defined by a forelock-tugging deference, so they subvert blunt Marxist categories of class struggle.

It is for this reason that Edward Thompson, that most subtle of historical materialists, has presented eighteenth-century social relations as operative within a self-limiting 'field of force'. Thompson argues that, despite witnessing the occasional riot or receiving some anonymous threatening letter, as a class, the early Georgian gentry felt reasonably secure.[51] The old paranoid willingness to detect a levelling conspiracy in lower-class agency could still be prompted; but unlike in earlier years, this was not a defining feature of elite culture. Similarly, although the lower orders had every reason to be watchful of their customary rights, and although 'the tetchy sensibilities of a libertarian crowd defined, in the largest sense, the limits of what was politically possible' for the established elite, Thompson found strong evidence of a constantly cautious 'reciprocity in the relations between rich and poor'. He went on:

> There is a sense in which rulers and crowd needed each other, watched each other, performed theatre and countertheatre to each other's auditorium, moderated each other's political behaviour. This is a more active and reciprocal relationship than the one normally brought to mind under the formula 'paternalism and deference'.

Early modern social relations were conducted within limits that were tacitly accepted on both sides. Thompson sees eighteenth-century social relations as 'structured' by a 'cultural hegemony' exercised by the gentry.[52] By this, he refers to the capacity of the gentry to maintain their dominant place within what he calls the 'field of force' of social relations. Noting that the eighteenth-century plebeian crowd was rebellious without being revolutionary, he goes on to show how lower-class appeals to custom allowed for a large measure of local confrontation and negotiation without ever developing into a fundamental challenge to the status quo. In his account, both crowd demonstrations and individual acts of insubordination were alive with politics; but even at its most incendiary that politics remained circumscribed by the public domination of the elite. In extreme moments, this power had much to do with the existence of a standing army; but then, 'for purposes of internal control this was often a small and emergency force'. More typically, however, the social power of the gentry rested upon their cultural authority.

In Thompson's account, popular culture forms the key arena within which the domination of the gentry was exercised. In the legal system in particular, the willingness of the magistracy to grant apparently irrational dispensations and pardons to suitably recalcitrant plebeian criminals seemed to confirm the reasonable, flexible nature of the law.[53] Informal acts of personal charity and patronage by the gentry also helped to oil the machinery of social relations, especially where these were conducted from a safe distance. Most importantly, Thompson argued that the limited aims of popular politics meant that plebeians became complicit in their own subordination. Hence, as eighteenth-century crowd actions pushed magistrates into enforcing legislation against greedy corn merchants, they also reaffirmed the basic justice of the social system. What emerges from Thompson's formulation is the sense that the Hanoverian labouring classes were held in subordination through their rulers' domination of the terms of political culture and social relations. Fundamentally, what Thompson proposed was a model of ideological domination, or 'cultural hegemony'. This concept is full of implications for how we understand the state, social power, resistance and rebellion, and as such is central to the concerns of this book.

The concept of 'cultural hegemony' originated with the Italian Marxist revolutionary Antonio Gramsci.[54] Following his imprisonment after the Fascist seizure of power, Gramsci concentrated his mind upon the underlying reasons for the failure of socialist revolution within Italy. He scribbled his deliberations into his censored notebooks, which survived his death in 1937 to become a classic work of cultural theory. Gramsci came to the conclusion that, while in the final analysis the state relied upon force, it represented much more than merely an armed body of men. Rather, the state comprised:

the entire complex of practical and theoretical activities with which the ruling class not only justifies and maintains its dominance, but manages to win the active consent of those over whom it rules.[55]

Hence, culture became a field of power relations over which successful states exercised a special force. In order to secure its cultural hegemony (a euphemism, in Gramsci's censored writings, for ideological domination), the dominating class had to grant a certain autonomy to subalterns (another euphemism: this time for the Marxist concept of the exploited class), such that they became complicit in their own subordination. This hegemonic trick was pulled off by granting to subalterns a narrow province of popular rights, thereby pulling them into its defence and distracting them from the larger empire of elite domination. In Gramsci's analysis, the challenge for the revolutionary was to convert the everyday, defensive struggles of subalterns into a much more ambitious political project: an assault upon the entrenched power of the dominating class. This was to be effected by working within hegemony: simultaneously defending the small rights granted to the popular classes, while pushing popular politics towards a more ambitious, revolutionary set of claims.

A variety of social historians have adapted Gramsci's speculations to their own ends: the contents of his prison notebooks have influenced historical interpretations of popular religion in Renaissance Italy, slave society in the pre-civil war United States, and social relations in post-Chartist industrial Lancashire.[56] The strong advantage of the Gramscian perspective has lain in its assumption that both everyday local-political conflicts and larger ideologies need to be studied in relation to their social and cultural context; and that political struggles comprise not only a struggle over space, institutions and resources, but also over meaning.

Gramsci's vision of cultural politics has heavily coloured recent historical interpretations of popular politics and social power in early modern society. Without always being conscious of their origin, early modern social historians have employed Gramscian concepts like 'subaltern' and 'hegemony' in their interpretations of popular culture, riot, social relations, custom and the law. A weak version of hegemony has been preferred by early modern social historians, in which subalterns are seen as consciously manipulating the terms of their apparent subordination. The cultural hegemony of the early modern gentry is understood to have operated negatively, by limiting the aspirations of popular politics. In particular, the notion that 'hegemony imposes an all-embracing domination upon the ruled' has been rejected.[57] Gramsci's broad interpretation of the state has proved especially influential in recent social historical analysis of the early modern state. In an important recent work, Steve Hindle has argued that during the late Elizabethan and early Stuart period, state structures were broadened, and state authority strengthened, due to the 'internalisation' of its values by village ruling groups. Although, as we shall see in Chapter 1, the implications of this broadening of the polity were never fully worked through within patriarchalism, a kind of hegemony was at work here. In return for their active participation within state structures, Hindle argues that 'the middling sort came to exercise a degree of political choice'. Thus, the 'political culture of the middling sort', while intimately connected to ruling ideas and state structures, developed within the relative autonomy of the small polity of the village. Hindle perceives in this the 'birthpangs of a participatory democracy' in pre-civil war England.[58] Central to Hindle's interpretation is an acknowledgement of the organising role played by the law and by legal institutions in the process of state formation. The next chapter is concerned with the relationship between contemporary elite perceptions of the polity, the law, legal institutions and popular politics. In particular, we will investigate the dangerous creative friction between popular politics and the state in early modern England.

1

AUTHORITY, THE LAW AND THE STATE

I   Political Theory and Popular Politics

The constitutional debates of the 1860s unsettled the slumbers of the Earl of Salisbury. Watched by his alarmed wife, the Earl seemed to struggle with some nightmare. Still sleeping, he walked to the windows of his ancestral home, Hatfield House. Finally awoken, Salisbury explained that, in his dreams, he had been fighting with the Mob, and that it had seemed that 'the forces of democracy were trying to break into Hatfield House'.[1] A similar set of anxieties gripped the waking consciousness of the early modern gentry and nobility. Writing to the Earl of Salisbury's distant ancestor in the winter of 1590, the Essex gentleman Sir John Smyth combined immediate fear with comparative history. He worried that in failing to hang plebeian criminals in sufficient numbers, the magistrates of Essex, 'under pretence of pity and mercy or favouring of life (as they call it)' were leading 'this realm to great danger'. That danger loomed within his historical consciousness:

> I will only make mention of the *bellum servile* that gave the Romans so much to do in the time they flourished most, the *Jacquerie* of France, and the dangerous rebellion of the peasants of Hungary . . . Commonly, the beginnings are very small and therefore lightly regarded, but once begun, they suddenly grow great, and then turn all to fire and blood.[2]

Such black fears of popular chaos contrasted sharply with the idealised, static, hierarchical image of early modern England upon which the gentry and nobility built their public values. That worldview was replicated in standard contemporary descriptions of the early modern polity. Works such as Sir Thomas Elyot's *Boke Named the Governor* (1531), Sir Thomas Smith's *De Republica Anglorum* (written between 1562 and 1565) and Edmund Dudley's *Tree of the Commonwealth* (1509) were structured around a set of unchallengeable assumptions: that the social order mirrored the natural and divine order in its perfection and immutability; that all social and familial authority flowed from the Crown; that to rebel was ungodly; that in rebellion, the lower orders displayed their lack of a rational politics, seeking as they did the destruction of all gentlemen and property.[3] In this section we shall see that some published interpretations of the polity were more sophisticated than this simplistic social authoritarianism implied. But a more flexible and realistic theory of government could only be developed within the interstices of such standard patriarchalism. During the 1640s, things changed rather drastically. Yet even after the Restoration, this authoritarian, patriarchal worldview continued to hold great power within elite culture.

Running through classical hierarchical theory was an obsessive concern with order, coupled with an anxiety about, and disavowal of, popular politics. Hence Sir Thomas Elyot explained in the opening chapters of *Boke Named the Governor*, how the social and political arrangements of his England mirrored the supreme order of the divine and natural world. Elyot felt himself to comprise part of a divinely ordained whole. Deploying the conventional language of social classification in description of the heavenly order, he demanded of his readers 'Hath not [God] set degrees and estates in all His Glorious works?' Elyot noted how the elements were hierarchically graded and 'set in their places'. So too with nature: 'Behold also the order that God hath put generally in all His creatures, beginning at the most inferior or base, and ascending upward.' And finally with humanity:

> A public weal is a body living, compact or made of sundry estates and degrees of people, which is disposed by the order of equity and governed by the rule and moderation of reason.

Within this organic whole, some were born to command and some to obey. Borrowing from Latin, Elyot named those at the base of his social world the:

Plebs [which] in English is called the commonalty, which signifieth only the multitude, wherein be contained the base and vulgar inhabitants not advanced to any honour or dignity.

The authority of 'the gentle and noble men' was based upon a combination of economic power and cultural capital:

they which be superior in condition or haviour [that is, property] should also have pre-eminence in administration, if they be not inferior to other in virtue ... where virtue is in a gentleman it is commonly mixed with more sufferance, more affability, and mildness, than for the more part it is in a person rural or of a very base lineage.[4]

And so in the social order of Elyot's England, as amongst animals, elements and angels, 'everything is order, and without order nothing may be stable or permanent'.

The grandiose social theory articulated by Elyot lived well beyond the chronological range of this book. In 1509, Edmund Dudley had been of the opinion that the commons 'may not grudge nor murmur to live in labour and pain', but should rather accept their subordination as divinely ordained. In 1671, the Duke of Albemarle wrote with similar ease of how 'the poorer and meaner people have no interest in the commonweal but the use of breath'.[5] But darker forces moved at the edges of the hierarchical vision. Elyot denied politics to the *plebs* because he assumed that should they gain access to government, chaos would ensue. Basing this conclusion upon his reading of the history of Republican Rome, he argued that:

The popular estate, if it anything do vary from equality of substance or estimation, or that the multitude of people have over much liberty, of necessity one of these inconveniences must happen: either tyranny ... or else ... the rage of a commonalty, which of all rules is most to be feared.

Since the commons were innately irrational, their nature led them to rebellion. Hence, government must ensure that the commons 'feel some severity', such that 'they do humbly serve and obey'.

Elyot's description of his social world represented a prescriptive ideal rather than a neutral dissection of contemporary social relations. This is not to dismiss the significance of Elyot's writing: as we shall see, his elaborately authoritarian anti-populism represented one powerful and enduring impulse within elite culture. For Elyot, government existed in order to prevent the formation of a popular politics. For this reason, he disliked the term 'commonweal', feeling that it carried the flavour of democracy in which 'everything should be to all men in common, without discrepance of any estate or condition'. The pervasive elite fear that popular politics implied a community of goods was most shrill during the 1640s. Two months before the outbreak of civil war, Sir Simonds D'Ewes warned the House of Commons that

> all right & propertie all *meum* and *tuum* must cease in civill warrs: & wee know not what advantage the meaner sorte alsoe may take to divide the spoiles of the rich & noble amongst them.

In the Putney debates of 1647, the same assumption formed the basis for Henry Ireton's case against the extension of the franchise to labourers and smallholders. After the Restoration, the gentry's social memory of the 1640s encouraged their maintenance of social authoritarianism. As we shall see in Chapter 4, Section VII, during the Exclusion Crisis of 1678–81, Tory propagandists dwelt upon the 'late Experience' of civil war, in which the gentry had 'submit[ted] their necks to the Yoke and Government of their own Slaves'.[6] Descriptions of plebeian crowds of the 1640s highlighted their repellent, disordered, unnatural characteristics: the 'many-headed monster', 'the Beast', or 'The Mouth'. Alternatively, they were known as the 'Mobile', referring to the collective mobility and instability of the crowd. By the 1680s, the word had been truncated into a new label: 'the Mob'.[7]

Throughout our period, authoritarian social theorists depicted popular politics in very similar terms. Much of the harsh advice proffered to Charles II upon his Restoration in 1660 by the Duke of Newcastle might have come from Sir Thomas Elyot. Newcastle advised the young monarch to display the outward countenance of authority at all times, for:

> Ceremony, though it is nothing in itself, yet it doth everything... ceremony and order, with force, governs all...and keeps every man and everything within the circle of their own conditions.

Like Sir Thomas Elyot, the Duke of Newcastle saw the gentleman's body as an emblem of social authority, and he suggested the restoration of the old sumptuary laws, which had defined appropriate dress according to social place:

> for certainly degrees of apparel to several conditions and callings is of great consequence to the peace of the kingdom, for when the lower degrees strive to outbrave higher degrees, it breeds envy in the better sort, and pride in the meaner sort, and a contempt by the vulgar of the nobility, which breeds faction and disorder, which are causes of civil war.[8]

Unlike Elyot, Newcastle had lived through a civil war and his advice to his new monarch bore the scars of that conflict. In Newcastle's interpretation, civil war had resulted from a fatal division of the gentry, which had allowed 'the people' on to the political stage. Yet he had the sense to see that 'the people' had not burst suddenly into political life in 1640. Rather, Newcastle's analysis of popular politics during the English Revolution gave causal primacy to long-term social and cultural factors. In his interpretation, the early modern gentry had failed to maintain a proper distance from the 'vulgar'. Newcastle argued that after the Reformation, social mobility and religious dispute had undermined a hitherto static social order. As the 'vulgar' had became overly conscious of their rights, so popular litigation increased, fuelled by an expanding legal profession. Popular litigiousness grew from the expansion of literacy, which had diminished respect for traditional values: 'The Bible in English under every weaver's and chambermaid's arms hath done us much hurt ... when most was unlettered, it was much a better world.' Popular chaos was most apparent in towns, where the indiscriminate distribution of the parliamentary franchise had created the preconditions for civil war: 'The truth is that every corporation is a petty free state against monarchy.' The restoration of the lost world of social hierarchy therefore lay in the reordering of popular culture:

> May games, Morris dances, the Lord of May and the Lady of May, the fool and the Hoby Horse must not be forgotten ... these divertisements will amuse the people's thoughts and keep them in harmless actions which will free your Majesty from faction and rebellion.[9]

The failure of patriarchal thought to cope with the realities of economic change, social conflict and political revolution mattered little. Like most dominant ideologies, the authoritarian social theory of Newcastle and Elyot spoke more to the ruling elite than it reconciled subordinates to their place. As we shall see in Chapter 4, Section II, this became most apparent in the last months of peace in 1642, when Royalist propagandists were able to rebuild support for the King amongst the gentry and nobility through an appeal to social authoritarianism. Representing the Long Parliament as the creature of plebeian London crowds, Royalist propaganda portrayed the Crown as the best guarantor of social order. Authoritarian social theory therefore represented the dominant fiction of its age, providing a conceptual framework for England's governing elite that was simultaneously reassuring and fantastic. Yet this ideology represented only one of a number of ways of conceiving of social relations and political power.

On the surface, Sir Thomas Smith's *De Republica Anglorum* seems to restate the standard formula followed by Newcastle and Elyot: that 'the defining characteristic of the "rascallity" was political impotence'.[10] But like Shakespeare's Jack Cade, Smith's political theory was full of fascinating contradiction. Smith's account was simultaneously structured by patriarchalism and in conflict with it. The central dividing line in Smith's England was office-holding, which guaranteed participation within the political nation. Hence, women, unless they were 'absolute' [that is, unmarried] rulers, were denied any public voice in the commonwealth.[11] But unlike Elyot, Smith perceived that political authority did not correspond neatly with social structure. Rather, institutional power was distributed in a surprisingly profligate manner. The recognition of this profligacy grew from the complexity of Smith's vision of Tudor society: 'We in England divide our men commonly into four sortes, gentlemen, citizens or burgesses, yeomen artificers, and laborers.'[12] The first two of these 'sorts' had ready access to institutional authority. Smith's discussion of the third 'sort', the yeomanry, was more ambivalent. He saw that this increasingly wealthy but nonetheless non-gentle 'sort' held local power within their own villages and towns, and so must 'be exempted out of . . . the rascabilitie of the popular'. But the implications of this exemption were too large to be explored fully. Instead, Smith fell back into a facile assumption of deference. Although Smith's yeomanry held office, they did so at the instruction of the gentry:

> [they] tend to their owne businesse, come not to meddle in publike matters and judgements but when they are called, and gladde when they are delivered of it, [and] are obedient to the gentlemen and rulers.

The same hesitation is apparent in Smith's discussion of the 'The fourth sort of men which doe not rule'. Moving closer to standard authoritarianism, Smith began his discussion of the 'fourth sort' by aligning their social subordination with their political powerlessness:

> The fourth sort or classe amongest us, is of those which the olde Romans called *capite censii proletarij* or *operae*, day labourers, poore husbandmen, yea marchantes or retailers which have no free lande, copiholders, all artificers, as Taylers, Shoomakers, Carpenters, Brickemakers, Bricklayers, Masons, &c.

Moving on from this lumpish categorisation to a discussion of the lack of authority held by such men, Smith began his next sentence:

> These have no voice nor authoritie in our common wealth, and no account is made of them but onelie to be ruled, not to rule other . . .

And then Smith hesitated. All too aware of the complexities of local political participation, Smith broke his seamless, conventional account of the subordination of the *proletarij* with the following extended caveat:

> and yet they be not altogether neglected. For in cities and corporate townes for default of yeomen, they are faine to make their enquests of such manner of people. And in villages they be commonly made Churchwardens, alecunners, and manie times Constables, which office toucheth more the common wealth, and at the first was not imployed uppon such lowe and base persons.[13]

Sir Thomas Smith's hesitations have recently acquired a special historiographical significance. In his influential inaugural lecture of 1989, Patrick Collinson used Smith's description of the fluidity of political relations to initiate a discussion of the 'social depth' of early modern politics. Collinson observed the common set of political assumptions and institutional arrangements which linked men and women of Sir Thomas Smith's class to those lower down the social scale. That relationship was one of 'active complexity', and was built upon a wider sense of politics than had conventionally been allowed in traditional political history.[14] Dwelling upon the example of the 'principal inhabitants' of the Wiltshire village of Swallowfield in 1596, Collinson showed how they possessed a strong sense of public duty, given institutional form in their town meeting.[15]

The politics of that association was to be found 'living and breathing' in the relative autonomy enjoyed by the town meeting over village life; 'in the distance created between these "cheiffe inhabitantes" and their social inferiors, the poor'; and in 'the formal . . . republican parity' which prevailed amongst the ruling group of the village. For Collinson, therefore, politics was constituted within institutional and cultural forms, within a socially capacious public sphere that comprised both the Swallowfield meeting and the High Court of Parliament.[16] Nonetheless, for all its careful subtleties, Collinson's discussion of Sir Thomas Smith's analysis of the Tudor polity leaves one fundamental question unanswered. If, as Collinson has argued, the role of villagers was so central to the operation of the early modern state, why was Smith's discussion of that function so ambiguous?[17]

Sir Thomas Smith's hesitations hint at both the social depth of the early modern polity and at the conflicts that seethed within it. For, as readership of any contemporary authoritarian tract reminds us, the place of village ruling groups within the body politic was both contested and unacknowledged. The habit of rebellion, as we shall see in Chapter 2, gradually died out amongst the 'chief inhabitants' of places like Swallowfield; but their capacity for organised political action did not. And as the social basis of the early modern state expanded, so it rubbed against the continuing appeal of authoritarian and patriarchal ideas within elite political culture. That Smith's otherwise smooth account should stumble at the very point that Collinson identifies as so important points to the difficult position of even the upper echelons of 'the commons' within the early modern polity. As to those below the 'chief men' of the parish, for all that Collinson assures us that the 'poor were also political animals', a wide vein of contemporary elite opinion was more likely to characterise them as brute beasts.[18]

One of the ugliest historical lessons taught by the twentieth century has been that cultures long conditioned by anxiety and hatred are more resistant to the exercise of reason than the academic mind might like to believe. The rational intellectual labours of Sir Thomas Smith may have meant rather less to the isolated country gentleman, anxiously watching his under-nourished labourers for signs of conspiracy at times of high food prices, than the gross simplicities of Sir Thomas Elyot. Schooled in the vindictive lessons of a selective classical education, the Tudor and Stuart gentry knew that in ancient times the many-headed monster of social disorder had been a terrible beast.[19] The quasi-classicism of the English Renaissance merely reinforced such prejudices. Historical accounts of the risings of 1381 and 1450 emphasised the violence of the lower orders when in rebellion. Closer memories of the rebellions of 1536–7 and 1549 were forced into the same template.[20] For all its grandiose pretence, authoritarian social theory was therefore shot through with anxiety about popular politics. Despite the formal separation within modern historiography between legal history and the history of political thought, that anxiety also crept into legal definitions of popular politics.

II   Treason, Sedition and the Representation of Popular Politics

On the 26th of November 1549, Robert Kett and his brother William stood trial for their lives before the Court of King's Bench.[21] The indictments proffered against the two men accused them of levying war against the King:

> Deum prae oculis suis non habens, sed instigatione diabolica seductus, et debitam legianciam suam minime ponderans ('not having God before [their] eyes, but seduced by diabolical instigation, and not weighing [their] due allegiance').

Although the two men were better schooled than most of their neighbours in their home town of Wymondham (Norfolk), it is doubtful whether either Robert or William understood much of the arcane Latin of their indictment. In one sense, this scarcely mattered. Neither had any agency within the legal proceedings, the outcome of which was a forgone conclusion. Both indictment and trial were formulaic. It mattered not at all that during the rebellion Robert Kett had prevented the murder of those gentlemen who fell into rebel hands. Robert and William Kett were found guilty upon an indictment that stated that the rallying cry of rebellion had been 'Kyll the Gentlemen'. The indictment of the Kett brothers echoed that drawn up against the leaders of rebellion in 1381, who were alleged to have intended the slaughter of the knightly class, the greater lords and the King. And yet the rebels of that year had claimed the King's sanctions for their actions; moreover, in 1381, as in 1549, rebel violence against the gentry had been deliberately discriminating.[22] The injustice of the allegations contained in the Kett brothers' indictment offends modern senses of truth. But the indictment needs to be understood in historical terms, as a textual product of a particular set of interests. Why was it so important to the framers of the indictment to maintain that the Kett brothers had intended the destruction of the gentry?

As we saw in the previous section, patriarchal theorists saw the prevention of popular politics as the defining role of the early modern state. Daniel Defoe's characterisation of 1715 might as well have been written two centuries earlier:

> The Reason and End, and for which all Government was at first appointed was to prevent Disorder and Confusion among the People; that is, in a few words, to prevent Mobs and Rabbles in the world.[23]

This instinctual hostility to popular politics expressed itself to greatest practical effect within the legal system. Over the course of the sixteenth and seventeenth centuries, legislators and judges developed a body of law designed to prevent popular political expression, either in individual speech or in collective action. This legislation built upon the earliest treason statute, that of 1352, which had made it an act of high treason (amongst other things) to 'compass or imagine' the death of the monarch and to levy war against royal government. Over the fifteenth and early sixteenth centuries, the range of activities by which the monarch's death could be 'imagined' was expanded to include verbal and written criticism of royal policy. Magical prophecies predicting future political developments fell under the expanding aegis of the 1352 statute, together with criticism of the monarch's personality and the spread of political gossip. Royal attorneys defined all of these activities as treasonable on the imaginative grounds that they 'were intended to destroy the cordial love that his people had for the king and thereby to shorten his life by sadness'.[24] Such interpretative innovation was known as 'constructive treason'.

In contrast to earlier practice, Tudor monarchs extended the body of statute law concerned with treason. Whereas between 1352 and 1485 there had been less than ten new treason statutes, Tudor parliaments added a further 68 treason statutes. The extent to which this represents a real discontinuity remains debatable. In many respects, the Tudor statutes merely clarified existent practice based upon construction and precedent. But it is clear that the new legislation also dealt with concerns specific to the early modern period. Henry VIII's break from Rome, with its concomitant decline of ecclesiastical jurisdiction over religious dissidence, required jurists and legislators to define new categories of secular treason. The changes of religious policy over the reigns of Edward VI, Mary and Elizabeth led monarchs and privy councillors to encourage legislation against distinct categories of treason, due in part to a desire to limit lawyers' autonomy in making constructions upon existent statutes.[25] The precise purpose of this legislation was to prevent religious and political dissidence, regardless of the social place of the dissident. Treason legislation intruded into the political worlds of the court, the parliament, the gentry and the nobility just as much as it did into those of the artisan, farmer and labourer. But it did so to different ends. Whereas the new legislation was designed to regulate elite politics in such a way as to ensure its conformity to the interests of the monarch, its operation upon popular politics was more extreme.

The passage of the Treason Act of 1534 marked a significant shift in the logic of such legislation. The Act came at a time at which popular criticism of royal policy seemed unprecedented, due to the royal divorce and the break with Rome.[26] In response, the Henrician Treason Act established certain forms of speech as treasonable. Adding to the 1352 statute and its later constructions, the 1534 Act rendered treasonable not only such deeds as were intended to depose the King, but also words and writings which were critical of his policies. Similarly, pronouncing Henry to be a heretic, schismatic, tyrant, infidel or usurper of the Crown became treasonable. Although the statute lapsed upon Henry's death in 1547, later legislation of 1552, 1554, 1571 and 1585 followed similar principles. Despite the differing religious politics of Tudor monarchs, the legislation passed in their names presumed that the central state ought to exercise control over political speech, writing and publication. The primary target of the sixteenth-century treason and sedition legislation was therefore the public sphere of political speech and action.

The tone of Tudor treason and sedition legislation was draconian: the preamble of the 1555 Treason Act laid down a hierarchy of punishments for speaking 'false, sedicious and sclaunderous news, rumours, sayeinges and tales' and concluded that 'we ar[e] forbidden to thincke evill and muche more to speake evell'.[27] In 1543, as the Henrician reformation entered its most conservative stage, the parliament of that year passed a new 'Acte for the advauncement of true Religion and for the abbolisshment of the contrarie'.[28] In establishing a statutory hostility to radical protestantism, the 1543 Act reversed the doctrinal direction of the 1534 Treason Act; nonetheless, it operated from similar assumptions about popular politics. The 1543 Act encouraged the 'noble man and gentleman' to read the vernacular Bible publicly to his household, and allowed

to the 'marchaunte man' the right 'to reade to himselfe privatelye the
Bible and New Testament'. These were 'the highest and moste honest
sorte', whose loyalty to the Crown had been (legislators hoped) deepened by their engagement with printed scripture. In contrast, 'a great
multitude' of the King's subjects, 'moste speciallie of the lower sorte have
so abused [access to the printed scriptures] that they have therebye
growen and increased in divers naughtie and erronyous opynions'.
Hence, the Act specified that:

> no woomen nor artificers prentises journeymen serving men of the
> degrees of yeomen or undre husbandemen nor laborers shall
> reade...the Byble or Newe Testament in Englishe, to himselfe or any
> other privatelie or openlie upon paine of oone monethes imprysone-
> ment for every tyme.

The early modern English state was always punching beyond its weight.
Its real capacity to supervise popular politics and to control print and
speech was always weaker than legislators and privy councillors liked to
recognise. Yet it remained important that the state was seen by the only
social class whom patriarchal theorists recognised as political actors – the
gentry and the nobility – to be 'imprynting' authority 'in [the] hartes' of
its plebeian subjects.

The study of early modern political thought has developed at a considerable distance from historical research into crime, law and punishment in the same period. This is unfortunate, since the criminal trial
could provide legal force to the abstractions of patriarchalism. The
treason and sedition legislation of the Tudor period combined with a
basic elite antipathy towards popular politics. Francis Bacon warned
that, due to the tumultuous irrationality of the commons, rulers should
watch constantly for insurrection: 'let no prince measure the danger of
[insurrections] by this: whether they be just or unjust; for that were to
imagine people to be too reasonable'. The control of both speech and
resources lay at the heart of his analysis. Since 'the rebellions of the belly
are the worst', then 'the first remedy or prevention [of sedition], is to
remove by all means possible that material cause of sedition...which is
want and poverty'. As we shall see in the next section, Bacon was therefore
especially concerned to see that popular complaints were rectified.[29]

Throughout our period, privy councillors required magistrates to
listen for 'murmering' against the regime, both amongst the gentry and
amongst the commons. But if magistrates had to watch for dissent

amongst their peers, then they were to be doubly observant of the lower orders. First, because the commons were supposed to be credulous and irrational and so were easily led into commotion; secondly, because the plebeian insubordination might grow into levelling fury. Bacon counted 'Libels and licentious discourses against the state, when they are frequent and open' as one of the 'signs of troubles' in a state. For Bacon, the control of speech represented the maintenance of order: 'seditious tumults, and seditious fames, differ no more, but as brother and sister, masculine and feminine'. He was not alone in this opinion. One Devonshire Justice opined to Robert Cecil that the 'vulgar sorte . . . ar[e] carried more by rumours without an head, then by the truth of thinges'.[30]

Repressive legislation sought to control collective organisation as well as speech. The Act of 1553 'againste unlawfull and rebellyous assemblies' made the organisation of riotous gatherings by 'speaking or uttring of any woordes . . . or by setting upp or casting of any billes . . . or writinge' a capital felony. By implication, it also made a capital felony out of the collective organisation of complaint against enclosure, high food prices or excessive rents, in that meetings of more than twelve people concerning such issues were deemed riotous.[31] The Court of Star Chamber was heavily concerned with the prosecution of riots. It also held jurisdiction over the dissemination of seditious or defamatory hand-written libels and over breaches in press censorship. One relatively common form of communicating grievances – that of the anonymous threatening letter – was therefore rendered illegal. Writing mocking rhymes against one's superiors was also punishable before Star Chamber. Coupled with the power held by the Stationers Company (established in 1557) to search the premises of printers and booksellers for seditious works, effective controls were also maintained over the printing press.[32] We shall see in Chapter 4, Section II how the abolition of Star Chamber in 1641 resulted in the temporary collapse of press censorship and the flowering of popular political journalism. Despite Restoration legislation designed to stifle such dangerous liberty, Chapter 4, Section VII shows how the later Stuart period saw continued conflict over the communication of political ideas through the printing press.

The treason and sedition legislation of the sixteenth century therefore established precise legislative authority for magisterial attempts to disable popular politics. The exact status of 'seditious' speech remained controversial within legal opinion and after 1628 common law courts accepted that seditious words could not constitute a form of high treason. Until the Restoration, therefore, sedition was understood as a crime of misdemeanour, to be punished by flogging, pillorying, imprisonment or fines. We shall see in Chapter 4, Section VII how the Restoration regime constructed a legislative monolith against religious and political dissent. Throughout our period, governors strained to hear the voice of popular politics, whether spoken in public sites such as the marketplace or the guildhall, or murmured in the alehouse, the street or the field. At times of economic or political crisis, popular criticism was often treated as though it represented a challenge to the political order. And political critique, however reasoned, might therefore seem all the more threatening when spoken within a common dialect. The yeoman Henry Elliott realised this to his cost when he was sentenced to be hanged, drawn and quartered in 1600 after the Assize judges heard report of his intelligent analysis of contemporary foreign policy:

> The Queene writeth hirselfe Queene of England, France and Ireland, but the [queen] is thrust out of France already and shortly she will also be thrust out of Ireland.[33]

To return to our organising question: why did the indictment of the Kett brothers in 1549 take such an exaggerated form? After all, Robert and William Kett had led a popular insurrection and had taken up arms against the Crown. Was this not sufficient evidence to sustain a charge of high treason? The question highlights a further mismatch; this time, between the hostile representation of the rebellion and the real rebel agenda. We shall see in Chapter 2, Section III how Kett's rebellion presented itself as a popular rising *on the behalf* of the monarch, *in support of* the old social status quo, and *against* an oppressive gentry. Recent historians of popular rebellion have shown how this limited agenda reflected the ordered, conservative village politics that dominated early modern popular political culture.[34] The gentry of Tudor England could not be so coolly dismissive. The actual restraint of Robert Kett had been one thing; the implications of his rebellion quite another. For, in barging into the seemingly closed halls of Tudor government, Kett had demonstrated both the capacity of the lower orders for orchestrated political action and the extent of their self-discipline.

The social authority of the early modern gentry depended upon their internal political integration. This was especially important in the mid-Tudor period, at a time of deep religious fissure. Fear of the levelling, many-headed monster of plebeian disorder helped to close the ranks of

England's ruling elite. With the defeat of Kett's rebellion came the opportunity to redefine the 'commotion time' as a bloody Jacquerie. And so the hegemonic claim that the gentry were born to command an irrational plebeian mass bore heavily upon the indictment of Robert and William Kett, generating the fiction that their rallying cry had been 'Kyll the Gentlemen'. Legal documentation did more than simply reflect a bureaucratic process of indictment, trial and sentence; it also formed a powerful textual representation of transgression, authority and punishment.

III   Legal Definitions of Riot

Some contemporary elite characterisations of popular politics were subtler than the rudimentary precepts of patriarchalism might imply. At times of relative stability, members of the gentry and nobility were willing to think beyond the simplicities of authoritarian anxiety. In his discussion of seditious rumours, for instance, Francis Bacon noted a contradiction:

> Neither doth it follow, that because these fames are a sign of troubles, that the suppressing of them with too much severity would be a remedy of troubles. For the despising of them many times checks them best: and the going about to stop them, doth but make a wonder long-lived.

Sharply aware of the danger that the 'poorer sort' might join with the rulers of their villages, Bacon warned that 'the danger is evident and great' when 'the better sort be joined with a want and necessity in the mean people'. In the 1597 Parliament, which met in the aftermath of a failed popular insurrection against enclosures in Oxfordshire, Bacon led proposals for new anti-enclosure legislation. His thoughtful consideration of the relationship between authority and popular politics extended into his discussion of economic disorders. For Bacon, 'the surest way to prevent seditions' was 'to take away the matter of them'. Hence, since government possessed legitimate authority over economics, it should maintain industry, repress waste and idleness, moderate taxes and the 'tributes' taken by lords, and regulate prices.[35]

There was nothing novel in Bacon's proactive vision of governance. Rather, he sketched a standard paternalist model of magistracy that was simultaneously patriarchal and authoritarian, while remaining open to popular complaint. The flexibility of that concept, combined with a growing legalism amongst the commons, created the ground rules for a contradictory, fluid pattern of social relations. Early modern governors defined themselves in opposition to popular anarchy, while simultaneously granting a restricted space within which plebeian complaint could be articulated. Plebeians contributed to this difficult concoction by mixing deferential appeals for paternalist protection with an occasionally vicious language of class, and by demonstrating in crowd actions an ostentatious restraint and regard for legal form. The resultant brew was always unstable. That in the later Tudor and early Stuart period it boiled over only rarely is therefore all the more remarkable. After 1549, it was only towards the end of our period, with the passage of the Riot Act of 1715, that protracted crowd actions were likely to lead to heavy repression. The occasional hangings that followed eighteenth-century food riots were almost unheard of in the preceding century.[36]

This, then, was the hegemonic terrain within which popular politics operated. Assessed upon the basis of its coercive powers, a relatively weak state confronted a popular politics which, while often riotous, only rarely contemplated outright rebellion. Up until the 1640s, there was no standing army within England. In repressing disorder, Tudor and early Stuart governors possessed only a limited range of options. Following its establishment in 1558, they could raise the county's militia. But as lord lieutenants were to discover during widespread anti-enclosure riots within the West Country in 1628–31, and as Charles I became even more painfully aware during the crowd demonstrations which drove him from his capital in January 1642, militiamen were rarely willing to use force against their neighbours. Alternatively, under the sanction of *Posse Comitatus*, magistrates could command subjects to take part in the physical suppression of disorder. During periods of very serious disorder, such as in 1549 and 1569–70, martial law might be imposed upon an area, and large numbers of executions might result. But it is significant that in the case of the 1549 rebellions, the government was forced into extensive reliance upon foreign mercenaries and bands of armed and mounted gentlemen.

The vast majority of cases of crowd disturbances that came before law courts were punished with financial penalties, brief imprisonment or with whippings. In the case of more serious disturbances, executions occasionally resulted. After the passage of the Riot Act in 1715, army officers were more willing to use violence in the suppression of crowd disturbances, and magistrates more confident in handing down capital sentences upon rioters. Throughout our period the treason and sedition legislation provided a last reserve of repressive legal force. At times of political crisis or extensive economic hardship, the treason laws might be brought into action. The would-be rebels of Oxfordshire of 1596, for instance, were tried for high treason. The same recourse was had against the Midland rebels of 1607, whose large-scale enclosure riots, although they had involved no violence against the person, had spilt across several counties. Subsequent legislation, in particular following both the Restoration in 1660 and the Glorious Revolution in 1688, extended the treason and sedition law to cover specific types of anti-monarchical criticism.

The flexible response of the authorities to perceived disorder helped to extend the creative engagement between popular politics and the law. In the aftermath of the 1549 rebellions, Edwardian parliaments anticipated Francis Bacon and passed a body of legislation that combined repression with paternalism. New statutes regulated the cloth industry; the protection of cottagers' rights; the prevention of enclosure; and the organisation of charity for the poor. At the same time, verbal politics was further restricted by legislation against seditious speech and prophecies; protestant reformation was strengthened by an act against 'divers books and images'; and in November 1549 the Parliament passed an 'Acte for the punyshment of unlawfull assemblyes and rysinge[s]'. Further Acts of 1553 and 1559 modified key provisos of the 1549 Act; but the essential spirit of the legislation was retained.[37] The mid-Tudor legislation of 1549–59 deserves special attention, as it highlights the flexibility allowed to early modern magistrates in dealing with crowd politics.

The 1549–59 statutes clarified earlier common law definitions of riot and rebellion by establishing a sliding scale of riotous offences. The legislation assessed the gravity of riotous offences according to the following criteria: the number of people involved in gatherings; their intent; whether they had been commanded by a magistrate to depart; the longevity of the disturbance; and the seriousness of the threat represented by the riot. Most importantly, the legislation defined certain kinds of crowd action as felonious (that is, a serious crime which as capital felony carried the death penalty). For instance, under the 1549 Act, if 40 or more people gathered to break enclosures for two or more hours in defiance of a magisterial order to depart, they were deemed guilty of treason. The Marian and Elizabethan statutes reduced the same offence to capital felony, but also decreased the requisite size and longevity of the disturbance to cover crowds of more than 12 people, gathered for more than an hour. The legislation of 1549–59 therefore allowed magistrates to discriminate between small-scale riots and more threatening disturbances. The 1549–59 legislation was allowed to lapse upon the death of Elizabeth I.[38] Thereafter, and until 1715, courts returned to the prosecution of riotous offences according to the common law principles discussed below. In 1715, following a protracted wave of anti-Hanoverian riots across much of Britain in the wake of the accession of George I, a new Riot Act was passed by Parliament.[39] Much of the rioting of 1714–15 had been directed against the chapels and meeting houses of protestant dissenters, who were deemed by Jacobite crowds to favour the fragile new Hanoverian regime. The 1715 Act therefore strengthened magistrates' powers against large-scale disturbances, indemnified the military from any deaths caused in the suppression of illegal assemblies, and made the riotous destruction of churches and dissenting chapels a capital felony.

The legislation of 1549–59 and 1715 complemented a longer-running common law definition of riot. According to common law principles, a riot was considered to have occurred where three or more persons assembled in a violent and tumultuous fashion, under their own authority, with the mutual intent of committing a breach of the peace. 'Violence' could be interpreted loosely, to embrace intimidating words spoken by people bearing offensive weapons. The definition of an offensive weapon was equally flexible, and in complaints against enclosure rioters was often be taken to include spades carried with the intention of filling in enclosure ditches. 'Combination' could also be interpreted widely, to include the collection of funds amongst rioters (known as 'common purses') intended to finance their legal defence, as well as plans to take collective action. As in the legislation of 1549–59 and 1715, some riots were judged more harshly than others. A riot that involved no interpersonal violence, was short in duration, involved only slight damage to property and carried no overt implications for state politics might be deemed to constitute a simple misdemeanour and face only light punishment, typically involving financial penalties. Courts made a centrally important distinction between private and public disputes. If the inhabitants of a place came together to break enclosures upon common land upon which they claimed an interest, this constituted a private matter between encloser and anti-encloser. As such, the case could be prosecuted as trespass or affray and might result in an aggrieved party suing in their capacity as a private individual. The offence was punishable before local criminal courts, and the accused might lodge cross-suits in other courts in order to demonstrate the legality of their actions. Such small-scale crowd actions accounted for the bulk of riotous cases heard by courts. But if rioters in one place combined with their neighbours in another to break down enclosures on land on which they had no private interest, this was taken to constitute a general attack upon enclosures. Such an act was deemed to levy war against the Crown and as such was punishable as treason. Thus, for instance, the labourers and artisans who took part in the Midland Rising of 1607 were prosecuted as traitors because they had destroyed enclosures across a wide area.

The legal discrimination embodied in both statute and precedent allowed magistrates to respond flexibly to crowd actions. It also provided an incentive to rioters to limit their actions. We shall see in Chapter 3, Section III how early modern plebeians often took crowd action in defence of common rights or to assert a 'fair price' for food. They were less willing, however, to confront state authority. The discriminating application of legal definitions of riot both exploited and deepened the legalism of popular culture. It allowed plebeians a certain space to develop tactical, short-term and local responses to perceived threats, while discouraging them from any larger challenge. A standard tactic of enclosure rioters, for instance, was to divide into individuals or pairs in order to break down fences. In so doing, they risked prosecution for the minor offence of trespass, but avoided indictment for riot. By such subtle means, the law therefore contributed to a diminution in the scale of public disorder.

IV   Law Courts and the Early Modern State

The law occupies a central place in the historiography of riot, rebellion and popular politics for four reasons. First, legal definitions of riot, sedition, treason and rebellion reflected elite anxieties about popular politics while providing a flexible law code for its containment or repression. Secondly, the inclusive, incorporative character of the English legal system allowed the law to operate as an arena of conflict resolution. Thirdly, plebeian political cultures were highly legalistic in their own right. Popular opposition to enclosure, for instance, often combined crowd action with litigation against the encloser. This litigiousness stemmed from both a close sense of tactics and from a deeper popular legalism, in which considerable weight was placed upon notions of custom, order and continuity. Fourthly, social historians of popular politics remain heavily dependent upon the records of litigation and prosecution at law courts for the description of their subject.

With important exceptions, the early modern English state operated in a highly legalistic form. Save for extreme situations such as the repression of the rebellions of 1536–7, 1549 and 1569, early modern rulers could not simply string lower-class dissidents up from the nearest tree.[40] Instead, rebellious plebeians had to be arraigned before law courts, thereby generating written records of their prosecution. Such archival material has survived in surprising bulk and, when combined with the record of popular litigation, has allowed historians to analyse many aspects of popular political speech and collective organisation. Historians have exploited the records of local manor courts, for instance, to show how ideas about custom and the law operated within local popular culture. The rather weightier archives of central equity courts have also been explored in search of plebeian politics. Such material provides evidence of riot and confrontation, while also implying something of the relationship between popular politics and the law. In order to appreciate the significance of that relationship, we must first sketch the salient features of the early modern English legal system.

Differing perceptions of land rights lay at the heart of much social conflict in early modern England. Tenants did not own land in their own right, but rather let it from a lord. In the case of freehold land, that tenure was so strong that, aside from the payment of rent, freehold was close to our modern concept of private property in land. In the case of copyhold tenure, rights varied from one manor to another according to local custom. In one manor, the tenurial rights of copyholders might well be almost as strong as freeholders. Within a neighbouring manor, copyholders might be more easily dispossessed; their rights to take timber or dig for minerals might be non-existent; their rents might be set at the lord's whim; and so on. Such factors helped to limit local popular agency, such that it seemed to one contemporary that the poor tenant's 'religion is a part of his copyhold, which he takes from his landlord and refers it wholly to his discretion'.[41] By the end of the seventeenth century, the amount of copyhold land had diminished, due in part to lords' attempts to undermine copyhold tenures in favour of weaker leasehold tenancies. One recurrent theme in this book, therefore, concerns the relationship between land, law and power in early modern England.

A major cause of conflict throughout our period concerned access to and rights over common land. Such commons typically lay on the

margins of the cultivated area of a manor, and were often more extensive in regions of poor soil and pastoral agriculture (fens, forests and
moorland areas, for instance) than in corn-producing, arable regions.
Ostensibly, local manorial courts both maintained the customs according to which copyhold land was held and regulated access to the
commons. Just as copyhold tenure varied from one manor to another, so
the extent of common right was also subject to significant local variation.
In some manors, common rights were restricted only to landed
inhabitants; in others, the freeholders might dominate to the detriment
of copyholders and the landless; in still others, common rights were
exercised by both landed and landless. Most importantly, despite claims
that custom represented long-established ancient practice, definitions of
common rights were ever changing. A manor where common rights
were exercised in an open, democratic manner in 1500 might, for a
variety of reasons, have become much more restricted by 1700.[42]

In many villages, the manor court remained an important focus
for local conflicts, either as a forum for the settlement of disputes or,
occasionally, as a focus for anti-seigneurial resistance. Yet over the
course of our period the authority of manor courts was in retreat. Lords
often overrode inconvenient decisions made by manor courts, or chose
complaint tenants as jurors. In the case of those villages where the lord
was absent (many villages included no gentry at all), manor courts
might fail to represent communal interests for a different reason.
Some manor courts became the focus for the aggressive pursuit of the
material interests of wealthier villagers against the landless and near-
landless. Long-term processes of social polarisation – in particular the
expanding economic power of wealthier villagers, especially within the
agrarian south and east of England – connected to such micro-
political developments. The development of the civil parish in later
Elizabethan England also contributed to the marginalisation of manorial
institutions. In place of the manor court, the village often fell under
the control of a relatively exclusive, landed, office-holding 'better sort'
or 'chief men'. The local institutional expression of the authority of
'the chief men of the parish' often took the form of a self-selecting parish
vestry, which assumed responsibility for setting poor rates, appointing
village officers, and ordering the 'little commonwealth' of the village.
Such 'middle people' did not fit easily into the hierarchical vision of
authoritarian social theory, being neither gentry, nor exactly 'vulger
plebeians'. Neither did this 'better sort' slot neatly into the early modern
polity: central as they were to the local exercise of power, they

remained anomalous within a political nation that was supposedly
defined by gentility.[43]

Even if poorer rural inhabitants had no direct access to the manor
court or the parish vestry, the operation of such institutions embedded
knowledge of legal form, precedent and local custom deep within local
culture. This consciousness ran alongside the growing authority of secular courts and magistrates in law-enforcement. Very minor offences,
such as brawls in alehouses or trespass, might be prosecuted at the local
manor court. By the later sixteenth century, especially in southern England, they were more likely to be heard by the Quarter Sessions. These
met every three months within local divisions of counties and held jurisdiction over a range of criminal offences, including small-scale riots and
seditious gossip. Trials were held before jurors who were characteristically selected from amongst the 'better sort' of male householders. The
magistracy of the Quarter Sessions (known as Justices of the Peace, and
referred to collectively as the county bench) was appointed by the Crown
to a county's Commission of the Peace. Membership of the bench was as
much a social statement, identifying its members as the cream of the
county's gentry, as it was a magisterial office. The most serious crimes
tried before the Quarter Sessions overlapped with those heard before
the Assizes. This court restricted its criminal jurisdiction solely to felonious offences. Hence, the records of Assize courts often form an important source of information about large-scale riot and serious political
sedition. Judges were professional legal men, but were recruited from
the same social milieu as the county bench. Juries once again were
selected from amongst the propertied, 'best sort' of male householders.
Assizes were organised in 'Circuits', covering a number of adjacent
counties.[44]

Many towns and cities held some form of exemption from the authority of county Quarter Sessions and Assize circuit judges. Some urban
centres enjoyed legal autonomy as enfranchised boroughs, which
carried the right to elect their own member of parliament according to a
locally specific franchise. That constitutional autonomy was symbolised
by the authority of the mayor, bailiffs or leading aldermen (the precise
arrangements varied from town to town) over lesser criminal matters.
Hence, minor urban riots were often prosecuted before local borough
courts. Larger conurbations such as London, Norwich or York held City
status. This granted to the town's ruling group (the precise constituency
of which again varied from one place to another, but which typically
comprised the mayor and leading aldermen) a jurisdiction equivalent to

that of the Quarter Sessions of the surrounding county. This meant that large-scale crowd disturbances and serious political sedition occurring within the boundaries of cities were typically prosecuted before borough courts. The continuity of borough government has meant that urban records tend to be richer and more extensive than those of manors, parish administration and Quarter Sessions. In the case of cities like Norwich, where the borough courts possessed a jurisdiction equivalent to that of a combined Quarter Sessions and Requests court, the result has been to preserve a unique archive of information about crime, protest, rebellion, seditious speech and popular politics. We provide a fuller assessment of the peculiarities of urban politics in Stuart England in Chapter 4, Section I.

We might chart two statistical curves in Elizabethan and early Stuart England: an apparent downward trend in the scale, ferocity and frequency of organised crowd protest and riot; and a rapid increase in litigation at central equity courts. The relationship between these trends cannot be specified with any certainty; but their coincidence seems more than accidental. Historians are beginning to appreciate that the formation of the early modern English state was closely related to the growth of popular litigation, especially before central courts.[45] A bewildering range of such courts, many of which practised law according to abstract rules of equity rather than common law precedent, met within and around Westminster Hall: the Courts of Requests, Common Pleas, Exchequer, King's Bench, the Duchy of Lancaster. The jurisdiction of these institutions overlapped with common law courts, with one another, and with two other central courts who sat elsewhere within the metropolis: the Court of Chancery, which took its name from its location on the edge of the City of London at Chancery Lane; and the Court of Star Chamber. All of these courts heard cases concerning such matters as the enclosure of common land, manorial and parochial custom, the parliamentary and local franchise, and the authority of local officers. But social historians of popular politics have had a special interest in one court in particular: the Court of Star Chamber.

The Court of Star Chamber met within the precincts of the palace of Westminster, in a room whose ceiling decoration gave the court its name. Star Chamber had its origins in the late medieval period, as the Privy Council's traditional role of hearing petitions and issuing judgments on the grounds of abstract fairness (or 'equity') became formalised. An Act of Parliament of 1489 clarified the court's jurisdiction as including, amongst other matters, the punishment of riots.[46] Uniquely for a central court, its judges were not senior lawyers, but rather comprised a selection of the monarch's privy councillors. In blurring distinctions between executive and judicial authority, the court had enormous potential as an arm of central state power. The Star Chamber's usefulness as an instrument of royal policy was only fully realised under the early Stuarts, especially during the years of Charles I's personal rule (1629–40), when the court imposed a series of highly controversial and draconian punishments upon leading critics of royal policy. The use of the court as an arm of prerogative power in the 1630s led to its abolition by the Long Parliament in 1641. For a while during the 1640s, the House of Lords claimed final jurisdiction over riotous offences. Upon the abolition of the Lords in 1649, the Court of King's Bench (or the Upper Bench as it was designated during the Commonwealth) claimed jurisdiction over riot. Yet the King's Bench never achieved the preeminence which Star Chamber had held over riot.

Given the slipperiness of legal definitions in the early modern period, it should not be surprising to find that Star Chamber's definition of 'riot' was a wide one. This included both large-scale, protracted disturbances and a wide range of lesser collective breaches of the peace. Furthermore, the Act of 1489 also granted authority to Star Chamber over the publication and dissemination of seditious libels and over conspiracy. In consequence, the Star Chamber was in a powerful position to censor a wide range of plebeian political activities. In addition to hearing cases concerning large-scale riots and insurrections, or the publication of seditious tracts, Star Chamber also dealt with (for example) small-scale enclosure riots; rent strikes against landlords; collective assaults on bailiffs; the collection of 'common purses' to fund legal action at rival central courts; and the drunken rendition of bawdy rhymes against local authority figures. Prosecutions were initiated from two sources: private individuals, or public prosecutions in the name of the Attorney General or Solicitor General. In the case of the former, many complainants were of gentle or noble status; but a surprising number of wealthier yeomen were also able to muster the funds to organise a complaint. Litigation was an expensive business. Moreover, poorer complainants were unlikely to receive an unbiased hearing before the court, as one ruling of 1593 made clear:

No man of base condition, such as an apprentice, horsekeeper, or such-like, should be a plaintiff in this Court before he had [found] sufficient surety to perform the order of the Court.[47]

In the case of the latter, the Attorney General and Solicitor General initiated public proceedings (or took over private prosecutions) where it was believed that an alleged breach of the peace was of such gravity as to threaten the stability of the state.

England was therefore formed as a polity through a complex network of local and supra-local legal institutions. In order to function effectively, these institutions relied upon a wide degree of popular participation. Of special importance in this respect was the propertied, adult male householder of 'middling' status. The indiscriminate crudities of official patriarchal social theory positioned such men within the 'vulgar commons'. Yet the 'middling' male householder was much more than just another object of governance. He played a dynamic role in the administration, expression, mediation and extension of authority: in his capacity as a member of a village court, a vestryman, an elector, a jury-man, or a constable, the early modern state came increasingly to depend upon him. This variety of roles gave him the potential to represent personal or collective grievances to those in authority, and even on occasion to organise resistance to lords, magistrates and gentlemen. We should not, therefore, be surprised to find that the 'middling' male householder often formed the leadership of popular protest in early Tudor England. His growing disinterest in that leading role, first manifest within parts of agrarian England from the later sixteenth century, is therefore of supreme interest to the social historian of popular politics. That implied shift in political allegiance and social relations is a recurrent theme in the next chapter.

2

REBELLION IN SIXTEENTH-CENTURY ENGLAND

I   The Pilgrimage of Grace of 1536 and the Rebellions of 1537

Sir Geoffery Elton once remarked how 'it is of the essence of the poor that they do not appear in history'. Yet even the most high-political histories of Tudor England have been forced to allow the large-scale rebellions of 1536 and 1549 into their accounts.[1] Once present within such narratives, popular insurrection is difficult to contain. For the sudden intrusion of rebellious plebeians into conventional histories of government, court faction and administration ruptures the assumption that politics stemmed only from the central state and the 'political nation' of the gentry and nobility. A different interpretative approach is demanded: one that emphasises the shifting place of rebellion within pre-existent popular political cultures. For the forms and outcomes of popular rebellion are only explicable when set within the context of the low politics of riot, resistance, negotiation and litigation. In this chapter we shall see how such a perspective allows us to reassess the forms taken by Tudor rebellions; the extent of popular autonomy in such rebellions; the changing ideology of rebellion; and the reasons for the decline of rebellion in Elizabethan England.

The most prominent cause of rebellion in pre-Reformation Tudor England was taxation. The preference of early Tudor government for assessing taxation on the basis of the land and income of individual households rather than upon the wealth of a community as a whole led to a heavier tax burden falling on the poor. Taxation was the central cause of rebellion in Yorkshire in 1489 and in Cornwall and Somerset in

1497. Public leadership in both insurrections came from the local gentry, but closer study of the 1497 rising has also revealed the important organisational role played by attorneys and wealthier villagers. Whereas the 1489 rebellion involved relatively little violence, rebellion in 1497 ended with significant bloodshed. A rebel army of some 15 000 marched on London, where they were defeated by a royal force. Although some initial executions occurred, the Crown preferred to impose heavy fines on rebel villages and towns.[2]

It was not until 1525 that further large-scale trouble developed over taxation. In an attempt to fund Henry VIII's foreign adventures, Cardinal Wolsey devised a new tax, the Amicable Grant. Financially exhausted by the payment of Lay Subsidies of the previous year, the population of the midlands, the south-east and East Anglia demonstrated against the new levy. In Kent, Essex and Suffolk opposition to the Grant bordered upon rebellion. Gathering in thousands at the clothworking town of Lavenham (Suffolk), weavers and labourers agreed to rise 'at the sounding of bells'. Only the negotiating skills of the local magnates, the Dukes of Norfolk and Suffolk, combined with the secret removal of the great bells of Lavenham by a loyal clothier of the town, prevented outright rebellion. Although the Court of King's Bench imposed fines upon the would-be rebels, ducal intervention prevented harsher punishment by Star Chamber. Meanwhile, the Amicable Grant was 'quietly dropped'.[3] So far, we ought to note two patterns to early Tudor rebellion: the relative lack of violence from rebels; and the willingness of the central authorities to moderate their actions when faced by rebellion. Both factors were present in the next major rebellion of the early sixteenth century; but in this case, the Crown's willingness to negotiate was less impressive than its subsequent enthusiasm for repression.

In early 1536, Parliament passed an act dissolving all minor monastic houses in England and Wales. Prior to its passage, rumours had circulated amongst the population of the 'putting down' of the monasteries and of the imposition of new taxes upon christenings, marriages and burials, sheep, cattle and basic foodstuffs. Some even said that the King's councillors intended to carry religious change as far as the destruction of all parish churches. At the same time, most householders were being assessed for the payment of new taxes. The planned removal of the minor monastic houses seemed, therefore, to confirm a wider set of popular anxieties concerning the growing ambitions of the central government. In early October 1536, the 'commons' of Lincolnshire rose in armed demonstration against such policies. Although public leadership came from the greater gentry of the county, the main movers of rebellion were men such as Nicholas Melton, known as 'Captain Cobbler': relatively prominent, prosperous villagers. Far from providing the real leadership to the rebellion, 'the first many of [the Lincolnshire gentry] knew of the rising was when their own bailiffs, tenants and serving-men confronted them with the demand that they swear the rebel oath'.[4] Rebel hosts marched behind banners bearing the 'Five Wounds' of Christ, proclaiming their piety and affection for traditional religion. The chancellor of the Bishop of Lincoln, held responsible for the local implementation of the Henrician reformation, was murdered, the city of Lincoln was seized by 10 000 armed rebels, and a list of complaints was submitted to the King. A substantial force was led north by the Duke of Suffolk, who had orders to refuse to negotiate with a rebel host in arms. Faced with royal intransigence, the Lincolnshire gentry refused to lead the rebels any further, and the commons were persuaded to return home by the royal representatives.

Meanwhile, similar events were unfolding in the north. Even prior to the Lincolnshire rising, rumours in the West Riding of Yorkshire concerning the Crown's desire to destroy parish churches had led commoners to swear oaths to defend their established religion. The arrival of copies of the Lincolnshire rebel demands inspired a much larger, co-ordinated rising of the counties of Yorkshire, Westmorland, Cumberland and Lancashire. Over three weeks in mid-October 1536, a large-scale rebellion was mounted, organised via Hundreds (the administrative entities into which counties were divided), from which men were mustered into nine large rebel hosts. Parishes, one of the key spatial units of early modern popular politics, formed the basis for the organisation of rebellion. The rebel hosts that besieged Carlisle and Skipton Castle, where loyalist gentry sheltered from the angry commons, were maintained by parish subscriptions. In some areas, the local gentry proved willing to lead the rebels; in others, gentlemen had to be forced into this role; while in the Lake Counties loyalist gentry were singled out as the rebels' main target. By late October, the rebels had sent their main force of some 28–35 000 men south to Doncaster to face the smaller royal army led by the Duke of Norfolk.[5]

Like the Lincolnshire rebels, those in the north marched behind banners depicting the 'Five Wounds' of Christ, and presented themselves as pilgrims, seeking their monarch's grace to maintain their established religion. The rebels swore oaths to maintain the commons, the King and the Church against the 'enemies of the commonwealth' (that is, the

King's advisors), and circulated handbills and ballads which were attached to church doors, market crosses, or were sung aloud in alehouses and on the march. These ballads and handbills reflected both the micro- and macro-politics of the rebellion. While including many complaints specific to local areas (in particular concerning the oppressions of manorial lords, who were felt to have broken 'the good and laudable customs of the country'), they were defined by a common concern over taxation, religion and social change. Upon the establishment of a council at York, rebel demands were homogenised around a set of complaints addressed to the Privy Council.

By this point, the northern gentry had assumed leadership of the rebellion. A compromise settlement was negotiated between the main rebel leaders and the Duke of Norfolk. In defiance of his instructions, Norfolk allowed the rebels to present their grievances to the Crown while still in arms. Further negotiations over these grievances were dragged out until December, when the rebels were promised a pardon in return for a free parliament at which their complaints would receive consideration. At first, the rebel hosts refused to accept this compromise; but in the face of persuasion from their most prominent leader, the lawyer Robert Aske, the rebel hosts dissolved. Henry VIII refused to honour his commitments under the negotiated settlement, and, following scattered uprisings amongst the embittered northern commons in the late winter and early spring of 1537, he launched what Fletcher and MacCulloch have called 'a systematic policy of punishment'.[6] Prominent rebel leaders, including Aske, were executed; Norfolk's declaration of martial law in the rebellious regions ensured that they were joined by many less well-known individuals.

The Duke of Norfolk's repression received enthusiastic sponsorship from the northern gentry, who were anxious to distance themselves from allegations of treason stemming from their forced participation in the 1536 risings. Hearing news of large rebel gatherings near Carlisle in February 1537, Norfolk wrote to Sir Christopher Dacre, advising him to 'spare not frankly to slay plenty of these false rebels to prove my old savings that Sir Christopher Dacre is a true Knight to his sovereign lord, and a hardy Knight, and a man of war'.[7] Dacre took the hint and led a force of mounted gentlemen in a decisive attack on the rebels near Carlisle. Allegiance in the border counties in 1537 was based upon explicit social division: a hostile eyewitness noted that there was 'never a gentleman amongst' the rebels. The subsequent description of that division illustrates how authoritarian social theory functioned within elite culture. The rebels were presented as a large, indiscriminate social group: 'the commons'. Sir Christopher Dacre saw off this plebeian rabble with the zeal expected of a man of his class: he 'showed himself a trewe noble Knight by riding down on the rebels with his own force':

> They came forth with speares substantiall
> Well horsed in array following in a chase
> By whome they lost their crosse their standard principal,
> And had three hundred taken within a little space
> The others fled away as shepe with wolves chased
> Some oppressed, some spoiled, some with lamentation,
> Thus five thousand by five hundred were utterly defaced
> Hunted like dogs for their abomination.[8]

That such organised, violent encounters between the gentry and the 'plebs' were, in historical fact, extremely rare mattered less than the character of their representation. Such accounts bolstered authoritarian impulses amongst the gentry, preparing them for the imagined moment at which they would ride down their social inferiors 'like dogs'. This was the social logic that underpinned the legal force of the *Posse Comitatus*, rendered historically transparent in the dominant cultural forms of the Tudor age. Given the presence of such values at the heart of elite culture, we are therefore left with the question of why the commons wished to secure the public leadership of the gentry in the rebellions of October 1536. It was with good reason that the former Captain Cobbler reproached himself while in jail after the extinction of the Lincolnshire rising: 'What whorsones were we that we had not killed the gentlemen, for I thought allwayes that they would be traytors'.[9]

A strong current of social conflict moved through the events of 1536–7. Despite the desire of the rebels for public leadership from the gentry, suspicions of their motives remained strong. In his communications with the Privy Council over the winter of 1536, the Duke of Norfolk observed how unwilling were plebeian rebels to allow their gentry leaders to converse in private, for fear of betrayal. Such fears were most powerful amongst the rebels of the border counties, where an earlier history of intense conflict over rents and seigneurial dues reproduced itself in popular anxiety over the role of the gentry in the rebellion. 'We do accept no gentlemen of our council', explained one of the rebels' letters, 'because we be afraid of them as yet'. Such hostilities were fundamental to the scattered but more venomous rebellions of January–March 1537, in which the local gentry were singled out as targets for their perceived betrayal of the Pilgrimage of Grace. One bill circulating in the Leeds area in January 1537 placed a heavy emphasis upon the duplicity of the gentry:

> Commons, keep well your harness
> Trust you no gentlemen,
> Rise all at once.

As in Lincolnshire, the grassroots leadership of rebellion in 1536 had been drawn from 'well-off peasants', 'minor gentlemen', and 'substantial yeomen'. Perhaps most importantly, although the October 1536 rebellion involved all social ranks, it presented itself as a rising of the 'commons'. In the border counties, the rebel host was led by four anonymous 'Captains', one of whom took the name 'Captain Poverty' and was said to represent the 'estate of poverty' or the 'commonalty'. The formulation was similar, if less stark, elsewhere. Encountering a group of rebels near Pontefract, one royal representative asked them why they were armed. They answered that they 'were for the commonwealth', and that if they failed to act 'the common[ali]ty and the church should be destroyed'. Another gentlemen was forcibly reminded both of where the real leadership of the rebellion lay, and of how 'the commons' understood their political role. Caught by a group of rebels in October 1536, the gentleman Henry Sais was ordered to swear the rebel oath to be true to God, the King and the 'true' commons. Answering that he would swear to the first two, one of the rebels retorted 'and not to us?' Sais was then warned 'If ye do not swear thus, to be true to God and to the king and to the commons, thou shalt lose thy head.'[10]

II   Religion and the Language of Popular Politics: the Western Rebellion of 1549

The strong evidence of social conflict in the 1536–7 insurrections acts as a warning against monocausal interpretations of popular politics. Historians have sometimes attempted to distinguish between 'religious' and 'secular' motivations in the Pilgrimage of Grace. 'Secular' issues are seen as relating to economic and social concerns, as though religion existed in a separate realm from the 'material' world.[11] Where religious factors are detected, they are often presented in derogatory terms. Hence, one historian describes the religious faith of the border rebels of 1536–7 as 'rather naive'.[12] Less attention has been given to how religious language and imagery united economic and political complaints into a coherent set of ideas. Similarly, while the Western rebellion of 1549 has been seen as largely 'religious' in its motivation, the risings of the same year in East Anglia and southern England are traditionally seen as expressing 'economic' grievances. But the rebellions of that year resist such secure categorisations. While the Western Rebellion contained important undercurrents of social conflict, so the rebellions in East Anglia and southern England were about much more than simple class conflict.

Like the rebellions of 1536–7, those of 1549 took place against a background of abrupt religious change. In the last years of Henry VIII's reign, partly as a consequence of increasing popular criticism, the Henrician reformation entered its most conservative phase.[13] Upon the accession of the young King Edward VI, however, authority passed into the hands of a Privy Council dominated by the Protector of the monarch, the Duke of Somerset. Like other leading members of the Council, Somerset was an evangelical protestant with a strong interest in social reform. His protectorate was characterised by two reformist impulses: the renewed protestantisation of the English Church; and an attempt to reverse the perceived cruelties of recent social changes. But Somerset and the Church reformers were no twentieth-century liberals. The reform agenda of these 'commonwealthmen' was an authoritarian and, in some respects, a conservative one.[14] This 'commonwealth' programme both overlapped and conflicted with the heterogeneous rebel agendas of 1549.

Between 1547 and 1549, protestant reform gained velocity. In demonstration of the civic virtue and piety of the godly elite, schools, hospitals and charitable institutions were established; chantries were abolished; 'superstitious' images were destroyed; and in 1549 the Archbishop of Canterbury, Thomas Cranmer, oversaw the introduction of a new prayer book, backed by an Act of Uniformity which provided statutory backing for liturgical change. This Edwardian reformation had a far greater parochial impact than the religious changes of 1529–39.[15] But like the Henrician reformation, it was anticipated by the spread of rumour, in which religious reform was often seen in broader, socio-cultural terms. Public opposition to religious reform was most vehement in the West Country. In 1548, a Cornish crowd led by a priest had murdered the leading local advocate of religious reform, William Body. In a smaller prequel to the events of the following year, some 3000 people gathered in western Cornwall to demonstrate their hostility to religious change. Yet on this occasion, neighbouring areas were willing to serve against the rebels, and the demonstrations were eventually suppressed.

A much fuller confrontation occurred in spring 1549, following the introduction of Cranmer's new prayer book.[16] That Easter, armed rebels from across Cornwall established a camp at Bodmin, where the gentleman Humphrey Arundel agreed to act as leader. Priests helped to prepare lists of articles that they would set before the government. By June, the Cornish rebels had besieged Plymouth and marched into Devon. Aided by insurrections within Devon, the rebel force swelled and soon Exeter was also besieged. The besieging rebel host was organised into camps, led by a council comprising three Devon gentlemen, three Cornish gentlemen and three commoners, and further articles were prepared for the attention of the government. Rebel demands included a return to Henrician religious practice until Edward VI reached the age of 24; the inclusion of leading religious conservatives amongst the King's advisors; the limitation of the number of servants whom a gentleman could maintain within his retinue; and the use of former monastic and chantry lands to maintain places where 'devout persons' could pray. Importantly, the demands assumed the permanence of the Henrician reformation, while disavowing further reform.[17] Yet the symbolism of the Western Rebellion bore closer resemblance to the Pilgrimage of Grace in 1536: once again, the 'Five Wounds of Christ' became an emblem of insurrection.

For six weeks, Exeter lay under siege before the arrival of royal forces under Lord Russell. The Mayor had been approached prior to the commencement of the siege and asked to support the rebellion, but had refused. Thereafter, Exeter's magistracy worried over the political loyalties of the City's poor. In this case more than in any other, the politics of provisioning manifest themselves. In his account of the siege of Exeter, the protestant John Hooker emphasised how the City's magistracy prevented internal insurrection through the equal division of food amongst the besieged inhabitants, and by ensuring that the wealthiest citizens were seen to provide substantial gifts of money to the poor as a weekly dole.[18] Hooker reminded his readers what every Tudor and early Stuart magistrate had drummed into him: 'no force is feared, no lawes obeied, no magistrate obeied, nor common societie esteemed, where famine ruleth'. Lessons learnt in peacetime conditions of dearth were therefore applied in wartime conditions of siege.

Lord Russell's royal forces in Somerset finally moved into the rebellious counties in late July 1549. Fighting a series of battles, they lifted the siege of Exeter on 6 August. Following Somerset's relatively lenient instructions for the punishment of the rebel area, Russell executed those leaders who had fallen into his hands, but pardoned rank-and-file rebels. Strengthened by reinforcements fresh from crushing rural insurrection in Oxfordshire and Buckinghamshire, Russell pressed into Cornwall in mid-August. The main rebel force was caught at the village of Sampford Courteney, where terrible slaughter was done upon both sides. The remnants of the rebel forces slipped away through north Devon, only to be driven to ground at Kingweston (Somerset). Summary executions followed, this time including both middle-ranking rebel leaders (including many priests) and ordinary rebels. The main rebel leaders were sent to London for trial and execution.

As with the Pilgrimage of Grace, the presence of some gentry amongst the rebel leadership did not preclude the expression of social antagonism in the rising. Early on in the rebellion, the rebels' reported rallying cry was 'Kill the gentlemen! We will have the Six Articles [the established Henrician liturgy] up again and ceremonies as they were in King Henry VIII's time!' This remark comes from a hostile source, as does the suggestion that the rebels were a 'band of thieves who would have no state of any gentlemen'. But other sources, and a more careful scrutiny of the prejudiced printed histories, also suggest that social conflict was an important stimulant of rebellion. The majority of the Cornish gentry were careful to distance themselves from the rising. In return, like their counterparts of 1536, the rebels took a predictable delight in plundering gentry mansions, and in imprisoning and humiliating those gentlemen and gentlewomen who fell into their hands. B. L. Beer has found that 'the behaviour of the rebels leaves little doubt that the gentry were [their] principal adversaries ... From beginning to end the Western Rebellion found the commons fighting on one side and the leading gentry families on the other'. Helen Speight concurs, finding a 'widespread animosity towards the gentry in Devon'. Following the defeat of the rising, Lord Russell was instructed to inquire into the causes of rebellion. He heard complaint of how the Cornish gentry, 'especially the meaner sort' of the gentry, had 'spoiled' and 'impoverished' the 'whole commons' of Cornwall. The rebel articles produced outside Exeter were heavily scripted by clerical interests, and like other rebel complaints of 1549, present only a partial sense of insurgent politics. But the inclusion of an article critical of the gentry's maintenance of extravagant households suggests that the Western rebels felt as aggrieved by the apparent increase in gentry wealth as other 'commotioners' in that year.[19]

One of the problems faced by the historiography of the Western rebellion has lain in the arbitrary division between religious grievance (the introduction of the prayer book; the dissolution of the chantries) and social complaint (the perceived avarice, arrogance and increased wealth of the gentry). The evidence of rebellion in 1549 and 1536–7 suggests that these categories were rather more fluid than has often been appreciated. John Hooker's account of the origins of the insurrection in Clyst St Mary (Devon) affords us a glimpse of the unifying significance of religious politics for the Western rebels. By the time that Clyst St Mary rose in rebellion, Devon and Cornish rebels had already united at Crediton (Devon) where the first major battle of the Western rising was fought. In the course of this engagement, Crediton was burnt. News of the destruction of Crediton reached Clyst St Mary (about 12 miles distant) on the same holy day that the local esquire Walter Ralegh encountered an old woman of the village. Seeing that she was carrying rosary beads, Ralegh criticised her devotion to the old religion and warned her that the recent passage of the Act of Uniformity meant that 'there was a punishment by law appointed against hir' if she continued to fail in her religious duties to her monarch. Hooker's account places no immediate response into the old woman's mouth; instead, he tells us that, frightened by Ralegh's aggressive enthusiasm for the new religion, she fled into the parish church of Clyst St Mary. A service was at that moment under way, and much of the parish was gathered there. Here, the old women poured out some

> verie hard and unseemlie speeches concerning religion saieing that she was threatned by the gentleman, that except she would leave hir beads, and give over holie bread and holie water, the gentlemen would burne them out of their houses and spoile them.

Enraged by this, a group of parishioners fortified the village and prepared to join the main rebel force.[20]

It seems reasonable to assume that the villagers of Clyst St Mary understood the threat to burn their village within the context of the recent destruction of Crediton. But there was another, less specific, possible interpretation of Ralegh's words. The threat represented by Ralegh's speech to the established religion of the villagers may have been understood as an attack upon the physical and cultural fabric of the parish church itself. That threat came from an aggressive, outside force: a protestant gentleman, backed by a protestant state. We do an injustice to the complex logic of Tudor popular politics if we simply characterise this as a 'religious' complaint and move on. For we have here chanced across an important aspect of the ideology of popular rebellion in Tudor England: the willingness to believe that outside forces intended the 'destruction' of the commons. This fundamental assumption, which identified 'the commons' and their enemies as large, macro-historical forces, seems surprising given the geographical limits of Tudor rebellion. After 1497, the geographical ambition of rebellion was at the best regional in its scale. Risings focused on important regional capitals – Exeter, Lincoln, York, Norwich – from which seemingly passive appeals were produced for the attention of central government. But the sub-national character of rebellion should not blind us to the willingness of plebeians to site their political culture within a larger conceptual and geographical space.

In the 1536–7 rebellions, plebeian rebels had overtly connected the defence of the Church with the defence of the 'commonwealth' and the 'commonality'. The state's increasing fiscal demands were open to being conceived of in religious terms. Rumours and bills posted on to doors in Richmondshire in early 1537 claimed that the Crown intended to introduce heavy duties upon christenings and marriages. If actualised, such taxes represented an attack upon the most vital point at which the Church touched the social world of the commons. As M. L. Bush has recognised, these rumours raised 'the horrendous prospect of the children of the very poor being condemned, by virtue of their parents' poverty, to spend eternity in limbo'. Amongst the rumours which had led to rebellion in Lincolnshire was the claim that 'visytors wuld com and take awaye the church good[s] and put down the churche'. Religious reformation represented an assault upon the material culture of medieval Christendom in which parishioners had invested so much money and meaning. The beneficiaries of that material deprivation appeared to be the very class who seemed to be gaining from the economic changes of the early sixteenth century: 'rich men', gentlemen, merchants, and most despised of all, 'gentry new come up'. The political equivalents of 'gentry new come up' were those men of 'low birth and small reputation' who were felt to have intruded into the monarch's council. The removal of church plate in 1536, the sale of former monastic estates, the dissolution of chantries and the sale of their assets after 1547, were all felt to benefit a vague class of 'rich oppressors' while simultaneously depriving 'the commons' of cultural identity, spiritual salvation and material succour. In the words of the Kendal rebels of 1536, all of this represented 'the utter undoing of the commonwealth'.[21]

Importantly, such anxieties were felt across England, and had a special resonance for those of non-gentle status. This is not to suggest that the Reformation was given a uniformly hostile popular reception. On the contrary, the English Reformation was defined by its uneven geography.[22] Travelling through Colchester (Essex) in December 1536, for example, one Yorkshireman was asked: 'How do the traitors in the north?' to which he retorted 'No traitors, if ye call us traitors we will call you heretics'.[23] Broadly speaking, protestantism found a warmer reception within East Anglian and southern towns than in the Yorkshire Dales or the northern border counties, where monastic houses represented such an important economic and cultural force. But that did not mean that the population of East Anglia and the south was uniformly welcoming of protestantism; or that the attitude of committed protestants to religious change was not coloured by the perception that the Henrician and Edwardian reformations implied the 'oppression' of 'the commons'.

Like the 'commonwealth' writers who influenced Protector Somerset's domestic policies, the surviving complaints of the Norfolk rebels assembled on Mousehold Heath anticipated a more active, godly Church.[24] Historians often contrast the protestantism of Kett's rebellion with the religious conservatism of the Pilgrimage of Grace or the Western rebels of 1549. But while the conclusions reached by the authors of the Norfolk commons' complaints differed from those of the Western rebels, both implied a critique of the Henrician reformation. Other sources indicate that the gap between the Western rebels and those in East Anglia was less wide than has traditionally been assumed. Prosecutions of former rebels for seditious speech at the Norwich Mayor's Court and the City Quarter Sessions, for instance, suggest that plebeian dissidents resented the sale of former monastic and chantry lands to the 'rich men'. This sense that the 'rich churles' were 'thieves' who had stolen both common land and church goods helped to define the contradictory politics of the 'commotions' in East Anglia.[25]

III   Kett's Rebellion and the 'Commotion Tyme' of 1549

The 1549 rebellions represented the largest and most sustained popular challenge to the authority of the English gentry and nobility during the early modern period. Although twentieth-century historiography has tended to focus upon the rebellion in central Norfolk and Norwich led by Robert Kett, contemporaries were well aware of the widespread geography of disturbances in the spring and summer of that year.[26] Contemporary accounts differ as to whether the rebellions had their origins in Somerset, Hertfordshire or Kent.[27] Trouble had been brewing since the spring of 1548, as anti-enclosure riots were triggered by rumours that Protector Somerset's reformist government would establish a commission to remove recent enclosures. In June 1548, the anticipated government proclamation establishing an enclosure commission was issued. This both reiterated the widely held view of enclosure as a moral evil and assumed that the commons and the government had a mutual interest in its suppression. Local commissioners were required to solicit information concerning enclosures and to see that 'covetous' enclosers were punished.[28] Official anti-enclosure rhetoric therefore dovetailed with popular perceptions of agrarian change.

In retrospect, it seemed to John Hales, who headed the 1548 midlands enclosure commission, that trouble in that year had first started at Cheshunt and Northall (Hertfordshire), prior to the announcement of the Commission. In the spate of large-scale rioting that followed in 1549:

> the first rysinge...was in Somersetshire, From Somersetshire it entred into Gloucettershire, wylshire, hampshire, Sussex, Surrey, worcestershire, Essex, hertfordshire and dyvers other places.[29]

In some cases, rioters claimed that they were enforcing official anti-enclosure policies. Protector Somerset did not welcome such popular intrusions upon governmental authority. On 21 August 1548, he wrote to John Hales in Buckinghamshire, complaining of how Hales' enthusiasm for the removal of enclosures had stirred the commons into a 'marvellous trade of boldness', some of the commons saying that 'if other remedy be not presently had... for the reducing of farms and copyholds to the wonted state, there shall not fail among themselves by a common assent the reformation thereof to be attempted'. The Protector recognised the link that was forming between the defence of common land and the reassertion of the old religion when on 11 June 1549 he wrote of how:

> In most parts lewd men have attempted to assemble and, seeking redress of enclosures, have in some places, by seditious priests and

other evil people, sought restitution of the old bloody laws, and some have fallen to spoil.

That in Oxfordshire and Buckinghamshire, priests should be prominent in the leadership of anti-enclosure riots in 1549 seemed to confirm that the rebellions were about more than agrarian discontent.[30]

By the late spring of 1549, disorder was widespread south of the Trent. Crowds of rebels said to number hundreds or thousands knocked down recent enclosures. The houses of unpopular gentry were plundered; wine cellars were emptied; estate archives selectively cleared of documents that prejudiced tenants' rights; deer parks were denuded by mass poaching. A letter of 25 May 1549 written by the gentleman John Paston to the Earl of Rutland gives some sense of the scale of rebellion, the character of popular grievances and the elite anxieties that it provoked. Paston reported the news in London: that 'a grete number of the commonse' were 'uppe abowte Salyssebery in Wylleshere'. The fences of deer parks had been pulled down and enclosures destroyed, but they had done no 'harme' to any of the gentry.

> Thay saye thay wylle obaye the Kynges maj[e]st[i]e and my lord Protector with alle the counselle, but thay saye thaye will not have ther commonse and their growndes to be inclosyd and soo taken from them . . . Ther is noyther gentylle man nor yet a man of any substaunse as forfurthe as I can lerne amoynge them.[31]

The most discriminating analysis of the 1549 rebellions has come from Diarmaid MacCulloch. He has shown that there were two 'distinct phases' to the pattern of insurrection in that year. The first phase, in the spring, represented a continuation of the earlier troubles of 1548. The second phase was precipitated by Somerset's fatal decision to issue a second enclosure commission on 8 July 1549. This was responsible for the spread of insurrection into East Anglia.[32] By then, the leading gentry of the region had been called away to Windsor, probably to discuss the Crown's response to rebellions elsewhere in the country. The first rebel camps within East Anglia were formed in western Suffolk, possibly by late May. By July, rebel camps had been established in Norfolk at King's Lynn, Downham Market, Norwich and Hingham, and in Suffolk at Ipswich, Melton and Bury St Edmunds. In Essex, there may well have been a camp at Colchester. Urban insurrections failed in Cambridge and Yarmouth.[33] By mid-July 1549, therefore, the camps had effectively closed off East Anglia to the reach of central government. It was from these camps, rather than from the name of Robert Kett, that the rebels took their name: the 'camp men'. And for a generation, the East Anglian rebellions were remembered as the 'camping tyme' or the 'commotion tyme' rather than as 'Kett's rebellion'.[34]

The names of Robert and William Kett do not enter our narrative until early July 1549, when open rebellion began near the Norfolk market town of Wymondham.[35] In Norfolk, as elsewhere, festivity provided a cover for insurrection. Between the sixth and the eighth of July, a crowd gathered at Wymondham for the traditional holiday and plays associated with the dissolved Abbey. According to the later published histories of the rebellion, in the course of these celebrations crowds marched out of the town to knock down recent enclosures. Robert Kett, a prosperous yeoman farmer and tanner whose wealth placed him on the borders of the gentry, was responsible for some of the enclosures. Kett agreed with the rioters that his enclosures should be removed, and offered to lead them (according to Woods' 1615 translation of the 1575 history of the rebellion) in an attempt to 'subdue the power of Great men'.[36] As Holinshed's *Chronicles* took up the story:

> Hereupon was Ket chosen to be their capteine and ringleader, who being resolved to set all on six and seven, willed them to be of good comfort, and to follow him in defense of their common libertie, being readie in the common-welths cause to hazard both life and goods.[37]

Marching on Norwich, the Wymondham rebels were joined by contingents from other villages. On their way, they destroyed enclosures, captured and humiliated unpopular gentlemen, and plundered mansions for food and weapons. The growing rebel host reached the outskirts of Norwich on 10 July, where what Woods called 'the scum of the City' greeted them. Like Colchester, Yarmouth and Cambridge, mid-sixteenth-century Norwich was a city divided against itself, riven by social and religious conflicts between a wealthy merchant class and a poor 'commonality'. In particular, the recent partial enclosure of the City's common fields had divided rich from poor. In Woods' account, the poor of Norwich joined with Kett's rural rebels in the destruction of the enclosures upon the City's commons:

> complaynting that they were common pastures (as they were indeed) and that they would not suffer any longer common pasture to be

inclosed, and were carried with so blind rage from all judgement and reason: as that which (by the providence and industry of their betters) was inclosed to common profit, they would pull downe with their owne hands.[38]

Kett asked permission from the Mayor of Norwich to march through the City to Mousehold Heath, a large expanse of moor on the eastern edge of Norwich, which in 1381 had been the site of an earlier rebel encampment. When the Mayor refused, the rebel host bypassed the City, arriving at Mousehold on 12 July. Here, a council was established, comprising a representative of each Norfolk and Suffolk Hundred from which the rebellion was drawn. Sitting under an oak tree – later to become known as the 'Oak of Reformation' – the council issued warrants as 'the king's friends and deputies' to assemble food, cattle, weapons and people at Mousehold Heath.[39] Captive gentry were imprisoned in Surrey Place, the former mansion of the recently executed Earl of Surrey. This stood on the edge of Mousehold Heath and offered commanding views over Norwich. Ensconced upon a powerful defensive position, Kett began negotiations with Protector Somerset's government.

Up until this point, the course of the rebellion within central Norfolk and Norwich had followed a similar pattern to elsewhere. MacCulloch has argued that the speed with which the Wymondham riots turned into a large-scale insurrection, combined with the outbreak of rebellion elsewhere in Essex, Norfolk, Cambridgeshire and Suffolk at the same time, is suggestive of 'co-ordinated planning throughout the [East Anglian] region'.[40] There can be no doubt that attacks on gentlemen and the formation of camps were widespread across East Anglia in July 1549. Rebellion within and beyond the region tended to take similar forms. Well-ordered camps were established alongside important urban centres, maintained by parish subscriptions and supplied with food from the nearby villages. Life in the camps was far from the anarchic carnival imagined in later chronicle accounts, but rather reflected the orderly politics of village elites. The camps were led by wealthier villagers and townsmen, whose interests dominated the complaints that were submitted to Somerset's government. The precise nature of complaints varied from one camp to another. MacCulloch suggests, for instance, that the articles issued from the Mousehold camp downplayed the enclosure of common land in favour of other agrarian complaints, such as the overstocking of commons by lords and the increase of rents. This was because large parts of Norfolk were already enclosed by 1549, and conflict had shifted instead to the lords' imposition of sheep flocks on to the enclosed fields of tenants. The enclosure riots that occurred in the course of Kett's rebellion, MacCulloch argues, all took place in the wood-pasture parts of the county, where enclosure remained a hot issue.[41] Such local variations in the nature of rebel complaints once again remind us of intense localism of popular political cultures. Yet the insurrections in the south and the east followed similar patterns, were directed against similar enemies, were defined in similar language, and articulated their complaints to the same person: Protector Somerset.

Thanks to his military difficulties elsewhere, and perhaps also influenced by a sympathy for the rebel demands, over the course of July 1549 the Duke of Somerset was drawn into comprehensive negotiations with the southern and eastern rebels. Royal heralds, local gentry and enclosure commissioners carried letters between the Protector and the leaders of rebel camps at Mousehold Heath and Thetford in Norfolk, St Albans in Hertfordshire and unspecified camps in Oxfordshire, Essex, Hampshire and Suffolk. It was in the course of this correspondence that the rebels drew up their lists of complaints, of which only the articles from Kett's camp at Mousehold Heath have survived.[42] A close analysis of Somerset's correspondence has recently allowed Ethan Shagan to conduct a radical reassessment of the mid-Tudor polity. In Shagan's analysis, this held a far greater potential for a 'dynamic interplay between rulers and ruled' than historians had hitherto supposed. For Shagan, the concentration of Tudor political historians upon administration, dynastic politics and court faction has blinded them to the 'extraordinarily promiscuous relationship between "popular" and "elite" politics' in 1549. Somerset emerges from Shagan's analysis as a tragic figure, caught between the active politics of a rebellious commons, the guarded hostility of the gentry and nobility, and his own authoritarian reform agenda. Somerset's letters therefore illuminate both his personal dilemma and the wider fault-lines running through the mid-Tudor polity. Most obviously, the style of the letters conflicts with their content and context. In his letter to the Norfolk rebels, for instance, Somerset compares them to 'inferiors to brute beastes'. Yet in defiance of the dominant norms of social authoritarianism, the correspondence shows both the government and the rebellious commoners tailoring their demands and arguments to meet the other's perceived interests.

In his earliest letters to the rebels, Somerset assumed that they were led by 'naughtie papist priests'. On receiving extravagant declarations of the Essex and Norfolk rebels' protestantism, the Protector expressed scepticism. Yet in spite of Somerset's reluctance to see the rebels as protestants, Shagan shows how the rebels 'internalised' the language of Lutheran protestantism 'and turned it back on the government, ostentatiously using the new Prayer Book [which had provoked such trouble in the West Country] and loudly proclaiming the Gospel as a way of legitimating their social and economic grievances'. In Shagan's analysis, Somerset 'came dangerously close to envisaging a political partnership between government and commons'. In a key concession, the commons were to appoint representatives who would present a 'bill' of their complaints to Parliament. Equally important, Somerset stated that the commons were to appoint enclosure commissioners in their local areas. Under the force of his declarations of 1548 and 1549, these plebeian commissioners would be authorised to remove recent enclosures. Effectively, this amounted to the exclusion of the noble and gentle power brokers through whom Tudor monarchs had previously governed, and the construction of a populist alliance between Crown and commons.[43] As such, it also provides a quite different context to the rebels' willingness to identify themselves as the 'king's friends and deputies' and the gentry as the 'traitors'.

Taking the rebel articles together with the records of Somerset's correspondence allows us some insight into the stated politics of the rebel leadership. As in earlier Tudor rebellions, that leadership came from those just below gentle status: those bailiffs, headboroughs and constables who were singled out in a Privy Council proclamation of 22 July 1549 as 'the very ringleaders and procurers' of the risings.[44] The surviving Mousehold articles seem to have been hurriedly composed, and comprise something of a random shopping-list of demands. Yet in spite of the articles' appearance, a strong logic underlay them. Fundamentally, the demands drawn up at the Mousehold camp articulated a desire to limit the power of the gentry, exclude them from the world of the village, constrain rapid economic change, prevent the over-exploitation of communal resources, and remodel the values of the clergy. Summarising the rebels' overall logic, MacCulloch concludes that they 'sought to exclude the gentry and the clergy from their world; they wished to recapture an imaginary past in which society consisted of watertight compartments, each with its own functions and each interfering as little as possible with the others'. Yet as MacCulloch points out, 'It would have been a very tidy world, too tidy for the rebels' ultimate comfort, for the articles were heavy with disapproval of social mobility in any direction.'[45] Like the articles of the Essex rebels, which have not survived but which are strongly hinted at in Somerset's correspondence, the Mousehold complaints echoed Somerset's religious radicalism. They wished to see the clergy adopt an educative, preaching ministry and to withdraw from speculation in land. While the demands assumed the continued existence of a limited seigneurialism, lords were to be excluded from common land and prevented from dealing in land. The Crown was asked to take over some of the powers exercised by lords, and to act as a neutral arbiter between lord and commoner. Rents were to be fixed at their 1485 level. In the most evocative phrase of the Norfolk complaints, the rebels required that the servile bondmen who still performed humiliating services upon the estates of the Duchy of Lancaster and the former estates of the Duke of Norfolk be freed: 'We pray thatt all bonde men may be made Fre[e] for god made all Fre[e] with his precious blode sheddyng'. The language of economic complaint might never have been less materialistic, nor more imbued with moral and religious implication.

Rebellion, then, was a means of opening a dialogue. Over July 1549, Somerset's representatives travelled across southern and eastern England, carrying offers of pardon as bargaining chips in negotiations with the rebels. Somerset heard growing complaint from other privy councillors against his appeasement of the rebels. Sir William Paget wrote to the Protector on 7 July to recommend a Henrician policy of repression:

> The law is almost nowhere used: the commons are become king. You should have followed the first stir hotly and used justice to the terror of others, and then granted a pardon . . . follow the example of others, of Henry VIII. He kept his subjects in obedience by the maintenance of justice. Force is necessary.

Reliving the early modern gentry's darkest nightmare, it seemed to Paget that England was experiencing its own version of the German Peasants' War of 1525:

> In Germany, when similar trouble began, it might have been appeased with the loss of twenty men, or afterwards of one or two hundred. But it was thought nothing . . . by allowing the matter to run so far it cost one or two thousand lives.[46]

Negotiation was therefore combined with intimidation. Military forces were sent to strengthen Lord Russell in the West Country. Lord Grey was dispatched into Oxfordshire with 1500 men to quell rebellion there, leading to an anonymous but bloody engagement somewhere in the county at which the rebels were run to ground. The King noted in his journal of how Lord Grey, 'coming with th[e] assembling of the gentlemen of the countrie, did so abash the rebels, that more than hauf of them rann ther wayes, and other that tarried were some slain, some taken, and some hanged'.[47] And the Marquis of Northampton was sent into East Anglia at the head of a small royal host of 1500. It seems that his purpose was to overawe would-be rebels, rather than to force combat. The progress of Northampton's force was smoothed through Essex and Suffolk by the success of prior negotiations with the local rebels, who had been granted pardons in return for consideration of their grievances. In Norfolk, however, the rebels were less willing to disarm.

The arrival of a royal herald at Kett's camp on Mousehold Heath on 21 July proved to be the moment at which negotiation turned into open warfare in East Anglia. The herald carried with him terms for a general pardon, which he read aloud at the Oak of Reformation. According to the later histories, some of the rebels fell to their knees and accepted this pardon, but Robert Kett refused, saying that they had offended no laws and required no pardon. The herald then denounced Kett as a traitor. The fiction of royal sanction having been exposed, the Norwich authorities closed the City to the rebels. The rebels stormed Norwich on the following day. Opposition was no more than symbolic and the City passed easily into rebel control. The mayor was seized and forced to set his name to Kett's demands, while other leading aldermen were imprisoned with the gentry captives in Surrey Place. By the time that Northampton's army arrived at the gates of Norwich on 31 July, the Mousehold rebels had therefore already distinguished themselves from 'commotioners' elsewhere by their refusal of the royal pardon and by having stormed the second largest city in the realm.

The story of the ensuing battles can be told in brief. Northampton's force gained easy access to the undefended City. That night, the rebels launched heavy attacks. In the morning, Kett's main host attacked. In confused fighting, Northampton's second-in-command, Lord Sheffield, was killed and the royal force was routed. In spite of this victory, over the next three weeks of August the Mousehold rebels were progressively isolated. The camp at Thetford broke up, while that near King's Lynn was suppressed, apparently with heavy losses. Two rebel attempts to seize Great Yarmouth ended in failure. The Essex and Ipswich rebels had dispersed following the grant of pardons. With the defeat of insurrections in Cambridge, Yarmouth and Lynn, by mid-August the camp on Mousehold Heath was left isolated. Meanwhile, a considerably larger force of perhaps 14 000 men, including a substantial force of mounted gentlemen and mercenaries, had been assembled under the leadership of the Earl of Warwick.

Warwick's army arrived at Norwich on 23 August. A herald, offering pardons to such rebels as were willing to disarm, preceded its entry into the City. According to Woods' 1615 history of the rebellion, some rebels flung down their arms and declared their loyalty to the King. Others denounced the herald as a traitor and cried:

> that pardon in appearance seemed good & liberall, but in truth would prove in the ende lamentable & deadly, as that which would be nothing else but Barrels filled with Ropes and Halters.

One final act of rebel contempt closed the negotiations:

> It happened that, before [the herald] had made an end of his speech, that an ungracious boy, putting down his breeches, shewed his bare buttockes & did a filthy act: adding thereunto more filthy words.

This so enraged one of the soldiers accompanying the herald that he killed the boy. Taking this as confirmation of the royal forces' treachery, a crowd of rebels raced about Robert Kett, holding his horse's bridle and preventing him from crossing into royal lines: for Kett had been 'minded to have spoken with Warwicke, face to face'.[48] So ended the last attempt at negotiations.

Three days of intense fighting commenced within the narrow streets of Norwich. On the evening of 25 August, Warwick came close to acknowledging defeat. But the arrival of fresh mercenary forces on 26 August tilted the balance. On the following day, with their supply lines to the countryside cut, the Mousehold rebels took heart in the passage of a prophecy amongst their ranks, which seemed to speak of the victory of the rural commons:

> The country grooffes, Hob, Dick and Hick
> With clubbes, and clouted shoon,
> Shall fill up Dussyndale
> With slaughtered bodies soone.

Dussindale is a low, flat valley lying a couple of miles south of Mousehold Heath. Unlike Mousehold, which was rugged and steep, Dussindale was perfect terrain for Warwick's cavalry. Having heard the Earl of Warwick's call to 'repute and take the company of Rebels which they saw, not for men, but bruite beasts', the mercenaries and mounted gentry broke the rebel lines. Another popular rebellion ended, therefore, with the physical assertion of elite superiority, as mounted gentlemen rode down their defeated social inferiors like 'wild beasts'.[49]

Kett escaped the general slaughter, only to be captured the following day. The histories of the rebellion are unanimous that great slaughter was done at Dussindale. During the initial pursuit, Warwick granted a pardon to those rebels who surrendered. But thereafter, a steady stream of executions followed in the wake of rebel defeat.[50] Robert and William Kett were removed to London to stand trial for treason at the King's Bench. As we saw in Chapter 2, they stood accused of intending the destruction of all gentlemen. Meanwhile, in a palace coup in October 1549, the victorious Earl of Warwick toppled the Duke of Somerset. In December, the Kett brothers were returned to Norfolk for their execution. William was hanged from the tower of Wymondham Abbey and Robert was hanged in chains from the wall of Norwich Castle. His body was visible from the City's marketplace, 'and there hanged for a continuall memory of so great villainie untill that unhappy and heavy body through putrifaction consuming . . . [fell] downe at length', as Woods gloated in 1615.[51]

The postscript to Kett's rebellion has a special significance for the conceptual relationship between the historiography of mid-Tudor politics and the practice of early modern social history. Conventionally, the fall of Protector Somerset in October 1549 is seen as the result of Somerset's progressive alienation of every major interest group within the closed 'political nation' of mid-Tudor England. There is much truth in this analysis. As we have seen, elite support for the Protector was ebbing away in July 1549, and with Warwick's defeat of the Norfolk rebels and his return to London, it was only a matter of time before Somerset was pushed aside. But that story misses an important dimension of mid-sixteenth-century politics. The rebellious commons, having kicked their way into the halls of government, wished to claim squatters' rights. Hearing of Warwick's coup, Somerset sent messages into the country for support. As a result, some four thousand 'peasants' gathered before Somerset and offered to die in his cause. Anonymous bills circulated, denouncing Warwick's supporters as intending 'the utter undoing of the commons' and naming 'lords and gentlemen and sheep-masters' as the enemies of the King, the Protector and 'the poor commonalty of England'. In the event, Somerset declined the bizarre opportunity to lead a state-sponsored popular insurrection against his own class.[52] Thereafter, political power passed to the Earl of Warwick, who was further dignified with the grant of the title Duke of Northumberland. Over 1550 and 1551, Northumberland's Privy Council continued to hear news of threatened insurrections and large gatherings of the rural commons, while jittery urban magistrates inquired into seditious speech given out in streets, alehouses and doorways about the 'treachery' of the 'rich men'.[53]

In 1553, Edward VI died suddenly. The succession of the catholic Princess Mary to the throne, over the Duke of Northumberland's protestant candidate Lady Jane Grey, has long been the stuff of standard, elite-centred political history. But once again, political division amongst the elite created new opportunities for popular politics. In Suffolk, where following Northumberland's coup some of the leaders of the 1549 rebellions had been executed, popular support for Mary's bid for the throne was strong. When the protestant gentry of the county announced their support for Queen Jane, it was the 'common people' who objected 'with murmers of discontent and great indignation'. In Great Yarmouth (Norfolk), the commons had their revenge upon the protestant merchant elite of the town, and were enthusiastic in their support of Mary. Even overt protestant opinion in East Anglia was consistently pro-Mary, so powerful was 'the memory of Northumberland's commanding role in the destruction of the Mousehold camp four years earlier'. This time, popular support for Northumberland's opponent proved decisive, and culminated in the Duke's execution as a traitor. It was bitter social antagonism, not religious loyalty, which brought the East Anglian commons out to support Mary Tudor's bid for the throne.[54]

IV   State Formation and the End of Rebellion in Elizabethan England

The great French medieval historian Marc Bloch once observed that 'agrarian revolt is as natural to the seigneurial regime as strikes, let us say, are to large-scale capitalism'.[55] The historian of popular politics might disagree. Large-scale capitalism seemed dominant in late-twentieth-century Britain; yet strikes were at a post-war low. Similarly, although it was changing in its form, seigneurial authority seemed secure within much of Elizabethan and early Stuart England; yet popular rebellion and large-scale riot diminished. If we are to explain such radical discontinuities in patterns of social conflict and popular politics, we have to avoid the temptation to see 'objective' conditions of exploitation as leading inevitably to resistance and rebellion. Rather than being spontaneously generated by the opposition of material interests, popular politics depends instead upon a collective sense of agency consciously fostered within communities of common interest. Where that community is undermined from within or successfully assaulted from without, popular politics can fail and die. That was surely the experience of many trade unionists and socialists in Britain after 1979, and it seemed also to have been true of the tradition of open popular rebellion in later Tudor England.

The central irony of the history of the 1549 rebellions is that so many of the rebel leaders were beneficiaries of the very economic changes that the rebellions sought to prevent. After 1549, that contradiction became less stark, as the successors of Robert Kett placed an increasing distance between themselves and the rural poor. We shall seen in Chapter 3, Sections I and II how the changing geographical pattern of enclosure rioting after the middle of the sixteenth century can be related to larger social, cultural, political and economic changes in southern and eastern England. As wealthier villagers and townsfolk, hitherto the traditional leaders of popular rebellion, gradually removed themselves from the articulation and organisation of protest, large-scale, open riot diminished and poorer plebeians lost public political agency.

Social change in the later sixteenth century also helped to undermine the capacity of the gentry and nobility to organise effective armed rebellion against the Crown. Tudor nobles often imagined themselves as independent-minded, baronial figures. Some landed themselves in hot water as a result of loose speech concerning the strong local loyalty which they believed was owed to them by 'those within [their] rule', by which they meant 'gentlemen in [their] country . . . honest and wealthy yeomen who were ringleaders in good towns . . . tenants and servants.'[56] Yet the record of noble revolt in Tudor England was rather more dismal than such words suggest. Rebellious nobles who relied upon appeals to social hierarchy or who assumed automatic deference from their tenants typically recruited few followers even in the early days of their insurrections. The rebellion of the Northern Earls in 1569 is the most outstanding example of this more general phenomenon.

Following a summer of rumours, in early November 1569 the catholic Earls of Westmorland and Northumberland rose against the Elizabethan regime. Parroting the habitual cry of Tudor rebellion – that they were 'the Queens most trewe and lawful subjects' who only intended to preserve the monarch from her evil advisors – the Earls' proclamations emphasised religious and social conservatism. Hence, the re-established moderate protestantism of the English Church was 'a new found religion and heresie'; the Earls were risen in defence of 'the auncyent and Catholicke faythe' and the 'ancyent customes and usages before used'; the Privy Council was dominated by 'diverse new set upp nobles about the Quenes Majestie'.[57] The Earls quickly gathered a force composed of their tenants, servants and dependent gentry, supplemented by men hired for money. Over the course of November, Durham passed into their hands, together with the borders and much of the north-east. Parts of the North and West Ridings of Yorkshire also mustered for the Earls, although York remained loyal, where the Earl of Sussex gathered a royal army. Yet by mid-December, disappointed by the insignificant forces they had recruited and intimidated by the prospect of moving south, the Earls had disbanded most of their forces and retreated into Scotland. Intermittent border skirmishing continued into February 1570, but any chance of maintaining any significant insurrection within England had been lost.

More impressive than the Earls' military activities was the scale of the subsequent repression. The surviving records are unreliable, but executions certainly ran into the hundreds. Sir George Bowes, for instance, wrote on 23 January 1570 that 'six hundreth and odd' had been executed around the North Riding:

> so that now the auctors of thys rebellyon ys curssed of every syde; and sure the people [are] in marvelous feare, so that I trust there shall never suche thing happen in these partes agayne.

Twelve days later, Sir Thomas Gargrave suggested 'ther ys by marcyall lawe alredy executyd, above 500 of the poore sorte'. The intended targets of repression speak volumes about the social organisation of Tudor rebellion. On 28 December 1569, the Earl of Sussex wrote to the Secretary of State, Sir William Cecil, to inform him that he meant:

> to passe to Durham, here I intend to remayne some dayes, to take order for such of the comon people as shal be exequuted by the

martial law; emongs whom, I meane to exequut specially, constables and other officers, that have seduced the people (under colour of the Quenes Majesties service) to rebell ... ther shal be no towne that hath sent men to the rebells, or otherwise ayded them, but some of the worst disposed shal be exequuted for example: the number wherof is yet uncerten, for that I know not the number of townes, but I gesse it will not be under vi or vii hundred, at the least.

At least in part, the Tudor state operated through repression, intimidation, display and example. Yet Sussex's choice of victims also suggests how far both successful rebellion and successful government depended upon securing the loyalties of the same people: those 'constables and other officers' who in December 1569 seemed to Sussex to have 'seduced the people', but who in more normal conditions Sir Thomas Smith knew were not 'altogether neglected' by the state, but rather held such local office as 'toucheth ... the common wealth'.[58] Just how closely such village officers touched upon the state was only fully revealed at those moments at which state structures cracked open.

The Northern Earls' rebellion of 1569 therefore highlights a number of issues fundamental to the study of early modern popular politics. First, it further substantiates the argument made in Chapter 1: that the historian must constantly differentiate between how the state was represented, and how it actually functioned. Immersed in the clichés of authoritarian social theory, the gentry might persuade themselves that the early modern state was a closed entity, locked and barred against popular participation. But the loyalty of those wealthier plebeians whom Sir Thomas Smith 'exempted out of ... the rascabilitie of the popular' remained central to its operation. Secondly, Tudor government was rather more open to popular politics than its outward appearance suggested. One of the government's main sources of information about the Earls' movements over the winter of 1569–70 was the loyal protestant gentleman Sir George Bowes. His correspondence with Cecil and the Earl of Sussex indicates how important the control of information was to both the government and the rebel leaders. Like Protector Somerset in October 1549, the Northern Earls sought to appeal to a much wider political nation than their social conservatism would suggest. They did so by open appeal to popular opinion through the written and verbal declarations cited above. Prior to their rebellion, they had been accused of spreading 'bruts and rumours' against the Crown. Similarly, early modern government operated through influencing, regulating and controlling popular politics. In spite of outward statements of contempt about the irrationality of the *plebs*, individuals like Bowes were pre-eminently concerned with the content of popular politics.

Sir George Bowes' temporary proximity to popular opinion meant that it was not long before he deduced how completely the Northern Earls had failed in their attempt to access popular politics. He wrote on the 17th November of how 'the matter groweth very hot, and sure in my opinion requireth to be expedited; as what with feare, of faire speche, or moneye, they [the Earls] drawe awaye the harts of the people.' In their attempt to gather and maintain an army, coercion and cash were rapidly becoming as important to the Earls as their appeals to the old religion and ancient custom. In the same letter, Bowes observed how 'Masse was yesterday at Darnton; and John Swinburn [one of the Earls' officers], with a staffe, drove before him the poore folks, to hasten them to hear the same'. In particular, the Earls had difficulty recruiting volunteer footsoldiers. Such men, it is important to bear in mind, tended to come from the lower ranks of society. Like Charles I after them, there was therefore a sociological significance to the fact that the core of the Earls' force comprised a body of mounted men. Most of the rebels' infantry were hired for money or had been forcibly pressed into service, and had little stomach for the rebellion. As Bowes reported on the following day: 'The Erles be this night at Rippon, and ther horsemen be somewhat increased; but ther pore rascall fotmen, that for feare, come slowly on the one day, go away a pace willingly on the other.' By 20 November, Sussex could reassure Cecil that 'The Earles, as you wryte, be oulde in bloude, but poore in force'.[59]

One very powerful reason for the failure of the rebellion of the Northern Earls concerned the changing structure of northern society. Mervyn James and Lawrence Stone have both argued that as an aggressive fiscal seigneurialism was unleashed upon northern tenants, long-established feudal bonds were loosened.[60] In their accounts, a more individualist, commercial, 'modern' society ultimately emerged from the ruins of a 'traditional' social structure. For James in particular, this earlier world had been bonded by customary values accepted by lords and commoners alike. The central state and the law courts had hitherto been distant from this 'lineage society'. Before seigneurial relations had been loosened by the neutral hand of central equity courts, neo-feudal ties remained strong, such that 'dependants proffered their "faithful" service; while lordship was . . . "good lordship", involving restraint in the claims made on inferiors, and the provision of "favours" and maintenance in return

for service'. The peculiar conditions of the border counties and Yorkshire, where very large, composite estates had been ruled by the same
powerful families for generations, produced a heavy emphasis upon the
authority of the ancient nobility, and an exaggerated concern for deference and social stasis. This was summed up in 1569 in advice offered to
the inheritor of the Dacre title: 'The poor people favour you and your
house, and cry and call for you and your blood to rule them'.[61] I have
some quibbles with this interpretation. In particular, I would prefer to
see elite acceptance of wide popular customary rights (fixed low rents
and fines; extensive common rights; strong tenures and rights of inheritance) during the fifteenth and early sixteenth centuries as indicative of
the relative weakness of seigneurial power at a time of low population
pressure, easy access to resources and a weak state.[62] But Stone's and
James' suggestion that, motivated by a growing profit imperative, after
the early sixteenth century landlords took a new interest in the exploitation of their estates, leading to unusually intense conflict with tenants
and commoners, is strongly borne out by the evidence on many estates.

In 1569, it seems that the northern Earls and their gentry retainers
were fighting to preserve a world that had already been lost. Indeed,
like many powerful social ideals, it may never have existed. That the
rebels of 1536 had forced captive gentry into a leadership role still
speaks volumes about the tactics and rituals of early Tudor popular
politics, of course. But we have also seen that in the rebellions of 1536-7,
as in the smaller rural insurrections that had immediately preceded
them, the tenants of the border counties had exhibited a deep hostility to
their landlords. That hostility had been founded upon conflicts over
custom and tenurial rights which, decades before the 1569 rebellions,
were setting lord and tenant against one another. The Northern Earls'
temporary military strength at the beginning of their rebellion seems to
have been bought with cash rather than earned from paternalism. Sir
George Bowes had similar difficulty in raising a loyal force in Yorkshire,
complaining to the Earl of Sussex that 'the contreth of Yorkshire never
goeth to war but for wages'.[63]

The authority of the great lords of the north was replaced by the
growing significance of lesser gentlemen. The retainers of the great
families of the north were undermining the large lordships from within,
such that (according to testimony of 1569) 'the tenants ... stand not so
much in feare of his lordshipe and his officers as of other gentlemen ther
neighbours'. Social change combined with legal and cultural shifts to
dissolve the authority of the old great houses of the north. According to

Mervyn James, the growing force of the law, coupled with the increasing autonomy of notions of custom with local plebeian culture, smoothed 'the penetration of the common-law way of thinking into remote northern countrysides, and the conferment as a result of rights on those whose posture had previously been solely one of submission'.[64] Again, I would argue with James' periodisation of this legal/cultural shift: the insurrections in the north in the 1534–7 period had seen plebeians making powerful appeals to custom, commonwealth and the law in criticism of the actions of both the Crown and the gentry. But the fundamental point remains a strong one: tenant deference, never to be easily assumed, was in retreat before a peculiar (and accidental) coincidence of social change, popular assertion, fiscal seigneurialism and state formation. These forces were in creative friction with one another, and found their clearest expression in an increased recourse to central law courts.

During the later sixteenth century, the law came to develop a highly contradictory relationship with popular politics. On the one hand, central courts could operate in the most arbitrary fashion. The early Stuarts used the Westminster courts to marginalise customary rights and to increase rents on their own estates. Moreover, the judges at such courts had been inculcated in the same authoritarian values as the rest of their class. Elite complainants before central courts therefore often exaggerated the 'seditious' intent of rioters, or the 'levelling' character of local custom. But on the other hand, equity courts were expected to conduct themselves according to abstract rules of fairness. The fact that, throughout our period, tenants, commoners and labourers continued to litigate before such courts with some degree of success suggests that this represented more than a simple ideological sleight of hand.

We might, therefore, detect in the operation of the civil law a similar hegemonic logic to that which Douglas Hay has sensed within the early modern criminal law, whereby plebeians were reconciled to the rule of law as a result of its occasional ostentatious fairness. Jim Sharpe has written in a similar vein of how the law became a part of early modern popular culture. I have tried to extend his point, and have argued that the allegedly 'lawless' free mining communities of the Forest of Dean, the Derbyshire Peak Country and the Somerset Mendips defined their local political cultures in relation to the law. Despite the high levels of illiteracy and poverty within such mining villages, early modern free miners were highly litigious and conscious of the law, both in its local, customary form and in terms of its operation at central equity courts. Hence, English free miners formed their collective identities and public politics on the basis of appeals to notions of law, justice, custom and common right.[65] Although those keywords of early modern politics often meant different things to the labourer than to the gentleman, their mutual use of that terminology helped to form a shared political discourse within which an open argument between ruler and ruled could be conducted. Most importantly, central law courts also provided a seemingly neutral public arena within which plebeian complaint could be heard, conflict could occur, and reconciliation might be effected, largely free from dangerous allegations of popular sedition or conspiracy. One unintended consequence of this extension of state authority was to legitimate an already powerful popular legalism. State formation, as Steve Hindle has recently suggested, was therefore closely bound up with popular politics.[66]

The law, then, helped to reshape both popular politics and social conflict. This was a gradual, intermittent and contested process. It had its roots way before our period, and required constant sustenance throughout. Within the north of England in particular, Elizabethan central courts sought to undercut the social basis of noble rebellion. Tenants whose customary rights had been solidly established before central law courts in the face of opposition from their local lord were less likely to follow that lord in rebellion than those who held land according to loose, unspecified customs which could be revoked or manipulated at the lord's pleasure. The certainty of custom had powerful implications for the potential success of noble rebellion. In 1569, it was argued that many of the border tenants had been unwilling to join the Northern Earls' insurrection, since 'their duties and fines being certain . . . they will not be led . . . to rebellion'. In the first years of the seventeenth century, law courts continued to fix rents and fines in the interests of northern tenants. Hence, in 1607, the Judges in Chancery, issuing judgment in a case concerning the Barony of Kendal, recommended that rents should be fixed as the subject had become a running sore between lord and tenant.[67]

Lords responded to the loose alliance of interest that grew between the Elizabethan state and the border tenants by playing upon the dangers of fostering popular freedom. In 1581, the gentry of the northern border counties submitted a petition to the parliament criticising proposed pro-tenant legislation. The bill in question passed into law as the Act for Fortifying the Borders, and provided statutory support to the traditional protection afforded by the Crown to the border custom of tenant right. The Crown had long tried to guarantee strong tenurial rights in return for tenants' military service on the Scottish border. The border gentry's petition claimed that the bill had been inspired 'by the under-sort and tenants', and argued that were the bill to become law, it would encourage the tenants to become assertive, leading ultimately to plebeian rebellion in the spirit of Jack Straw and Wat Tyler.[68] Couched within the language of social authoritarianism, the gentry's case was characteristically overstated, but there was a grain of truth to it. Richard Hoyle has shown how the 'sophisticated and resourceful' Elizabethan border tenants habitually combined riot with litigation, negotiation and petition to defeat or limit their lords' attempts to break their 'ancient and laudable customs'. Although Elizabethan equity courts countenanced partial enclosure and rent increases, they 'accepted as a matter of course the claims of the tenants to have an inheritable tenure'. Importantly, tenants prosecuted their lords at Westminster courts because they felt that local Quarter Sessions juries had been selected by their opponents, and hence were 'hostile to the principles of tenant right and favoured lords against tenants'.[69]

The Elizabethan state did much to remould popular political culture. Lord Hunsdon's oft-quoted report in the aftermath of the 1569 rebellion that the commons of Northumberland 'knew no other Prince but a Percy' was anachronistic even in its own time.[70] Lawrence Stone has claimed that before 1569, the call '"A Percy! A Percy", "A Dacre! A Dacre!"' might be expected to 'evoke a Pavlovian response of unthinking loyalty among the gentry and peasantry of the North'. The evidence suggests, however, that early Tudor tenant deference was always more conditional and considerably more complex than Stone assumed. It is true that in 1536 the commons of Howden had gathered to the cry of 'Thousands for a Percy'; but there was a sharp irony to this. Thomas Percy had been forced to swear allegiance to the rebel cause on pain of his house being plundered. By 1640, the gentry deployed such formulations not in an appeal to popular politics, but in antagonism to that 'many-headed monster'. Following his son's rejection by the insufficiently deferential electorate of Ipswich during the elections to the Long Parliament, the Suffolk gentleman Sir Roger North led a group of truculent gentry through the town, assaulting sailors, whom they disdained as 'water doggs', and calling out 'A North! A North!' Only where the aristocratic name invoked in such cries connected with other political allegiances might the formulation still inspire a favourable response. The Duke of Monmouth was greeted on his landing at Lyme Regis at the start of his rebellion of 1685 by crowds crying out 'A Monmouth! A Monmouth!

The Protestant Religion!'.[71] Monmouth's rebellion was no dynastic rising, or baronial struggle. The Somerset farmers and Taunton weavers who rallied to the 'Protestant Duke' in 1685 did so out of loyalty to a protestant faith which they felt to be in peril, rather than out of any 'Pavlovian' loyalty to the Duke himself.

The roots of that popular protestantism are to be found in the late sixteenth century, and helped to define the changing relationship between the state and popular politics in early modern England. We saw in Chapter 2, Section II how religious language and imagery helped to unite disparate popular complaints in early Tudor England. In particular, criticism of the early Reformation identified the enemies of the Church as the enemies of plebeian community. During the early modern period, the *function* of religion within popular politics remained basically unchanged. As we shall see in Chapter 3, Section IV, the enemies of community continued to be characterised as unchristian, avaricious and individualistic, and to be stereotyped as Old Testament 'oppressors'. But over the course of Queen Elizabeth's reign (1558–1603), the *content* of religious belief underwent partial transformation. By the end of Elizabeth's reign, the moderate protestantism of the established Church was stepping into the hegemonic terrain hitherto occupied by the old religion. By the beginning of the seventeenth century, the twin extremes of puritanism and 'popery' were taken to represent alien threats to popular religious practice. Thus, when Laudian conservatives during the 1620s and 1630s attempted to introduce clearer symbolic distinctions between the minister and the laity, these were denounced as 'popish innovation'. The altar rails imposed within parish churches by Laudian bishops during the 1630s seemed to represent as great a threat to the (fictional) unity of the parish as the Crown-sponsored enclosures of common lands which were also taking place in many parts of England during that decade.

This basic alteration in the religious loyalties of the majority of the English people was initiated during the Elizabethan period. In recent years, historians have understood this fundamental development as a long, contested, process of 'protestantisation', rather than an abrupt shift in religious loyalty imposed from above.[72] This process was uneven in its geography and intensity. Puritans of the early seventeenth century, for instance, were convinced that many of the lower orders of the 'dark corners of the land' remained stubbornly 'popish'. Historians have been more discriminating, and have mapped out a series of local variables that influenced the speed and force of 'protestantisation': did a parish have a 'godly' minister? If not, did it fall into a puritan preaching circuit? Were local elites sympathetic, or antipathetic, to protestantism? How high were literacy levels? What was the pre-Reformation religious history of the area in question? Was the area in question urbanised, or was it remote from main centres of communication? Some historians, as we shall see in Chapter 4, Section III, have even proposed that arable, corn-producing parishes were more religiously conservative than pastoral, industrialised parishes, where a more individualistic approach to religion helped to foster puritanism.

The increasingly sophisticated historiography of popular responses to protestantisation has therefore highlighted the wide variation in regional responses to England's long reformation. But protestantisation had an important national history as well. Especially within the latter half of Queen Elizabeth's reign, protestant propagandists attempted to forge a link between protestantism and national identity. Through public preaching, the sponsorship of works such as Foxe's *Book of Martyrs* and the routine depiction of the link between secular and religious authority, protestant magistrates, ministers and writers attempted to remould popular religious loyalties. The reverse image of the loyal, protestant subject became that of the scheming papist. Although that task was never fully completed, by the early seventeenth century anti-popery had become a defining feature of popular political culture.[73]

In generating a moderate, populist protestantism, the English state laid the basis for a new set of political identities amongst its subjects. For all that they adopted the linguistic conventions of popular deference to the nobility, the collective exclamations that greeted the Duke of Monmouth in 1685 were products of the religious politics of the seventeenth century. The cry 'A Monmouth! A Monmouth!' might seem superficially to reflect an enduring tradition of noble rebellion. But it was the cry that followed – for 'The Protestant Religion!' – that held the greatest power over popular political culture in Stuart England.[74]

3

RIOT AND POPULAR POLITICS IN EARLY MODERN ENGLAND

I   The Geography of Enclosure Riot, *c.* 1509–1625

This chapter addresses the material sources of local-political conflict, dealing in particular with how social change affected popular political culture in early modern England. Chapter 3, Sections I and II describe the shifting chronology and geographical distribution of public, collective opposition to enclosure. In particular, we are concerned with the history of the enclosure riot. Section III focuses upon the changing nature of food rioting over the same period. In order to make comparisons with the earlier period, it strays into the history of food rioting in the 1740s. Finally, Section IV discusses some organising themes in early modern popular political culture: the influence of scripture; notions of community, custom, gender, neighbourhood, rights and duty; and the structuring role played by ritual in the organisation of crowd actions.

Probably the most common cause of riots during the sixteenth and early seventeenth centuries, was the enclosure of common land. Enclosure had a long and complex history of its own.[1] In some regions, especially within the agrarian south and east, much land had already been enclosed before the beginning of the sixteenth century. Many enclosures were uncontroversial and so often went undocumented. Only in a minority of cases did enclosure lead to riot. Enclosure could come from a number of sources. Recently arrived poor migrants might settle upon common land, establish a cabin, and enclose a small part of the surrounding land. In villages that enjoyed extensive commons and weak manorial control, and that were not subject to population pressure,

82

such migrants might be welcomed, and their small transgression upon common land forgotten. In places where such factors were not operative, however, the settlement of poor migrants upon common land was often a fiercely contested issue. This became especially true in the face of rapid population expansion in the later sixteenth century. Reacting in part to such demographic pressure, established villagers might take their own chunk out of the commons. Once again, such individual enclosures often went unopposed; in other circumstances, riot or litigation might result. Other established farmers sometimes resented such small-scale enclosures and were prepared to take action against them; moreover, the village poor frequently saw such infringements upon common land as threatening to their livelihood.

By the late sixteenth century, there was an increasing tendency on the part of established, wealthier farmers to come to collective enclosure agreements, either with one another or with their lord. In such agreements, common land would be divided amongst the landholders. In those enclosures conducted 'with the agreement of the most part of the better sort', the poor were sometimes offered some kind of compensation.[2] Once again, enclosure by agreement amongst landholders often went unopposed. As we shall see, the rural poor did not enjoy the same political agency as their wealthier neighbours, and when faced with the combined power of village landholders, could be intimidated into signing over their common rights. Finally, the lord of the manor sometimes imposed enclosure upon the fractured rural community. In the early sixteenth century, as lords attempted to extend their parkland and to create sheep-runs, an aggressive lord might push inhabitants off common land. By the early seventeenth century, lords were more likely to enclose commons in order to turn the land over to arable use. Seigneurial enclosure frequently faced the combined opposition of the whole village, and therefore remains the best documented. By the middle of the seventeenth century, however, lords were becoming increasingly successful at dividing the social basis of such protest. It became typical for wealthier tenants to be offered compensation for the loss of common rights, while the landless poor, whose common rights were often much harder to sustain at law, gained little or nothing in return.

The enclosure of common land ran alongside the decline of communal systems of agriculture and the marginalisation of other forms of communal entitlement. Customary rights sometimes extended into enclosed, privately held land. In many manors the rural poor claimed the right to glean for scraps of corn for a limited period after the harvest had been taken. Inhabitants might possess a collective right to take firewood or building materials from enclosed woods. In some mining areas, miners claimed a right of free mining, whereby they could dig for minerals on any land, regardless of its ownership. Such customary rights were often whittled away over the course of the sixteenth and seventeenth centuries leaving only a residue of popular entitlements by the early eighteenth century. Yet in spite of the residual nature of customary rights in early Hanoverian England, the intensity of their defence reveals much about the enduring economic and cultural significance of the commons to the rural poor.[3]

In recent years, social historians have grown increasingly sceptical of the value of the large-scale quantification of historical processes. As we saw in the Introduction, social historians have instead turned to the deeply contextualised micro-analysis of power relations and moments of contestation within which the study of language and representation has loomed large. We shall see in Chapter 4, Section IV how the analysis of the rhetorical and organisational forms of protest and rebellion illuminates important aspects of popular political culture. But earlier generations of social and economic historians were happier with quantifying historical phenomena such as riots. In particular, considerable effort has been invested in measuring the chronology and changing geography of food and enclosure rioting. The results of such research, if deployed with sufficient caution and a wider understanding of the context within which riots occurred, allow us to map some aspects of the shifting forms of popular politics and crowd actions in the period between (roughly) the Reformation and the early eighteenth century. Throughout, we address local and regional variations in patterns of riot from a long-term, national perspective.

Roger Manning deployed the records of litigation before the Court of Star Chamber in order to survey national shifts in the distribution and significance of large-scale disorder between 1509 and 1625.[4] Such labours have been paralleled in other studies, in particular of the geography of food riots, with which the next section is concerned.[5] Manning's study of litigation at Star Chamber was heavily orientated towards the prosecution of enclosure riots. The most important patterns he observed concerned the changing geography of enclosure riot; the leadership of enclosure riot; and the size and form of such riots. Surveying the records of the Star Chamber, Manning found that over the reigns of Henry VIII (1509–47) and Edward VI (1547–53), the court of Star Chamber heard some 75 enclosure riot cases from across England. Over the reign of

Elizabeth I (1558–1603), it heard a total of 88 such cases. During the rather shorter period covered by the reign of James I (1603–25), the court heard some 116 cases of English enclosure riot.[6] Most strikingly, Manning found clear evidence of a relocation of rural protest from East Anglia to the north midlands of England. Edwardian and Henrician East Anglians appear to have been much more willing to riot than their Jacobean descendants: Norfolk, Suffolk, Essex and Cambridgeshire accounted for 12 per cent of English enclosure riot cases heard by the Star Chamber during the period 1509–53. In contrast, Manning identified a mere 4 enclosure riot cases (3 per cent of the English total) which led to Star Chamber action within the counties during the reign of James I. If East Anglians were becoming more passive, the inhabitants of the West Midlands were becoming more riotous: 20 per cent of Manning's cases came from Shropshire, Staffordshire, Herefordshire, Worcestershire, Warwickshire and Gloucestershire between 1509 and 1553; the same region contributed some 33 per cent of the total in 1603–25. Elsewhere, geographical dislocations seem less obvious from Manning's figures. His 'southern counties', for instance, made up 20 per cent of the total in 1509–53 and 18 per cent in 1603–25. Similarly, Manning's 'East Midlands' made up 24 per cent in 1509–53 and 22 per cent of English cases in 1603–25.

Manning found that the leaders of Jacobean enclosure riots came from lower social groups than their predecessors. Whereas in the period 1509–53 some 50 per cent of enclosure riot cases heard by the Star Chamber named gentry or nobility as the leaders of riots, in 1603–25 that figure stood at 40 per cent. That reduction was less striking than the apparent growth of lower-class leadership of enclosure riots. In 1509–53, around 20 per cent of Manning's sample of enclosure riot cases were led by what he characterised as 'smallholders and craftsmen'. In 1603–25, such lower-class leadership had risen to some 53 per cent of the total. Most obvious is the increasing distance placed between the representatives of institutional authority and agrarian protest. Whereas the clergy led 8 per cent of enclosure riots in 1509–53, none could so be characterised in 1603–25. Manning also found that 11 per cent of enclosure riot cases were procured by manorial courts, municipal officials or Crown officers between 1509 and 1553, in contrast to a mere one such case (1 per cent) in 1603–25. This should not, however, be taken to imply that the opponents of enclosure were becoming more levelling. On the contrary, Manning detected a growing willingness on the part of enclosure rioters to combine direct action with litigation: 'one-fifth of the enclosure rioters in the Jacobean sample were accused of raising common purses to pay for the cost of litigation, as contrasted with 7 per cent of the Elizabethan sample'. None of Manning's Edwardian or Henrician cases included allegations that the opponents of enclosure had raised common purses. Manning detected an important discontinuity in this evidence, arguing that Jacobean enclosure protestors became 'more sophisticated than their . . . predecessors'.[7] This growing litigiousness seemed to be paralleled by a gradual decline in the size of rioting crowds. With important exceptions, such as in the riots occasioned by the drainage of the East Anglian fens in the 1620s and 1630s, or in the Midland Revolt of 1607, the period c. 1509–1640 saw a gradual diminution in the numbers involved in riots. The typical Elizabethan or Jacobean enclosure riot was short in duration, limited in its target, rarely involved interpersonal violence, and numbered between 20 and 40 people.

We might raise many objections to Manning's methodology and evidence (some of which, to be fair, Manning anticipates). Most obviously, the large bulk of riots which occurred in Tudor and Jacobean England probably went unrecorded. We are, of course, dealing with a small sample and a selective one at that: those cases where the complainant was sufficiently wealthy and confident of success to mount action at Star Chamber. Moreover, the Star Chamber archive has not been passed down to us in its complete form; there are many missing documents, especially for the earlier period. Other factors also need to be borne in mind. The increase in Star Chamber enclosure riot cases between the 1509 and 1625 points more to the willingness of the governing classes of England to use central courts in the settlement of disputes than it does to an increase in riot. In fact, the period c. 1509–1625 probably saw a diminution in large-scale riot. Beyond this, a series of further questions present themselves. How closely does Manning's regional breakdown correspond to the patchwork of economic and cultural regions in early modern England? His 'East Midlands' region includes, for instance, both the commercialised, grain-farming belt of central Lincolnshire and the upland, lead mining region of the Derbyshire Peak Country. His large-scale calculations therefore flatten out important differences within regional economies and popular cultures. And how reliable are his figures concerning the leadership of protest? We should not accept at face value the contemporary elite assumption that because a gentleman is caught up in an enclosure riot, he is necessarily leading it.

So, Manning's suggestion that the c. 1509–1625 period sees a gradual shift towards the lower-class leadership of rural protest needs to be qualified: rather, it sees the gradual shift towards the *public* leadership of such protest becoming increasingly concentrated amongst the rural lower classes *alone*. Finally, Star Chamber litigants tended to fling a variety of labels at their opponents, only one of which was 'rioter'. Star Chamber cases were notoriously complicated and often involved more than a single alleged enclosure riot. Rather, complainants presented such riots alongside allegations of treason, assault, trespass, libel or resistance to arrest. Manning's survey missed many cases of enclosure riot lodged in the Star Chamber's archive, mistaking them on initial inquiry to be concerned with issues other than rural protest, and hence not to be included in the sample. These caveats represent qualifications of Manning's argument, rather than a challenge to his basic assessment of the geography of enclosure riot.

Historians have conventionally understood the changing geography of enclosure rioting as indicative of long-term transformations in the early modern rural economy. From the latter third of the sixteenth century, the population of hitherto marginal pastoral regions grew much more swiftly than within downland, agrarian, corn-producing areas. Migratory workers were attracted to weakly manorialised, pastoral regions such as the Yorkshire dales, the West Country forests or the East Anglian fens by the availability of work in expanding cottage industries such as textile manufacture, small-scale mining, basket-making or the production of small wares. Industrial employment (sometimes for wages) was supplemented by access to large commons on unenclosed moors, wastes, fens or forests, and by the maintenance of an (often illegal) smallholding carved out of the common.[8]

All of these factors were especially powerful in the expanding mining regions of early modern England. Demand for coal from London and from regional urban markets drove the industrialisation of many coal-bearing regions of England, especially the northern coalfield near New-castle. Increased commercial demand for tin, copper and lead similarly attracted migrants into metal mining regions such as Cornwall, Devon, the Derbyshire Peak Country, the northern Pennines and the Mendips. One consequence of population expansion was therefore an intensifi-cation of local conflict over rights of tenure and common. In mining areas, attempts by lords and entrepreneurs to expropriate customary claims by tenants or free miners to the mineral rights of a locality became a further source of conflict.[9] In some cases, established villagers combined and drove newcomers out of their village. In other instances, lords saw the expanded population of such areas as a potential source of revenue and

sought to increase manorial tolls or deny common rights until cash
payments were offered by inhabitants for their confirmation. In both
cases, riot (sometimes combined with the establishment of a common
purse and the pursuit of legal action) frequently resulted. In particular
where lords or wealthier villagers tried to limit common rights or to
divide commons with enclosing stone walls, hedges or fences, notions of
custom, law and common right which became hotly contested. The
consequence was that pastoral-industrial areas not only experienced a
larger number of riots over enclosures, mining and common rights, but
also that their inhabitants came to be perceived of by their rulers as
dangerous and riotous inhabitants of 'dark corners of the land'.

In contrast to the growth of open conflict in pastoral-industrial
regions, the plebeian populations of arable areas are often presented
as relatively passive. In some downland villages, richer soils had long
fostered a firmer seigneurialism, as lords took a closer interest in the
administration of more profitable corn-producing manors. In other
villages, where the lord was not in residence, local authority often lay
with a relatively exclusive 'better sort'. The social changes of the
sixteenth century produced a new class of farmers on the border of
gentle status. It has been argued that this 'better sort' of villagers became
increasingly distant from their poorer neighbours as they acquired
larger landholdings, dominated village office-holding, achieved higher
levels of literacy and removed themselves from the leadership of popular protest.[10] As such men and women took to enclosing common land
and denying use-rights to the village poor, so the community of interest
which had sustained medieval and early Tudor traditions of popular
protest in agrarian England went into steep decline. Hence, whereas the
yeomanry of East Anglia had provided the leadership of popular rebellion in 1549, by the death of Queen Elizabeth they seemed to form the
leading edge of government.[11] It is within this socio-political context
that the decline of riot in arable East Anglia charted by Roger Manning
must be understood.

Once again, we are dealing with necessary generalisations. The
distinction between a rebellious pastoral-industrial zone primarily
located to the north and the west and a passive, deferential arable area in
the south and the east is, of course, massively overstated. It ignores the
inconvenient location of areas such as the industrialised, conflict-ridden
Weald in the south-eastern counties of Sussex and Kent, for instance.[12]
That basic ecological distinction has provided an important organising
focus for much of the historiography of early modern popular politics.

Yet we impoverish our subject if we lean upon that distinction too heavily. Riot was certainly the pre-eminent form of popular politics in many regions and villages. But not everywhere. The contestation of authority took many other forms than the open, public, daylight riots that pressed themselves upon the written record. We need not assume from the relative public quiescence of Jacobean East Anglia that labourers lived in deferential harmony with their lords or employers. Rather, public riot was one form of collective political agency which they had largely lost. Where we are charting shifts and changes in the forms of popular politics, we have, therefore, to listen to silences and to note absences. There was a politics to semi-public verbal dissent, muffled grumbling and anonymous threat as much as there was to open protest.[13]

II   The Decline of Enclosure Riot, 1625–c. 1720

Enclosure riots did not die out after 1625. But their geographical distribution does become harder for historians to chart. The Star Chamber's records for the pre-revolutionary period of Charles I's reign have survived only in scattered form. And with the abolition of the court in 1641 went the only means by which later historians could chart, via the records of a single institution, long-term shifts in the national distribution of large-scale riot. From the Caroline period up until the early eighteenth century, our picture of the geography of enclosure riot becomes still more circumspect. Certain qualifications continue to apply. Most obviously, we remain heavily dependent for our knowledge of the distribution of riot upon the records of law courts and of the institutions of central government. Such reportage often missed a great many occasions of riot and demonstration because, either due to poor record survival (especially important in the 1640s, when many law courts stopped functioning) or as a result of a decision not to prosecute rioters, the legal record is fragmentary. Similarly, central government was dependent upon reports from local magistrates and lord lieutenants, whose own information was often partial, and who might well have good reason to avoid the humiliating experience of reporting the breakdown of order within their locality. It is a bold historian, therefore, who sees in the records of central government 'a reasonably accurate indication of the chronology and topography' of riot.[14]

One very obvious discontinuity in the sources of rural discontent manifests itself from the second decade of the seventeenth century. The

Crown, always a large landholder, began to exploit its tenants with a new ruthlessness in the last years of the reign of James I. Hitherto, many of the Crown's manors had been only loosely administered. In the absence of a powerful manorial presence, tenants had frequently developed a wide range of customary freedoms. The wide customary rights and low rents on many Crown manors had often attracted the large numbers of poor cottagers. Finally, the Crown had also tended to protect forest rights in order to uphold chivalric traditions of hunting. The result was that popular freedoms in forests had often enjoyed a larger degree of latitude than elsewhere.[15] All of this changed during the reign of James I. In one Crown manor and forest after another, surveyors arrived to map the division of commons, inquire into how loose local customs might be limited, and search into the titles and rights held by inhabitants and tenants. The overriding purpose of such surveyors was to find new ways by which the Crown's revenues might be maximised. In this, the Crown's estate policies seemed to validate the harshness of seigneurial practice on other large estates. Coupled with the rapid decline of protective legislation for tenants and commoners after 1624, the seigneurial interest seemed to be on the offensive.[16]

When the Caroline Crown sold off commissions for the drainage of the East Anglian fens, it managed to forge a unity of interest between the wealthy cattle farmers of the region and the poor cottagers. Already apparent in earlier, less co-ordinated attempts at drainage late in Elizabeth's reign and earlier in that of James I, the capacity of poorer and middling sorts of people to unite in the defence of common rights upon the fens became a national political issue in the late 1620s and after. Similarly, upon the Crown's Duchy of Lancaster manors in the Peak Country of Derbyshire, the willingness of the Crown to back its patentees against the tenants and miners infuriated local opinion. Very similar social alliances formed the basis for popular protest in the forests of the West Country.[17] The geography of enclosure rioting in the 1620s and early 1630s reflects both this new aggression on the part of the Crown's estate managers and the capacity of local farmers, tenants, cottagers and industrial workers to transcend local social differences and to unite against a common opponent.

This new-found unity of action upon the Crown's estates and in the fens and the forests forms a powerful contrast with the dominant pattern of rural protest elsewhere in early Stuart England. Where wealthy farmers, poor tenants and landless cottagers were not united by the intervention of some disruptive outside force, village elites were more reluctant to place themselves at the head of popular protest. This was most obviously the case during the Midland Rising of 1607. Directed against recent large-scale enclosures carried out by the local gentry and the wealthiest yeoman farmers within Leicestershire, Warwickshire and Northamptonshire, the rising attracted few of the wealthier villagers who had traditionally led rural protest. Rather, the Midland rebels, mostly farm labourers, artisans and smallholders, produced an organic leadership from amongst their own ranks.[18] The local gentry suppressed the rising with (by the standards of the early seventeenth century) heavy bloodshed.

As we shall see in Chapter 4, Section III, the opponents of enclosure in forests, fens, Crown manors and on the large estates of enclosing nobility had their revenge in the years of the English Revolution. Intense enclosure rioting broke out between 1641 and 1643 and continued through the rest of the decade. The pattern of serious civil war disturbances is accessible through the records of the House of Lords, which assumed much of the judicial business of the Star Chamber until its own abolition in 1649. Yet in spite of the gentry fears that the collapse of civil order would breed a levelling anarchy amongst the commons, rural unrest tended to fit into the pattern established during the early seventeenth century. Although rioting crowds were often larger than their peacetime equivalents and were sometimes more aggressive in their actions, John Morrill and John Walter have stressed that elite fears of the 'many-headed monster' of popular disorder were without foundation. Violence against the person remained rare during civil war rural riots, and outbreaks of riot tended to occur only in those areas:

> where the radical challenge of enclosure to local economies prompted, and local social and economic structures permitted, the persistence of active, collective resistance. It was in the western forests and eastern fens and the larger estates whose royal, aristocratic and episcopal owners were associated with a discredited regime that riots were to be found.

Most importantly, 'The classic locus of earlier [that is, early Stuart] enclosure riot and rebellion, the fielden Midlands, remained remarkably still.'[19]

Enclosures destroyed in the 1640s were, in many cases, reconstructed in the 1650s. The Commonwealth regime, anxious to build loyalty amongst the traditional political classes and highly conscious of how successfully the Royalists had stigmatised it as the party of rebellion, was all too willing to garrison troops on rioting districts. The Commonwealth years also saw the triumph of the pro-enclosure lobby within government. In the Tudor period, enclosure had been condemned in successive Privy Council decrees and parliamentary statutes. The last anti-enclosure statute was passed in 1597 against a background of widespread dearth, scattered food riots, large-scale disturbances amongst the London apprentices, and an attempted rural insurrection in Oxfordshire. Thereafter, the pro-enclosure lobby gradually gained ground. In 1607, following the Midland Rising, Parliament met to consider fresh anti-enclosure legislation. The House of Commons was divided over whether to maintain anti-enclosure legislation. Whereas enclosed fields seemed to imitate the tidiness of social hierarchy and individual property rights, it seemed to one disputant that common land and forests, were 'nurseries of beggars'. By 1624, Parliament had passed its first pro-enclosure statute.[20]

In surveying and dividing common land, increasing rents and fines and restricting popular use rights, the pre-war Crown's estate managers only anticipated the actions of the Commonwealth. The estates of the Crown, the Church and the major Royalist noble families were broken up and sold off in the late 1640s and early 1650s. Parliamentary acts of 1653 and 1654 authorised the disafforestation and sale of most of what remained of the Crown forests. The Commonwealth authorities conducted major surveys of the Crown estates in 1649–50, in which commissioners inquired into the value of common lands and mineral or grazing rights hitherto exercised by inhabitants. These searches formed the basis for the sale of Crown lands and rights. Whereas the early Stuarts' attempts at enclosing and selling off common land had often faced bitter opposition from a broad front of local tenants, cottagers and the landless poor, in the 1650s local opposition was more muted. Partly, this was due to the larger repressive capacity of the Republican state, which did not hesitate to dispatch soldiers to suppress riots. Partly, it had to do with the changing intellectual environment, as what has been identified as a 'discourse of improvement' gained ground amongst both the gentry and richer farmers, helping to justify the division of common lands and the expropriation of common rights. But the lower levels of opposition also had much to do with the willingness of Commonwealth commissioners to exploit divisions amongst potential opponents of enclosure. Where common lands were divided for sale, richer tenant farmers were compensated for their loss of common rights with the grant of substantial chunks of the former commons. Such wealthier inhabitants were also often the beneficiaries of the sale of leases of use-rights to timber, minerals or other commercially exploitable materials that had hitherto been held in common. The effect was therefore to disrupt the capacity of local communities to unite against an outside encloser.

Very similar policies were adopted after the Restoration. The continuation of a standing army provided the later Stuart monarchs with a greater capacity to intervene against rural disorder than their predecessors had enjoyed.[21] The deepening elite appeal of mercantilist ideas strengthened the moral and intellectual case for enclosure and improvement, as commons came increasingly to be viewed as wasteful and commoners as lazy, sinful and rebellious.[22] Finally, the enclosure policies pursued both upon the Crown's estates and upon those of many large landowners tended to follow the strategy developed in the Commonwealth years: dividing wealthier landed inhabitants from their poorer neighbours by granting the former a proportion of the former commons.[23] The appearance of a decline in rural disorder in the later years of the seventeenth century might therefore be genuine, reflecting not the lack of a significant archive of information on the subject, but a genuine diminution of collective, public opposition to enclosure.

Within many areas where the plebeian population had hitherto been active in defence of common lands and common right, the later Stuart period seems to have been a dark one for the opponents of enclosure. It is difficult to argue from absences, but the lack of riots against the large-scale enclosure of commons and wastes in the Peak Country of Derbyshire during the 1670s, 1680s and 1690s, for instance, ought to tell us something about the decline of popular politics within that region. In the late sixteenth and early seventeenth centuries, enclosure had stimulated a large number of crowd actions and collective legal cases by tenants, cottagers and miners. Similarly, attempts by lords and entrepreneurs to dissolve the right of free mining by which independent miners made a living from digging for lead on both private and common land had generated large-scale riots and a tradition of popular litigiousness. In contrast, the miners of the post-Restoration Peak were almost silent before their growing marginalisation within the lead-mining industry. Such developments were related to local processes of social and cultural polarisation, which might be summed up in the life story of William Bagshawe, from the Peak village of Litton. In the 1630s, Bagshawe had been one of the leading opponents of the Church's claims to take a tithe of lead upon the local miners, and was a significant member of a network of miners, smallholders and yeomen who distinguished themselves as defenders of mining custom and as opponents of enclosure. By the 1660s, Bagshawe was a wealthy farmer and lead merchant. He

had taken to styling himself as 'Mr Bagshawe', was engaged in the enclosure of the commons of the neighbouring village of Hucklow, and
had acquired a lease of the very lead tithe which he had opposed so
vehemently thirty years before.[24]

Exceptions to this pattern seem largely to prove the rule. Rural areas
whose plebeian populations continued to demonstrate a consistent pattern
of sustained, public opposition to enclosure and to the commodification
of customary use-rights tended to share similar cultural and economic
characteristics. In the Forest of Dean (Gloucestershire), Cannock Chase
(Staffordshire), Gillingham Forest (Wiltshire), Deeping Fen (Lincolnshire) and the Isle of Axholme (Lincolnshire) post-Restoration attempts
at enclosure, disafforestation or drainage met with large-scale riot, often
backed by collective court action. In all of these areas, the landless poor
continued to form a significant element of the population. Such people
were often artisans or industrial workers. Despite the prejudices of elite
outsiders, the depositions they presented to law courts show that they
did not consider themselves to be shiftless paupers, but rather defined
themselves as part of an inclusive plebeian community. Hence, commoners emphasised that they paid rates for the maintenance of the parish
poor; that they inhabited ancient cottages that carried with them the
possession of common rights; and that they held a strong knowledge of
local custom.[25] Perhaps most importantly, in all of these areas the
experience of riot and collective litigation in defence of customary rights
was ingrained within local culture.

Enclosure riot in late seventeenth- and early eighteenth-century
England was no longer the 'pre-eminent form of social protest' which it
had been in 'the period 1530 to 1640'. Whereas Manning found that
Elizabethan enclosure riots were 'numerous and widely dispersed
throughout the realm', Andrew Charlesworth's chronology of enclosure
riot found the early eighteenth century to be 'the quietest [years] so far
encountered'.[26] Jeanette Neeson has qualified Charlesworth's national
generalisations, pointing to the enduring importance of common rights
to the inhabitants of pastoral-industrial areas such as Rockingham
Forest (Northamptonshire). We might add to the list: the miners and
commoners of the Forest of Dean, for example, continued to demonstrate their characteristic pugnacity in the defence of free mining and
commoning rights. In 1724–5 the poorer inhabitants of the Broadland
village of Stokesby (Norfolk) invoked exaggerated fears of a repeat of
the 1549 rising with their riotous defence of their customary rights of the
local marshes. And the inhabitants of the East Anglian fens continued to

smash drainage equipment, assault drainers and disturb the officials of the central state throughout the later Stuart and early Georgian periods.[27] Nonetheless, the larger pattern was clear: public resistance to enclosure had become restricted to a relatively small number of regions. Elsewhere, loud clamour against agrarian change seemed to have been replaced by bitten lips and closeted complaint.

III   Food Riots and the Moral Economy

The food riot is probably the form of crowd action most commonly associated with eighteenth-century England. The old image of the food riot as an explosion of senseless mob anger in the face of threatened starvation is now long vanished from the historiography of the subject. In its place, Edward Thompson's 1971 essay 'The moral economy of the English crowd in the eighteenth century' has established the dominant format for the study of food riots.[28] Thompson argued that 'the food riot in eighteenth-century England was a highly complex form of direct popular action, disciplined and with clear objectives', deeply rooted in a traditional and conservative plebeian culture. Food riot was often preceded by threatening letters to magistrates or grain merchants, warning of disorder unless prices were lowered, or by open collective appeal to the authorities. If no action were taken, crowds would impose what they regarded as a 'just' price upon stallholders. Alternatively, in the countryside, farmers' barns were searched for 'forestalled' food, which had been held back from the market in order to inflate prices. According to Thompson's model, merchants and farmers might be roughed up or humiliated by the crowd, but would be paid a 'just price' for any food which was taken. Rioting crowds attempted to inspire ameliorative action on the part of magistrates, who would see that prices were lowered and food stocks brought to market. To that end, the language of rioters was often heavily legalistic, sometimes even making reference to government proclamations against forestalling. Violence against the person was rare. As Thompson summed up the matter:

> What is remarkable about these 'insurrections' is, first, their discipline, and, second, the fact that they exhibit a pattern of behaviour for whose origin we must look back several hundreds of years ... The central action in this pattern is not the sack of granaries and the pilfering of grain or flour but the action of 'setting the price'.[29]

In their legalism, restraint, discipline and tactics, food riots therefore bear close similarity to enclosure riots. Like some enclosure rioters of the sixteenth and early seventeenth centuries, food rioters sought to bring their grievances to the attention of the established authorities (especially the county bench or the Privy Council). Riot (or, perhaps more properly, demonstration) therefore helped to foster a dynamic relationship between the crowd and the magistracy. Thompson and others have argued that the self-conscious discipline of food rioters demonstrated to magistrates both the depth of popular need and their desire to stay within the law. Although food riots were often laden with implicit threat, both magistrates and rioters tended to use very similar language in description of forestallers and profiteers. Both saw farmers and grain merchants as responsible for a 'dearth of victuals', in that producers and merchants were believed to hold back stores of food in order to inflate the market price. Hence, the logic of magistracy helped to sustain some of the founder-myths of popular politics.

In 1586, the magistrates of Gloucester received instructions from the Privy Council concerning the recent increase in 'the prices of all kyndes of corne'. The Privy Council understood the blame for the dearth of food to lie with:

> the farmors and such as use tillage, havinge sufficient quantities to serve the cittie and countrey, doe of greedines and to the ende they may advaunce the prices bringe little to the merchantes, wherby the poorer sorte of Her Majesties subjectes are in daunger to famishe.

Eleven years later, the Privy Council investigated a case of alleged seditious words that illustrates the correspondence between popular and magisterial attitudes. The labourer Robert Drewe was alleged to have committed sedition by claiming 'that the world would nev[er] be merrye untill there were a kinge. For there is never a noble man in England worth a pinne but in wordes.' Drewe explained to the anxious Privy Councillors that he had been 'talking of the Prise of Corne' and explained that his words had been as follows:

> If there were a Kinge he would come amonge the marchants and take better order for the prices therof And denieth that he spake anie wordes toutching the Lordes.[30]

Such language suggests not only that misogyny was a cross-class phenomenon in early modern England, but also that ruler and ruled shared common economic and moral assumptions about the market, duty and greed. Although the forms of magisterial concern over the supply of food changed over the course of our period, its basic content did not. Unlike official hostility to enclosure, which as we have seen gradually died out between the Midland Revolt and the English Revolution, it was not until the last third of the eighteenth century that magisterial attitudes to the marketing of grain began to change, and even then slowly. In the early and mid-sixteenth century, the Privy Council had encouraged local magistrates to look to food stocks and to ensure that the poor were supplied with sustenance at times of economic and political crisis. In particular, Tudor magistrates were expected to be *seen* to be acting against forestallers and corrupt market officials.[31] The intention was to prevent 'mutinies' amongst the poor by demonstrating an ostentatious, proactive concern for the supply of food.

Such practice was codified in the Book of Orders, first issued in 1587 in the aftermath of a severe dearth, a spate of food riots in the West Country and a threatened insurrection in Hampshire.[32] The Book of Orders was based upon a series of earlier royal commandments that originated in a proclamation of 1527 against forestalling. This proclamation had itself been issued in response to food riots in East Anglia and southern England.[33] The contents of the 1587 Book of Orders, which were printed and circulated to magistrates, required that commissioners be appointed to survey local stocks of food, to force farmers who held surpluses to bring their food to market, and to regulate the activities of middlemen. The Book of Orders was reissued in 1594, 1595, 1608, 1622 and in 1630. Importantly, these were not the only dearth years witnessed in the early modern period. Rather than await the arrival of the Book of Orders, magistrates were expected to be proactive. In local conditions of dearth, therefore, county Quarter Sessions and town authorities often put into action the contents of the Book of Orders, saw that the poor were set to work, and publicly announced that such measures had been carried out. Again, the objective here was to maintain a dialogue with potential rioters; and again we are reminded of the necessarily flexible and dynamic nature of governance within early modern society. After all, in order to see that grain was brought to market from the barns of hoarding farmers, magistrates were reliant upon information from the 'ruled'.

We should not, therefore, be surprised to find that grain rioters possessed an 'acute awareness of government policy' concerning food supply, nor that they were creative in their 'conscious exploitation' of that knowledge. The first dearth orders of 1527, for instance, were 'cited a year later by Huntingdonshire villagers opposing the export of foodstuffs'; Kentish rioters in 1631, when they cried out 'one half . . . for the K[ing] the other for them' while carrying off grain 'were making a precise reference to the reward offered in proclamations to those instrumental in preventing the illegal export of grain'.[34] It is for this reason that historians have often described grain rioting as a form of collective bargaining by direct action.

The sensitivity of early modern magistrates to popular attitudes meant that, in anticipation of trouble, local governors often imposed regulations upon food supply. Walter and Wrightson therefore note that the 'years of dearth in England in . . . [the sixteenth and seventeenth centuries] were not marked by widespread rioting'. In contrast, the supply of food was probably the most obvious cause of riot in mid-eighteenth-century England. As John Bohstedt has recently shown, this raises problems for Thompson's view that eighteenth-century food rioters followed a pattern established by earlier generations, and that in contests over food supply we see a conflict 'between an innovative market economy and the customary moral economy of the plebs'.[35] Rather than presenting food riots as forming an unbroken continuum from the sixteenth century to the late eighteenth, Bohstedt instead divides the history of the subject into three chronological phases. In each of these phases, both the geography and form of food rioting and the nature of governmental responses to dearth and riot differed significantly. In the first of Bohstedt's phases (c. 1550–1650), demographic pressures combined with growing rural industrialisation, urbanisation and regional specialisation to produce high levels of dependency within particular regions upon the supply of food from outside. England's population nearly doubled over that century, from around three million to perhaps five and a half million. This population increase was most apparent in urban centres and in poor, marginal areas such as fens, forests and upland regions, within which rural industry was increasingly located. Hence, growing numbers of industrial workers and urban inhabitants became enmeshed in market relations beyond their region. In years of harvest failure, as food-producing areas clung to their reduced surpluses of grain, food scarcity occurred within the poor and populous pastoral-industrial regions such as the cloth-producing and mining regions of the West Country.

Yet outside the West Country, this period saw relatively few food riots compared with later periods, since 'poor people typically petitioned magistrates rather than rioted'. The 'occasional riots' of the period prompted magistrates to take action against forestallers. Such action 'reaffirmed the beneficence of the social order'. Grain-producing regions experienced few riots since farmers were often willing to sell grain at reduced prices directly to their labourers and the village poor. Customary rights of gleaning enabled the rural poor to subsist upon shards of corn left over from the harvest. Seeming trivial to the modern eye, gleaning rights were often essential to the maintenance of the fragile domestic economy of the farm labourer's household, and reiterate the enduring significance of custom within local plebeian cultures.[36] Moreover, living-in servants and labourers were guaranteed food as part of their contract of employment. Similarly, wealthy gentry and noble families assumed a paternal role, dispensing food from their farms and cellars in ostentatious statements of their social pre-eminence.[37] We shall return to the politics of this relationship below.

In Bohstedt's second phase (c. 1650–1740), a steadily declining population reduced pressure upon the supply of food. Hence, 'rioting became rarer and, not coincidentally, so did market regulation'. In tune with the changing attitudes to enclosure observed in the previous section, later Stuart central government retreated from regulating the grain market and instead offered bounties encouraging the export of food. The prerogative power to suspend export of grain was not renewed after the Restoration and exportation was only suspended by parliamentary statute in 1699 and 1709. Bohstedt sees in this 'a major reversal of the Tudor-Stuart paternalism, but it seemed tolerable in a period of farm surpluses and low prices'.

Hence, in Bohstedt's third phase (c. 1740–1820), which he identifies as 'the golden age of food riot', traditions of food riot and of magisterial response had to be 'invented'. Bohstedt's third period lies beyond the bounds of our fuzzy periodisation.[38] Yet his argument is important for our interpretation of food riot traditions. Food riot in Bohstedt's third period resulted initially from the coincidence of two phenomena: a growing urban and industrial population and a governmental policy of encouraging food exports. Unlike in the sixteenth and early seventeenth centuries, which had also seen a rapid growth in rural industry and in urban population, 'the government did not act quickly to stop exports in times of crisis'. Moreover, farmers were cutting back on living-in servants and labourers and gleaning rights were being limited, thereby increasing the vulnerability of many rural workers to dearth.[39] Bohstedt sees mid-eighteenth-century rural industrial workers becoming freed from 'dependency networks of social control more common to agrarian communities' and beginning to develop 'solidarities that would give them a formidable if informal franchise in the politics of provisions' (by which he means food riots and their attendant negotiations). The overall result, in Bohstedt's rather cold phrase, was the establishment of an 'optimum degree of social independence to riot'.[40]

In 1740, Bohstedt argues, for the first time England experienced a national outbreak of food rioting. Further national waves followed in 1756–7, 1766, 1771–3, 1794–6, 1799–1801, 1810–13 and 1816–18. He sees the rioters of 1740–66 as a 'formative generation' who established a new tradition of food riot and contests the centrality attributed by Thompson to price-setting in the eighteenth-century food riot. Rather than setting prices, mid-eighteenth-century rioters directed their efforts against the bolting mills that produced finely ground flour for the export market. Rioters often tore down such mills and assaulted their owners. Hence, food rioters 'practised true Luddism by wrecking machines not because they were new, but as a way to stop production in a dispute'. Thompson's emphasis upon the lack of violence and respect for property of the eighteenth-century crowd therefore seems to Bohstedt to be misplaced. He is similarly sceptical as to the longevity of the food riot tradition. Bohstedt's rioters of 1740–66 did not cite the Book of Orders as Tudor and Stuart rioters had done; nor did they search barns for foodstuffs on the pretext of enforcing the law. This is all the more striking, since eighteenth-century plebeians were in other contexts all too willing to appeal to ancient legislation and (an occasionally invented) sense of hallowed custom. Yet Bohstedt follows Thompson in seeing riot as the heaviest weight which the labouring people of Hanoverian England could bring to bear in their difficult balancing act with their rulers. Where magistrates did ensure that food was brought to market and sold at reasonable prices, they did so out of fear of crowd action, or out of still deeper fear at its recurrence. Mixing metaphors, Bohstedt observes how, for magistrates, 'Riot made the milk of human kindness flow: riots jump-started *noblesse oblige*'.[41] So paternalism was conditional upon the possession of social power; and the distribution of social power stemmed from local-political conflict.

IV   Gender, Ritual and Community

The preceding discussion of food and enclosure riots has artificially separated the two outstanding causes of collective disorder in early modern England. For much of our period, access to food and access to land were conceptually intertwined. Tudor economic thought, whether elite or plebeian, conceived of the enclosure of arable land as both an economic and a moral evil, responsible for the dearth of food and the destruction of social order. By the early seventeenth century, that association between enclosure and high food prices was beginning to dissolve within the collective mind-set of the gentry and nobility. But that it remained lodged within popular culture helps to explain some elements of the idiom of rural protest. Underpinning the plebeian critique of enclosure and high food prices was a powerful language of rights. Fundamentally, popular conceptions of rights stemmed from two closely connected sources: secular notions of custom, legality and proper order; and an assertive reading of scripture. The fluid, creative relationship between custom, scripture and local-political conflict in plebeian culture is best illustrated by example.

In 1609, Janet Whappet of Waddingham (Lincolnshire) was accused by a local farmer of taking part with 40 of her neighbours in an enclosure riot. In her subsequent evidence to the Court of Star Chamber, Janet Whappet explained that she was a poor cottager, that her husband was a 'day labourer' and that they held a cottage with attached freehold rights. Their tenure of this ancient cottage meant that, like her neighbours, she enjoyed common rights over a long-enclosed field in Waddingham, upon which she grazed cows from Lammas Day (1 August) to Lady Day (25 March). 'Contrary to all equitie & righte', Janet had been prevented from exercising her pasture rights on the lands in question, and so she had broken down the fences which barred her from the land.[42] The Waddingham rioters' sense of rights was local in its focus and vested in custom. As inhabitants of freehold cottages, Whappet and her neighbours claimed to hold legally meaningful rights over the land, which they hoped to demonstrate with reference to local memory. But as their husbands were 'pore men', the women of Waddingham implied another source of rights: that of poverty. Although her rights as a freehold cottager held rather more legal authority, the status she claimed as one of the 'pore' gave a special moral and scriptural authority to Janet's claim.

The Bible was full of potential for popular politics. Readership of the Bible suggested that the encloser offended not only against local custom and (at least in the Tudor period) royal commandment and parliamentary statute, but also offended God. 'Accursed be he who removeth his neighbour's doles and marks', warned Deuteronomy. When on their yearly perambulation of the parish bounds, local inhabitants were reminded that God was numbered amongst the opponents of enclosure. Scripture was read aloud by the parish minister when the Rogationtide procession reached important turning points in the parish boundary: 'Thou shalt not remove thy neighbour's mark, which they of old time have set in thine inheritance', ordered Proverbs. Rogationtide perambulations provided an opportunity for the restatement of the ideal early modern community: homogeneous, socially stratified, patriarchal and small-scale. The Rogationtide homilies invited parishioners to 'consider the ancient bounds and limits' of the parish:

> be content with our own, and not contentiously strive for others, to the breach of charity, by any encroaching upon one another, or claiming one of the other further than that in ancient right and custom our forefathers have peaceably laid out unto us for our commodity and comfort.

The Rogationtide rituals and homilies defined a powerful fiction of community that could be deployed to a variety of ends. Religious conservatives and civil war royalists, for instance, exploiting puritan hostility to Rogationtide, saw in the ceremonies an affirmation of an ancient patriarchal culture.[43] The opponents of enclosure and the defenders of common rights drew a related set of meanings from Rogationtide, as the Norwich alderman George Cocke discovered upon purchasing the manor of Old Buckenham (Norfolk).

In 1619, Cocke explained to the Court of Star Chamber how, during the recent Rogationtide celebrations, eleven yeomen and labourers of Old Buckenham had broken down his fences and trespassed upon his enclosed demesne land. When he bought the manor, Cocke had learnt the role of the lord in the Rogationtide celebrations: to provide cheese, ale and bread for the perambulators upon their arrival at the manor house. In return, the parish minister would lead the congregation in singing psalms for their lord. On this occasion, Cocke had gone so far as to provide 'spiced cakes and good p[ro]vision fit for them and farr better then ever was p[ro]vided before that tyme'. Anticipating a ritual display of community and festive cheer, Cocke was to be sadly disappointed. When the parish procession arrived at his manor house, instead of hearing his tenants' psalms, Cocke watched as 'in disgracefull manner [they] did singe, looke out new Oysters, new Mackerells and such like uncivill sings and tunes'. The fences surrounding his manor house were broken down and the eleven riotous villagers returned to Old Buckenham, where they sat drinking in an alehouse, boasting of their deeds.[44] There was an obvious meaning to these events, in which the new lord was mocked as 'new Mackerell' at precisely that moment in the ritual year at which social harmony and hierarchy was meant to be restated.[45]

In reversing the Rogationtide rituals, the Old Buckenham rioters simultaneously humiliated their lord and defined a different vision of community. Trespassing upon the enclosed space of the lord's demesne land, breaking the fences around his manor house, refusing seigneurial hospitality in favour of the alehouse all spoke of a sense of community from which the lord was excluded. In refusing Cocke's gift of spiced cakes, the Buckenham men also denied him his social place. Perhaps these Norfolk villagers had some East Anglian equivalent of the old Gloucestershire saying that 'a great housekeeper is sure of nothinge for his good cheare save a great Turd at his gate'.[46] In any case, the celebration of Rogationtide at Old Buckenham in 1619 reminds us that the destruction of enclosures was often about much more than the simple removal of some walls and fences.

There was, therefore, a symbolism to popular protest. In breaking down enclosing walls and placing cattle upon land from which they had been excluded, rioters were not only physically reoccupying contested land; they were also symbolically reasserting communal control over space and resources. Such actions seem to have been quite deliberate. During enclosure riots in Gillingham Forest (Wiltshire) in 1644, John Phillips jumped his horse over enclosing walls, and rode 'from one close to another, [saying] ... I ryde in, and I ryde out of these grounds at my pleasure'.[47] Historians have often stressed the relative lack of violence in enclosure riots; yet such crowd action could be terrifying to witness. In the course of disturbances in Gillingham Forest during 1643, the estate steward Thomas Brunker watched as the size of rioting crowds increased from 50 people at the outbreak of civil war to about 300. To his terror, he noted that 'amongst them is 60 musketts and fouleing peices, besides Halbirts and other weapons'. The rioters had brought their armoury to Brunker's attention by brandishing them during their riots.[48] This was a characteristic feature of rural demonstration in the Tudor and early Stuart period. One purpose of riots was to intimidate opponents. When rioters gathered together in militia-style assemblies, with drums and muskets, but nonetheless did not attack their opponents, they conveyed a clear message: highlighting their own restraint, while communicating their potential physical power.

The meaning of crowd demonstration was sometimes, therefore, extremely obvious. In other cases, its meaning is less apparent to the modern mind. One dominant theme within the symbolism of popular protest was that of inversion. Historians have argued that rioters structured their protests in such a way as to communicate, through the symbolism of inversion, how their social worlds had been turned upside down by the disrupting effects of a given grievance. The idea that the world could be turned inside out, or upside down, was a recurrent theme within both medieval and early modern popular culture, and has received considerable attention from historians.[49] In particular, it is important to note that such inversive imagery was often deployed by the authorities in shaming punishments: John Stow recalled in 1598 how one Shrove Monday at Charing Cross he had seen 'A man carried of four men. And before him a bagpipe playing, a shawm, and a drum beating. The cause was his next neighbour's wife beat her husband'.[50] Since order was synonymous with 'quietness', inversive punishments were often attended by clamorous noise. Prostitutes, for instance, were led through streets, preceded by the 'ringing' of pots.[51] Given the extent of popular involvement in the law, it is unsurprising that such rituals should also influence popular protest, especially where crowd actions were directed against those who were felt to threaten the established, patriarchal order of the village. Hence, village constables sometimes led their neighbours in the collective mockery of husbands who were felt to have failed to maintain proper order within their households (where they were considered to have been cuckolded, for instance, or where they were regarded as having ceded too much authority to their wife). Similarly, men and women who were suspected of 'loose living', or of cohabiting out of wedlock, became victims of mocking rituals.[52] Magistrates and judges in Star Chamber were left to ponder whether such events constituted disorderly riot, or the proper punishment of offenders.

Although the precise characteristics of individual rituals varied from one village to another, and were subject to important change over time, certain features were common across western Europe. Mocking crowds gathered to the sound of clamorous noise from drums, trumpets, or the ringing of wooden spoons upon pots and pans. The victims might be set facing backwards on horses or poles. Men might dress as women, and women might dress as men. Masks might be worn, or faces painted black. In their essay on the subject, Alun Howkins and Linda Merricks observe the wide variation in the names given to such rituals.

Known in France as 'charivari', in Britain it had a variety of regional names, Skimmington (South West), Rough Music (Midlands), Tinging (East Anglia), Riding the Stang (North), Ran-tanning (North), Ceffyl Pren (Wales).

In all cases, the purpose of the ritual was to mark out its target as having offended a set of public, communal norms which were so well known as to scarcely require further articulation. As Howkins and Merricks put it

> Its target was an individual, couple or small group. Its aim was to persuade the deviant to conform to the norms of *communitas*, to leave the community or to compensate the community for transgression. In these respects it sought not change the world but to keep it the same.[53]

Perhaps the typical use of rough music lay in the maintenance of the patriarchal norms that constituted the public culture of the village. The politics of the skimmington ought to be obvious: it represented a mechanism by which the existent distribution of power within the village and household, threatened by some disrupting force (an assertive woman; an insufficiently patriarchal husband; an enclosing lord; an oppressive tax-collector) could be reasserted through public, collective demonstration.

In 1618, the young men of the Wiltshire village of Calne heard news that there was 'a skimmington' dwelling in the neighbouring village of Quemerford.[54] Organising themselves 'like soldiers, armed wth peices and other weapons', 300 of the Calne men marched to Quemerford, preceded by:

> a man riding upon a horse, haveinge a white nightcap upon his head, two shininge hornes hanging by his eares, & counterfayte beard upon his chine made of a deares tayle, a smocke upon the top of his garments, & he rode upon a red horse wth a paire of potts under him.

Others carried rams' horns (the traditional sign of the cuckold) and bells. Upon their arrival in Quemerford, the crowd invaded the house of Agnes and Thomas Wells. They dragged Agnes into the street, trod upon her, and beat her 'blacke and blewe'. It was their intention to take Agnes Wells and place her in the cucking-stool reserved for the punishment of female offenders: especially prostitutes and 'scolds'. Four aspects of the disturbance command our attention: the relatively unusual use of violence by rioters; their apparent belief that they were enforcing the law; the attempt to impose male authority upon a disordered 'skim-mington' household; and the implication that the riot was expressive of a local conflict between Calne and Quemerford. This latter point was confirmed by an abortive attempt to mount a similar incident a few days before the actual attack upon Agnes and Thomas Wells. Three or four men from Calne, accompanied by ten or twelve boys and a drummer, had come to the bridge at Quemerford and announced that 'there was a Skimmington dwelling there & they came for him'. Some men of Quemerford shouted back that the 'report of Skimmingtons dwelling in Quemerford was false'. A local conflict between the two villages then seemed to transform into a gender conflict:

> the women of the towne understanding that the drumer & his company came thither for a Skimmington... made towards the drumer & cutt a p[ar]t of his drume, whereupon he and his company departed towards Calne.

Just as plebeian men deployed a patriarchal language in justification of their intrusion into the public sphere of political life, or to explain their participation in enclosure riots, so plebeian women frequently employed a similar rhetoric. Women enclosure and food rioters, as we have seen, sometimes justified their actions in terms of the defence of their households. The imagery of inversion, deployed by the men of Calne in their attempt to restore Agnes Wells to domestic subordination, could also be deployed by women to justify their involvement in crowd actions. According to legal theory, women were less responsible for their actions than men. For this reason, judges in Star Chamber frequently interrogated women accused of riot in order to ascertain whether they had been 'led' into action by their husbands or fathers. But this logic could be turned on its head. Such legal reasoning only helped to strengthen the popular belief that women rioters could not be prose-cuted before the courts. On a variety of occasions, therefore, we find women announcing 'that they... were lawles creatures and that there was noe lawe to rule order or punishe them for... theire riott'. Some women enclosure rioters 'put off their seemely shamefastnesse, & apparel-ling themselves in the attire of men... they assembled in gret number, & in riottous maner pulled downe an enclosure'.[55] Ritual, then, helped to structure popular protest. It frequently did so in an ironic manner. Those in authority in early modern England had sometimes to develop thick skins when faced with the mocking rhymes and rituals that

expressed the occasionally burlesque voice of popular politics.[56] But
crowd rituals did more than provide vehicles for popular criticism. They
also helped to maintain notions of community, and to communicate
some of the politics of popular protest.

Bob Bushaway has described the Rogationtide perambulations as

> part of a holistic structure which, in the early modern period, embraced
> the administration of the open-field system and the common lands ...
> [in which] the perambulation of the parish represented a public
> affirmation of the physical and social boundaries of the community.[57]

That conception of the moral community of the village may have been
'holistic' as an ideal, but in reality it was shot through with contradiction.
Then as now, the claim to represent community was a very political one,
which necessitated the drawing of boundaries and the silencing of
dissident voices. The language of community was something over which
groups and individuals struggled. The 'inhabitants' of a place might
refer in one context to all those who lived there; while in another, it
might be more exclusive, referring only to those who held land, or had
resided there for twenty years or more. This was important, because
'inhabitancy' guaranteed access to parish poor relief, as well as to the
fuzzier entitlements of 'custom' and 'neighbourhood'. The 'parish'
might similarly refer either to all the villagers, or to only those who comprised a restrictive parish vestry. The struggle for a popular politics
therefore often took the form of a struggle over words.

'Neighbourhood', one of the most charged words in the lexicon of
early modern parish politics, might have been felt by some plebeians to
impose a direct political duty: in some cases, even to riot. The Jacobean
defenders of tenant right customs in the northern border counties drew
a clear distinction between their opponents – the 'landlords' – and themselves – the 'neighbours'. Hence, one of the leaders of tenant resistance
asked an uncommitted neighbour in an alehouse in Kendal 'will you goe
to your partners or the gentlemen?' Neighbourhood, custom and rights
blended together in Joan Perkins' appeal to her friend Alice Mitchell in
1604. The other women of their village of Shepshed (Leicestershire)
were already on the disputed commons breaking down enclosures made
at the order of the Earl of Rutland when Joan asked her if 'she wold not
gow wth her & the rest of her neighbours to throwe downe the said
ditches'. Alice joined with the crowd in order that 'they might enjoy their
Rights of comon ... as form[er]lie they had donne'.[58]

We have seen how in many regions over the course of our period, wealthier villagers and lesser gentry withdrew from the leadership of popular protest. But there were important exceptions to that long process. In some villages, community continued to possess a greater social depth than such generalisations might suggest.[59] This is most clearly illuminated in an account of an alehouse conversation between Mr Francis Devonish and the young labourer John Belman on the night of 27 April 1643. Mr Devonish, a lesser gentleman, had an estimated yearly income of £100; but like his poorer neighbours he felt a responsibility for the defence of Gillingham Forest (Wiltshire). Gillingham had been one of those West Country royal forests that had been forcibly enclosed by the Crown in the 1620s. Between 1628 and 1632, the enclosure had been opposed by the inhabitants, who combined collective litigation with large-scale riot. Trouble flared in the forest once again in 1641–2, as part of the widespread rural riots that preceded the outbreak of civil war (see Chapter 3, Section II and Chapter 4, Section III). In the second spate of riots, the enclosures that had been made in the late 1620s by the agent of one of the Crown's patentees Mr Brunker had been broken down. The rioting was renewed in April 1643, as the foresters took advantage of the civil war to drive out the newly established farmers.[60] Young John Belman had not taken part in the riots, and Mr Devonish had been sent to speak with him about this. Asked why he was not with the 'companie', Belman answered

> I have nothing to do with them I will not meddle with theire business, [Mr Devonish] said what will you bee against all your neighbours for the love of one man, hee answered Mr Brunker is my friend and if I do him noe good I will doe him no hurt, [Devonish] seyd Mr [Brunker] is but one man and will you loose the love of all your neighbours for him, he is amongst us but a stranger here today gone tomorrow the forrest wilbe throwne downe when tht is donne he is gonne, and where is your friend then, the townesmen wilbe yor friends alwayes if you goe with the rest and doe as they doe you must live by your neighbours, I wish yor mind might be turned or els you will be hated of all your neighbours lik[e] a doge.[61]

The case that Devonish put to John Belman rested upon an appeal to a set of emotive keywords: neighbours; company; townsmen; friends. These were the linguistic building blocks of the early modern language of plebeian community – yet we should note that it was a forest gentleman who articulated them before John Belman.

The language of community allowed rioters to constitute themselves as the upholders of a legitimate order in the face of 'innovation' from 'foreigners'. That terminology allowed morality and duty to transcend village and class distinctions. The 1643 letter which called rioters together from the rival villages of Gillingham and Meare announced how 'wee have joyned togeather for the good of o[u]r poore Inhabitants of both places . . . wee hath bin soe much wronged that wee will not suffer it any longer'.[62] The language of community, order and custom was also marshalled to contest hostile characterisations of popular politics. Jacobean complaints against fenland enclosure rioters, for instance, referred to their opponents as 'many pore and simple people' who together comprised an 'uprore and Tumulte of a multitude'. In their evidence, the fenland rioters deployed very different collective definitions: they were 'the company' and 'the townesmen'.[63] The use of communal labels at times of local conflict helped to integrate individual acts of opposition into a larger set of ideas and thereby to validate plebeian politics. By breaking fences or setting food prices, rioters knew that they were demonstrating their membership of a community: the 'neighbours'; the 'goodfellows; the 'parishioners'. The changing use of the word 'Digger' provides a vivid example of how such categories were deployed in local-political conflict. By the beginning of the seventeenth century, the term 'Digger' had come to refer to day-labourers, and carried with it a nasty sneer of contempt. In 1607, the labourers, artisans and smallholders of the midland counties of England rose in large crowds to break down enclosures made upon their commons. They referred to themselves at that time, and in the secret letters by which they had communicated their plans to rise, as the 'Diggers'.[64] As we shall see in Chapter 4, Section V, this was also to become the alternative collective title used in self-description by the 'True Levellers' who, in 1649–50, established communities of the poor upon common land.

Notions of community became especially intense during periods of dearth. We have seen in Chapter 3, Section III how farmers in corn-producing regions often prevented their labourers from starving by providing low-cost food as part of their wages. This was supplemented with large-scale charity from the more distant figures of the gentry and nobility. In the hard years of the 1590s, for instance, Sir George Shirley acquired 'the glorious title of father and nourisher of the poor' for 'relieving during the great dearth 500 a day at his gate'. We might be tempted to see such actions as the static expression of a power structure: one of Thompson's 'calculated occasions of popular patronage' which held the authority of the nobility and gentry in place. But John Walter suggests a different side to the story. The generosity of the rich 'was sometimes triggered by the threats of the poor'. Farmers did not always have full control over the charitable disposal of their surplus. Rights of gleaning may have been made more valuable by the pursuit of 'a deliberate policy on the part of harvesters: one Lancashire gentleman who criticised his harvesters for unclean reaping was asked "What shall we leave for the poor ones?"' After all, the early modern poor could draw succour from Boaz's words to Ruth: 'Let her glean and reproach her not.' At times of dearth, the poor who gathered outside the gates of their lords may have expected charity as a right.

The growing practice whereby charitable funds were established for the poor in recompense for their loss of pasture rights upon enclosed common land only strengthened such beliefs.[65] Begging, often a source of deep division within village society, might similarly be reconceived as a right: the Kentish labourer John Jenkyns was pilloried in 1598 for his opinion that:

> yf the Queene did putt downe begginge she is worse than Nan Bennett (meaning Agnes Bennett, widow, lately executed for witchcraft), which forsooke God and all the world.

The poor were never wholly powerless in early modern society. In Restoration Northumberland, the gentry wished to prohibit begging, but stood in fear of the Beggar's Curse. Enraged paupers spat this curse at those who denied them charity; and so the Northumberland beggars continued to receive their alms from the gentry, 'for fear of their curses'. Again, scriptural authority could be found for the Beggar's Curse: 'He that giveth unto the poor shall not lack; but he that hideth his eyes shall have many a curse.'[66]

Poverty, then, imposed responsibilities upon the wealthy. Wealthy villagers who denied charity to the poor thereby lost their place within the moral community. In hard years, such guilt was difficult to bear. Alan Macfarlane and Keith Thomas have suggested that witchcraft accusations grew from that guilt, as poorer villagers, denied informal charity, invoked the Beggar's Curse against their wealthier neighbours. Upon some ill-fortune befalling the cursed household, the curser might face an allegation of *maleficium* (that is, of causing malicious damage through magic) before a criminal court.[67] The desperate condition of the 'poorer sort' demanded a political response from those with greater power. The great achievement of the Elizabethan regime had been to channel the agency of such village rulers into the central state. Involvement in local systems of parish relief and law enforcement, hitherto perceived of as a duty to the small community of the village, was redefined by parliamentary statute, preaching ministers and active magistrates as a direct form of participation in state structures. In part, this attempt to draw wealthier office-holders into the central state represented a long-term response to the major rebellions of the mid-sixteenth century, which as we saw in Chapter 2, Sections I–III, were led by relatively wealthy, office-holding villagers and townsmen.[68] But the success of that later Tudor political project created a fundamental mismatch between the structural characteristics of the early modern state (incorporative, flexible and dynamic), and the authoritarian, hierarchical principles by which it justified its existence. That conflict between theory and reality was to become most obvious during the years of the English Revolution.

4

POPULAR POLITICS IN STUART ENGLAND

I   Urban Popular Politics in the Seventeenth Century

Towns have an appeal for the contemporary Western historian which
rural areas simply do not. Most living historians of early modern England have been brought up in societies that are dominated by the urban
experience. Transport networks, educational facilities, party politics,
economic organisation, population distribution and cultural identities
all seem in our social world to converge upon the town. This urban bias
does not equip us well to understand early modern society. Although
the English urban population was growing both in absolute size and relative significance between the early sixteenth and the early eighteenth
centuries, historical demographers have shown that even at the end of
our period the large majority of the population lived in rural areas. Yet
in spite of this, to the historian of early modern popular politics there
remains something seductive about the town. The very term 'early
modern' hints at things which (allegedly) have yet to come: class society;
large-scale industrialisation; mass literacy; print culture; the development of individualism, of national party identities and of a public sphere
within which political discourse might legitimately occur. All of these
factors help to constitute a notion of modernity which, in its fully mature
form, is assumed to lie beyond our period, but which is thought to have
first stirred between the sixteenth and early eighteenth centuries: and
so, our allotted bloc of the human past is now conventionally labelled the
early modern period.[1] Most germane to our subject, young modernity is
thought to have flaunted its flashy self most visibly within the town.[2]

For the historian of popular politics in particular, this perception of England's long modernisation is full of implications and dilemmas. It underlies many historians' willingness to assign to urban (and especially metropolitan) populations a vanguard role in the 'rise of political consciousness' or the 'politicisation' of the English people in the seventeenth century.[3] The late spring of that 'growth of political consciousness' is located in the English Revolution of the 1640s, with the flourishing of open political debate, the formation of factions both within and outside Parliament, and the free flow of printed polemics and newsbooks. Following a late hard frost between the Restoration of the Stuarts (1660) and the start of the Exclusion Crisis (1678–81), this 'political consciousness' was once again to bloom vibrantly after 1678. Firmly established thereafter within the rich soil of urban culture, popular politics was to prove itself a hardy perennial in the years that followed the Glorious Revolution (1688).

In recent years, historians have identified the town (and, again, especially the metropolis) as the site of the birth of a new 'public sphere' of political life. This sphere of political activity was constituted by a series of factors that had a special force within the town: relative freedom of political discussion; an easy flow of political news and ideas; the wide readership of printed news and propaganda; open political organisation and expression. Taken together, these factors are felt to have generated a qualitatively richer political culture, founded upon 'rational' political debate. The period c. 1678–1715 is therefore seen as a time of radical transformation in popular politics. We investigate this claim much more thoroughly in Section VII of this chapter. But in order to make sense of post-Restoration developments in popular politics, we must first form an appreciation of the basic conditions within which urban popular politics operated in the seventeenth century. As we have seen, there is a powerful urban bias to the idea that a 'public sphere' of rational politics emerged in the later seventeenth century. Certainly, urban popular politics operated within a qualitatively different environment from that of the countryside. In administrative, economic and cultural terms, the conditions of urban politics appear to have allowed for popular politics to operate both more forcibly and more publicly than was the case in rural areas.

Since the Anglo-Saxon period, towns had been constituted as self-governing units.[4] In the medieval and early modern periods, the monarch granted a town's political rights. The Crown could therefore extend, limit, suspend or revoke urban custom in an arbitrary manner that was not legally possible in the countryside. The authority of urban magistrates depended upon the provisions made within such royal charters: as we saw in Chapter 1, Section IV, in enfranchised towns the law was maintained by magistrates appointed by (and typically from within) the town's ruling group. But although many town charters assumed that a powerful oligarchy would dominate urban affairs, they also assumed that non-elite 'commoners', 'inhabitants' or 'citizens' (the precise meanings attached to such terms varied from place to place, and over time) also had a legitimate collective voice. Many medieval town charters therefore established tiers of representation, government and administration within the urban community. Classically, a common council was elected from amongst the town's male householders, and held jurisdiction over lesser, day-to-day affairs (minor affrays, for instance, or street cleaning). Above this body, a self-appointing council of aldermen, headed by a mayor or bailiffs selected annually from amongst their own number, set the town's policy and maintained control over its defences, archives, property, finances and external relations.[5]

Whereas in the countryside the authority of magistrates might seem distant, in towns and cities the reverse was often the case. Early modern towns were typically very densely packed. Parishes and wards were of small size. Poorer households lived cheek-by-jowl, packed into multi-occupancy buildings. Urban magistrates were easily recognised and sometimes widely disliked. Combined with these structural and cultural factors was a wider degree of formal political participation amongst the town's adult male householders. Towns almost always enjoyed a wider parliamentary franchise than counties; in Norwich in the 1690s, for instance, it has been estimated that some 30 per cent of the adult male population possessed the right to vote. The franchise was still broader in Preston (Lancashire), where all adult male residents, including those staying overnight in the town at the time of an election, were entitled to vote.[6] The legal peculiarities of urban government therefore reproduced and expressed a larger set of tensions that gave popular politics in the town an unusually powerful intensity.

Although the town seemed superficially to be an urban hybrid of the socio-political hierarchy which authoritarian social theorists assumed to be operative within the countryside, real relations between 'upper' (aldermanic) and 'lower' (commoner) parts of the urban body politic were rather more conflictual. In many cases, the nature of appointment to such bodies, the division of responsibilities, and the relationship between upper and lower councils had been worked out through conflict. The capacity of the Crown to rework urban custom added a further complication. In granting new charters, or in amending existent rights and relationships, the Crown could intervene decisively in such internal disputes. Alternatively, the grant of a new charter might provide grounds for new conflicts. The structures of urban administration and representation therefore served to focus conflict within the town. To give an example: early modern Colchester (Essex) had a well-established reputation for disharmony which was built into its constitutional arrangements.[7] Until the grant of a new charter in 1635, Colchester was governed according to a charter of 1462 that established 2 bailiffs as the head governors of the town. These bailiffs were backed by 8 aldermen, followed by a first and a second (or common) council, each made up of 16 members. The bailiffs and aldermen were chosen by 5 representatives of the four wards that together comprised the town. Although the town's freemen electors selected them, these representatives had to meet a restrictive property qualification. The bailiff and aldermen were responsible for selecting the first council. The members of the first council, the bailiffs and the aldermen selected the junior common council.

The grotesque gerrymander of Colchester's pre-1635 constitutional arrangements therefore produced a perfect administrative expression of the town's political culture. Divided against itself, Colchester's constitution allowed for the articulation of a popular voice, while ensuring maximum elite control over office-holding and policy. In spite of its subordinate place within the town's constitution, the freeman body of Colchester was both substantial (enfranchised inhabitants numbered between 500 and 1000 in the early seventeenth century) and assertive. In the early sixteenth century, trouble over the election of the Corporation had turned into riot. In 1595, in blunt statement of their lack of genuine choice of governors, the freemen had simply refused to select a Corporation. In 1612, more trouble occurred when the town oligarchs sought to further complicate and qualify the freemen's role in the election of the Corporation. Deploying rhetoric that highlighted the close connections between concepts of local and national rights, dissident freemen deselected those members of the Corporation who 'went aboute to take awaye their ancient lib[er]ties & customs'.

The nature of the town's constitution ensured that freemen were not only caught up in contests over the selection of their local governors. Ambiguity over the nature of the parliamentary franchise meant that the commonality and the Corporation ran into conflict over the right to select the town's two members of parliament. The matter reached a head in 1627, when 'the common sort of burgesses in general' refused to elect one of the two candidates whom their governors had selected for their endorsement, and chose their own member. The 'common sort of burgesses' petitioned Parliament to settle the dispute, which decided in favour of the freemen's independent franchise.

Within towns like early Stuart Colchester, therefore, the contradictions of urban administration and representation helped to foster internal conflict and to focus a popular politics which, in its concern with 'ancient liberties and customs' and its growing interest in parliamentary authority, stood in contradiction to the principles of authoritarian patriarchalism. It is therefore unsurprising to find that in 1635 the Crown granted a new charter to the town in which popular constitutional rights were severely curtailed. Yet far from proving the death of popular politics within Colchester, the new charter merely heightened local antagonisms: for urban popular politics, while it often thrived within the contradictions of urban institutional arrangements, did not depend upon them.

In towns and cities, popular politics seemed at its most heterogeneous, vibrant and disputatious. This had much to do with the cultural and material environment of the town. Due to the substantially higher rates of literacy prevalent amongst the urban population, the presence of printing presses in London and (later) in other major urban centres, the greater density of population and the closer proximity of established political institutions, immediate political information and religious controversy formed a more powerful element of everyday life than was the case in rural areas. This was much more a matter of relativities than absolutes. It was far from the case that the plebeian inhabitants of the early modern countryside were cut off from national and international political news. We have already seen how closely attuned the rural commons of southern and eastern England were in 1548–9 to news from the Edwardian Parliament and Court. We have also seen how keen Elizabeth I's government was to both monitor and influence popular opinion in the distant Yorkshire dales during the rebellion of the Northern Earls in 1569. But in towns, and especially in London, the immediacy of news, and the sound of the popular voice seemed much louder.

There was an intimate political geography to the early modern town, the significance of which social historians are only beginning to appreciate.[8] The buzz of news within the metropolis of early modern London did not respect administrative boundaries between the City, Southwark, Westminster and the privileged islands of the Inns of Court, any more

than it followed socio-political boundaries between elite and plebeian.
More than anywhere else, early modern rulers worried about gossip in
the capital. Rumours of instability heard about the Exchange might
imperil the fiscal security of the state; gossip spread from poor Southwark alehouses might threaten its political security; and the one flowed
into the other. 'Men will tell you more than all the world, betwixt the
Exchange, Pauls and Westminster', remarked a visitor to London in
1631. St Paul's Walk was supposed to be frequented by the wealthier
classes of the City: merchants, gentlemen, diplomats and ministers. But,
as Adam Fox's researches into political gossip have shown, such centres
of rumour 'were not entirely socially exclusive'. Just as the collective face
of the crowd was recalled in the elite imagination in terms of clamour
('a great shuffling ... a commotion ... a hurly burly'), so the spread of
news seemed to form the white noise against which popular politics took
shape. 'The noyse in it is like that of bees,' one commentator observed in
1628, 'a strange humming or buzze, mixt of walking, tongues and feet ...
It is the great exchange of all discourse, and no business whatsoever but
is here stirring and a foot.' The metropolis operated as a centre for the
homogenisation and reproduction of regional gossip. As Fox observes:
'London acted as a magnet, drawing in visitors and their news stories
from around the country and then radiating them out once again'.[9]

There were certain sites within the early modern town through which
the current of news flowed most powerfully. Most important were those
places where travellers paused or stopped, journeys began and ended,
and where goods were traded. For poorer travellers, this meant alehouses; for richer folk, it meant taverns. Junctions of main throughfares,
where visitors mingled with residents, were another important spot. But
the most significant place in the social and political geography of the
town was the marketplace. In the largest cities such as Norwich, York,
Bristol or London, the urban landscape was punctuated with a variety of
open markets. Small towns and even some larger villages possessed their
own marketplace. Fine medieval crosses that had long been sensitive
points within the political geography of the town often distinguished
main crossroads and the centres of marketplaces. By the early seventeenth century, some had become occasional preaching spots, from
which godly lecturers propagated the gospels. Likewise, they were the
place at which royal commandments or new urban by-laws were
announced by town criers.[10]

Crosses, marketplaces and crossroads were not only sites at which
authority announced itself; their centrality in the physical organisation

of the town meant that they became contested sites of popular politics. Just before the outbreak of the Midland Revolt of 1607, a crowd of 100 of the 'poorer sort' gathered in a blacksmith's shop in the small town of Ladbroke (Warwickshire) to hear a reading of libellous verses against the local gentry. This described the county's rulers as 'greedy', 'filthie', 'craftie' 'lowte[s]', and 'knave[s]' for their enclosure of common land. Having 'forgott' to provide alms, the gentry were no longer the 'poore mans freinde'. The next stage in the propagation of this scribal insubordination seemed obvious: literate members of the audience made copies of the rhyming libel which they read aloud at fairs, markets and in church, and which were fixed to the market cross in Southam.[11] In the same fashion, Derbyshire miners, organising crowd demonstrations against the Church's tithe upon the lead ore they dug, spread news of their gatherings in 1634 by means of notes fixed to Tideswell market cross.[12] There was, then, a deeper context to the anonymous papers that were found attached to St Paul's Cross in London in May 1629. Their politics was specific to 1629 – the libels accused Charles I of having 'violated' his duties as King – but their form and the meaning of their placement had a longer history.[13]

Urban authorities lived in fear of the moment at which seditious speech moved from the semi-secret climate of the alehouse to the public air of the marketplace. And so the Norwich magistracy took seriously the angry speech of George Fowler in May 1634. A poor labourer of the City, Fowler earned so little that he was paid only in farthings; but he found that the market traders refused to fiddle in small coins. The enraged Fowler exploded that:

> nowe he could not have any victualls for [his farthings] & therefore ... yf [the traders] would not take them to morrow ... in the m[ar]kett, That hee and half a score more would make some stirre in the m[ar]kett.[14]

Fowler's angry speech grew from his marginal place in the urban economy, and helped to reproduce the small change of daily popular politics. More dangerous were the actions of the 'dyvers boyes and Lewde people' who pulled down the gibbet in Leicester's marketplace in June 1607. This had been erected, at the commandment of the Earl of Huntingdon, in an attempt to scare the commoners of the town out of taking action in support of the rural rioters then destroying enclosures within the midland counties. In breaking his gibbet, Huntingdon felt that the 'Children' of Leicester had shown that the town was not 'a place of government . . . to be governed by men of rip[e] age and not by the unruly stroke of youth'. That the youthful insurrectionaries had then proceeded to destroy recent enclosures made upon the town's commons seemed only to confirm Huntingdon's anxieties.[15]

Authority, commonality and economics collided most publicly and routinely within the marketplace. Sudden increases in the price of food might stimulate plebeian muttering or physical confrontations between traders, farmers and consumers. Deliberate demonstration and riot over the price of food typically converged upon, or originated within, the marketplace. Urban authorities often attempted to impose themselves between the Scylla of the market and the Charybdis of moral economy, empowering city officers and magistrates to see that grain was sold cheaply to the poor, or that the Book of Orders was put in effect. And authority brandished itself in the marketplace in the everyday form of the whipping post, the cage and the stocks; or, in times of great trouble, the temporary gallows.

The marketplace was therefore a theatre for the everyday performance of domination, subversion, confrontation and resistance. In times of crisis, the marketplace was transformed into a site at which audiences gathered to witness the symbolic enactment of political struggle. In early 1643, in statement of its Parliamentarian loyalties, the Corporation of Norwich sanctioned the burning of 'scandalous' religious images in the City's marketplace. Ninety years earlier, Smithfield market in London had been the site for the incineration of opponents of Mary I's counter-reformation; and in 1681 an effigy of the Pope was burnt there.[16] There was an important calendrical element to crowd activity in the urban environment. Shrovetide remained a dangerous time for independent women in early modern London: some twenty-four of the years between 1606 and 1641 saw recorded riots by London apprentices against alleged prostitutes and 'bawdy houses'. Ritual violence could be turned to more openly political ends: in 1641 and again most notoriously in 1668, apprentices' Shrovetide riots provided the opportunity for significant protest against royal government.[17] May Day, another traditional time for festive misrule and the occasion for large-scale riots in 1517, was adapted after the Restoration as a time for riotous displays of loyalty to the Crown. On 1 May 1660, Parliament had voted to restore the Stuart monarchy. On that day, the news had been greeted with bonfires, the peal of church bells and the citizenry of London 'drinking of the king's health upon their knees in the streets'. The anniversary of the arrival of

Charles II in England, 29 May, was likewise entered into the calendrical cycle of crowd demonstration. By the early eighteenth century, as the calendar became increasingly politicised, the two commemorations of May Day and Restoration Day slipped into one another. After the Hanoverian succession, 29 May remained commemorated by excessive drinking and displays of anglican harmony designed to annoy or intimidate local Whigs.[18]

The urban landscape and the calendrical year were not, therefore, merely passive backdrops to political life. Instead, time and space were imbued with passionate, and sometimes conflicting, meanings. The heterogeneous diversity of popular politics was at its most turbulent in early modern London. On 2 February 1642, in the course of widespread attacks upon 'popish' images and architecture within London and elsewhere, crowds attacked the medieval cross at Cheapside. Felt by godly Londoners to represent an antique remnant of catholicism, the cross had become an emblem of both the post-Reformation politicisation of urban space and of the diversity of urban popular politics. As the godly iconoclasts set about the ancient structure, they were themselves assaulted by crowds of apprentices calling themselves the 'defenders of the cross' and denouncing their opponents as 'roundheads and Brownings'. Marketplaces also provided the forum for collective conflict. Opposing crowds clashed in Smithfield market on the Whit Sunday of 1642 as one side tried to erect a maypole. The opponents of the religious ceremony were not above playing upon charivaric forms in expression of their politics. In August 1641, a high church service complete with organ music was interrupted by an invasion of boys, led by a drummer, who (without removing their hats) proceeded to dance amongst the outraged congregation.[19]

Early modern London's most prominent streets and open spaces were charged with political electricity.[20] The courtyard outside Parliament House provided possibly the most important channel for street politics, where in the 1640s crowds gathered to demonstrate their political views, raucously cheer those members whom they supported, harass those they despised, and distribute printed propaganda. Lambeth Palace, the home of the Archbishop of Canterbury and the site of major tumults amongst the apprentices on May Day 1640, was another charged place. The Strand, which connected the City to Westminster and on to which faced the London residences of many leading noble families, often formed a channel for crowd movement and a static site for political demonstration and symbolic argument. Supporters of the Stuart regime attempted to light a bonfire there in September 1679 to celebrate the Duke of York's return from political exile, but found that some 'yong men' kicked out their fire. Charing Cross shook to 'great shouts of joy' from 'the people' in October 1660 when it was the forum for the execution of the regicide Thomas Harrison. In the winter of 1659–60, as the Republican regime wilted and died, London apprentices gathered in Cheapside, Fleet Street and St Paul's churchyard to hang Harrison's fellow regicide Colonel Hewson in effigy. Twenty years later, in 1679 and 1680, Temple Bar, the junction between the City and Westminster and a long-established site for demonstrations, saw the Pope burnt in effigy by large crowds of Londoners demonstrating their hostility to the allegedly pro-catholic policies of the Restoration regime. The demonstrators used the anniversary of Elizabeth I's accession (17 November) to spell out their own claim to legitimacy: that their politics represented continuity with the tradition of English protestantism. Like the iconoclasm in Norwich in 1643, the Pope was burnt along with collections of catholic relics, images and books hunted out from recusant households by a sympathetic Whig magistrate. The Pope's effigy and the 'popish' relics were carried through London's main thoroughfares with much mock ceremony, preceded and followed by men dressed as Jesuits, monks and devils. Colourfully loaded with harsh messages about religious conflict, the Pope-burning ceremonies attracted crowds of up to 200 000 people according to one (probably exaggerated) report.

The forms of urban crowd politics, then, drew upon the deep reservoir of population that defined the metropolitan environment. That population was radically variegated by religion and (towards the end of our period) by party loyalty. Political stereotypes were starting to turn into party identities towards the close of the seventeenth century. The formation of such new identities sliced into pre-formed elite ideas about the political homogeneity of the 'rabble' and has made later Stuart historians especially dubious about ascribing any fundamental characteristics to 'popular' politics. Hearing reports of how, in late 1681, a London crowd 'went to blows among themselves by the distinction of Whig and Tory', privy councillors could be forgiven for perceiving of the 'rabble' less as a many-headed monster bent upon the destruction of the social order than as a beast divided against itself.

The melange of urban popular politics grew from the cultural and economic diversity of town life. Although urban social structures were plotted within visible extremes of wealth and poverty, many towns contained within them significant numbers of wealthier artisans, traders and minor merchants who together comprised an important middle segment within the urban social hierarchy. Keith Wrightson has argued that this social category, hitherto referred to as the 'better sort' or as the 'able inhabitants', discovered a political label in the early 1640s as the 'middling sort' of people. Importantly, the term seems scarcely to have been used before the English Revolution. Wrightson shows that the term acquired a new value and ubiquity within London in the crisis of 1641–2 as the wealthier citizens who had formed the leadership of crowd protest against royal government tried to counter allegations that they formed the head of plebeian sedition. Linking their claims to independent political rights with their economic and social autonomy as relatively wealthy, self-employed male householders, pro-Parliamentarian demonstrators and pamphleteers identified themselves as part of an industrious, virtuous 'middle rank' or 'middling sort' within the realm. Simultaneously distant from the horrors of lower-class sedition and from the corrupt popishness of the court, this newly defined London 'middling sort' created for themselves a label which was soon attached to others of similarly ambivalent social position within both town and countryside.[21]

Yet locked into the identity of the 'middling sort' was an explicit denial of popular politics. In order to counter accusations of seditious mutiny, the Root and Branch petition of December 1641 was escorted to Westminster by the wealthiest citizenry of London dressed in their finest clothes. Their presence was intended 'to prevent the aspersion that was laid upon them that they were of the basest sort of people only which were that way affected'. Other London petitions were signed only by male heads of household, so as to undermine suggestions that a flood of 'popularitie' was overwhelming the patriarchal order. Yet this did not satisfy some members of parliament, who continued to assert that the mass petition 'tended to mutiny' and 'would bring on the cutting of throats' by the lower orders.[22]

The ideal urban 'middling' householder was not only protestant, sober, male and industrious: he was also office-holding and literate. The fact that the term 'middling sort' is largely to be found within surviving examples of print propaganda tells us much about the relationship between socio-political self-categorisation and the printing press in the English Revolution. As office-holders within urban parishes, or as members of the common councils of towns and cities, the precursors of the 'middling sort' of the 1640s had long formed the broad basis of governance within the town. It is significant in this respect that the selective parish vestry was an urban innovation. Arguably, the loyalty of this expanding social group to the protestant religion within the Tudor capital had helped to stave off major political instability in the late sixteenth century.[23]

Such 'honest' and 'able' householders represented the urban equivalent of those rural yeomen who, over the same generations, seemed to be distancing themselves from 'mutinous' popular politics. But like that rural 'better sort', the wealthier townsmen who participated so extensively in the government of corporations, guilds, companies and parishes were acquiring habits of political organisation and being exposed to a rhetoric of governance which could be used for more than one end. Divisions within some London parishes in the 1630s and early 1640s followed the same fault-lines as those within the Corporation, the Common Council and, eventually, the Parliament. Always a fraught subject in early modern London, disputes over the extent of the franchise and the nature of custom within London companies and guilds expanded and intensified in the early 1640s. Struggles within the companies and guilds against the 'arbitrary' power of masters seemed to their protagonists to represent micro-political mirrors of the simultaneous struggle within the national body politic. Importantly, however, whereas parish activists for the godly religion tended to come from the wealthier social classes, those involved in agitation over the franchise and customary issues within companies were not included amongst them.[24] Conceived of from the dizzy heights of patriarchal ideology as a unified and terrifying plebeian mass, urban popular politics seethed with contradiction and potential conflict.

The heterogeneity of urban politics seems to have been lost upon many pro-Royalist commentators in the early 1640s. Shocked by their humiliating defeat at the elections for the Short and Long Parliaments in 1640, pro-Court candidates were tempted to describe elections in the terminology normally reserved for riots and rebellions. Lord Maynard's notorious fulmination of 1640 against the county electors of Essex forms the ideal type of such rhetoric. He wrote in anger to Sir Thomas Barrington, the victorious candidate, of how 'rude vulgar people' had grown to 'insolencye' in denying him his seat in Parliament. Warming to his theme, the election crowds transformed in his account into 'popular assemblies whear fellowes without shirts challenge as good a voice as myself', leading 'to menacing of us all to pull us in peeces'.[25]

It was certainly true that in some areas the distribution of the parliamentary franchise offered great potential for the articulation of the popular voice. The late sixteenth and early seventeenth centuries saw a substantial increase in the size of the electorate, as inflation cut into the monetary qualification for the freeholder franchise in the countryside, and as an increasing number of towns acquired enfranchised charters which enabled them to send representatives to the House of Commons. More important still, as we have seen, the extent of the franchise laid down in such charters was often surprisingly wide, allowing a substantial proportion of the male householding population of towns and cities to participate in parliamentary elections.[26] But as Mark Kishlansky has argued, those possibilities for popular politics were only rarely realised before the late seventeenth century. Contested elections before 1640 were very unusual. County gentry and urban oligarchs met in advance of elections in order to select from amongst their number those who would be sent to Parliament. Such selections were based upon the perceived 'honour' and standing of individual gentlemen amongst their peers, rather than any overt ideological position. The selected candidates would then be presented to the election crowd for their passive acclamation. This seemed to offer Kishlansky confirmation of his view that 'In early modern England, political activity took place within the context of a hierarchical social structure and theocentric universe.'[27]

The result of the Essex county election of 1640 was certainly distasteful enough to Lord Maynard. But, as Ann Hughes has perceptively observed, what truly affronted Maynard was the fact that an election had occurred at all; as she points out, 'by counting each man's vote as equal', the poll had 'affronted all ideas of social hierarchy'.[28] The concept of the gentry county community represented a small-scale model of the national patriarchy imagined within authoritarian ideology. Moved by the defining anxieties of social authoritarianism, county gentlemen and urban governors tried to present the outside world with a unified whole; for division amongst the 'honour community' of the gentry was felt to open the doors to popular insurrection.[29] Hence, for Maynard, the division of the Essex gentry had created the possibility that 'fellowes without shirts' might 'pull us in peeces'.

Such elite anxieties reached boiling point in 1641–2; but they drew upon earlier characterisations of electoral politics. Contested Yorkshire county elections of 1625, in which the successful candidate Sir John Savile had played upon a populist, protestant, anti-Court rhetoric, were described by his defeated opponent as more like 'a rebellion than an election'. In a similar tone, the disputatious county elections of 1628 were likened to insurrections: 'very unruly'; candidates chosen by

'public outcrye'; elections themselves like the dreaded peasant 'fury'.[30]
Parliamentary elections, especially when set in towns like Halifax or
Colchester with their godly preachers and assertive clothiers and weavers, seemed to reproduce all of the darkest nightmares of the Stuart
gentry. Again, then, we are reminded of the extent to which patriarchal
authoritarianism was designed for internal consumption by the gentry,
rather than as a hegemonic ideology intended to pull upon the loyalty of
their social subordinates. But, while that body of ideas helped to maintain internal cohesion amongst the gentry, it blinded them to the deep
divisions that ran through popular politics. For generations, the gentry
had been schooled to believe that the division of their class in civil war
would lead to the emergence of a united popular challenge to the status
quo. Yet with retrospect what is most impressive about popular politics
in the English Revolution was its religious, cultural and regional diversity.
It is to that heterogeneity that we now turn.

II   Religion, Popular Culture and the Origins of Civil War Allegiance

Throughout the first civil war (1642–6), both the King and the Parliament
faced the problem of mustering popular support. Given that both sides
claimed to be upholding the traditional socio-political order, this placed
propagandists in a difficult position. For, according to traditional
authoritarian social theory, those outside the gentry and nobility had no
legitimate voice within the national polity. This problem was most
serious for the parliamentary side, due to Royalist accusations that it had
become the creature of the seditious lower orders. The charge had a
special force due to the strong support shown to the Parliament by demonstrating London crowds during the crisis months of November and
December 1641, and by major pro-Parliament crowd protests in many
towns and cloth-producing areas in the summer of 1642. This section
therefore surveys the ways in which print propagandists appealed to
popular opinion, and examines in particular the meanings given to 'the
people' and 'the middling sort' during the 1640s. It also examines the
deeper sources of popular allegiance: how did puritanism influence
popular politics in early Stuart England? Why were popular responses
to the outbreak of war so regionally varied? How did definitions of
popular politics change during the 1640s? But we begin with the most
obvious of questions.

When did the English Civil War start? For those assembled at Nottingham on 22 August 1642, the answer might have seemed self-evident. Watching the attempts to raise the King's standard over the town, observers would have recognised its significance: the King was demonstrating that he was in arms against his rebellious Parliament, and was calling upon the loyalty of his subjects. Keen to lobby popular opinion, that very day the King had set his name to printed declarations addressed to the truculent miners of the Derbyshire Peak Country, offering to exempt them from manorial duties if they joined his forces at Nottingham. Highlighting both popular involvement in the earliest stages of the civil war and the diversity of popular allegiances, 150 miles south of Nottingham, the 22nd of August saw large crowds marching out of Colchester to destroy the neighbouring mansion house of Sir John Lucas. Caught up in the anti-catholic fears washing around England that summer, the inhabitants of Colchester suspected Lucas of harbouring armed papists who, so the rumours went, intended the slaughter of loyal protestants.

In Nottingham, at Colchester, and in the mining villages of the Peak Country, it might have seemed that the war started on 22 August 1642.[31] But longer hindsight might suggest that the war really began on 15 July 1642, the day on which the Parliament appointed the Earl of Essex as the captain general of its forces. Military division, although not yet organised fighting, proceeded from that day. The early summer of 1642 saw both Crown and Parliament rallying support and mustering troops across England. Or perhaps the point at which war became certain was in December 1641. Looking back on the origins of civil war from the distance of the Republic, one anonymous commentator found significance in the location of Charles I's execution:

> neare (if not in the very same place) where the first bloud in the beginning of the late troubles was shed, when the King's cavaliers fell on the citizens, killed one, and wounded about 50 others.

Perhaps civil wars start when armed factions become identifiable. It was in the course of those notorious attacks that the term 'Roundhead' first entered into the lexicon of proto-Royalism.[32] The demonstrations and riots of December 1641 and January 1642 broke royal control over the streets and open spaces of London and Westminster. By 10 January, claiming that his family was no longer safe from the London crowds, Charles and his court left Whitehall palace for Windsor.[33]

Later Royalist propagandists were to argue that it was in January 1642, with the displacement of the monarch from his capital, that the civil war began. For, as the author of the massively popular *Eikon Basilike* was to interpret events from the distance of 1649:

> as swine are to Gardens and orderly Plantations, so are Tumults to Parliaments, and Plebeian concourses to publick Counsels, turning all to disorders and sordid confusions.

The people, acquiring their collective form as 'that unruly animal' the *mobile vulgus* (the vulgar in motion), had not only broken into the halls of government, but had ejected its main occupant. England's traditional ruling class were reminded by the royalist press that 'The security of the nobility and gentry depends upon the strength of the crown ... otherwise popular government would rush in like a torrent upon them.' In such accounts, it was therefore the entry of the *mobile vulgus* that marked the start of the war. Sliding over complexities of religious, local and social division within popular politics, later Royalist accounts were to depict civil war as class war, and the 'people' as a homogeneous 'Plebeian concourse'.[34]

Or perhaps the war began in speech and imagination. If so, then civil war first arrived in the Cheshire village of Holt in 1638, when the godly householder Alexander Powell found 'a beggar man' at his door. Powell turned away the beggar, saying:

> No Sirrah you shall have no Almes here for shortly you wilbe prest to warr, and then you will fight ag[ains]t us.

Powell's words proved eerily prophetic. Located beside a strategic bridge on the main road from North Wales into the Cheshire plain, Holt was fought over several times in the course of the first civil war, and by 1646 the village lay in ruins. Prior to the civil war, the leading inhabitants of Holt had established a reputation for puritanism. Back in 1638, the churchwardens of Holt had been accused of allowing a suspended puritan minister to preach in their church. Amongst those accused of attending such 'illegal conventicles' was Alexander Powell. As in the famously godly county of Essex, talented puritan ministers had long been at work within parts of Lancashire and Cheshire, securing a certain popular basis for puritanism.[35] Differing regional reactions to pre-war puritanism were to influence fundamentally wartime popular politics. It is this fact that has led some historians to define the English Revolution as a 'war of religion'.[36] But civil war allegiance was so complex as to deny any single causal explanation. Puritanism, for instance, represented a view not only upon the national politics of church doctrine and foreign policy, but also upon the local politics of social power, poverty and poor relief.

Puritanism encouraged its adherents to think in terms of cultural, religious and political conflict. The willingness of puritan preachers to dwell upon binary oppositions between godly, regenerate, able householders and profane, popish, alehouse frequenters helped to invest religious meaning in local economic divisions between rich and poor. Both David Underdown and William Hunt have argued that a long cultural conflict helped to push England into war in 1642. Within the material world, puritan ministers and layfolk had long sought to reform the manners of their poorer or more profane neighbours: closing down alehouses, scrutinising morals, cleansing popish habits. Within the spiritual world, the 'puritan mind-set' was founded upon the anticipation of apocalypse, divine judgement and the force of providence. If the last days seemed near at hand, Satan's forces were already mustering against the godly in the shape of popish courtiers and alehouse drunks: that multitude whom Richard Baxter, the godly minister of Kidderminster (Worcestershire) called 'the drunken riotous party of the town (poor journeymen and servants)' who rushed to the defence of the Royalist cause.[37]

Puritanism therefore grew within the conceptual cracks in popular politics. To its Arminian opponents, puritanism contained the dangerous germs of 'popularitie'.[38] Yet the relationship between puritanism and popular politics was more ambiguous. There is little doubt that godly religion helped to justify the articulate involvement of 'the people' in both parochial and national politics. Yet it did so by limiting the social breadth of that term, and by politicising its meaning. In part, the social force of puritanism came from its validation of the growing gap between richer and poorer villagers, such that 'the people' and 'the poor' became distinct and opposed categories. And so, when 'the people' entered politics, they did so partly to protect themselves from 'the poor'. The micro-politics of the village and the macro-politics of the realm seemed therefore to connect in Alexander Powell's reported remark to the supplicant beggar at his door in 1638. Perhaps to godly householders such as Powell it seemed reasonable to see in the poor beggar of today the armed soldier of tomorrow. Possibly, this proved to be a self-fulfilling prophecy. Certainly, the poor, illiterate and allegedly popish inhabitants of the Welsh hills which stood above Holt proved such a fertile recruiting ground for the Royalist cause that they became known as 'the nursery of the King's infantry'.[39]

Godly religion, then, provided an intellectual basis for the imagination of civil war. So, too, did the defence of the subject's rights. In his study of political gossip, Adam Fox provides a graphic example of how as early as October 1626, civil war had become a subject of conversation within one London tavern. Worries about Charles I's leading advisor, the Duke of Buckingham, considered by many to harbour both popish sympathies and tyrannical tendencies, led Thomas Bridiman into a remarkable set of speculations. He told his audience within John Brangston's tavern in Drury Lane how:

> now, the auncient men's cou[n]cells are refused and justice had not lawfull proceeding, and the papists encreased and grew bold, unto whom it is held the duke of Buckingham is a great patron ... if the state stood as it doth it would not continue long.

Asked what he thought might replace the current state, he replied 'It may bee a free state, or perhaps the Palatine and the Lady Elizabeth shall have it.' Turning to John Brangston, Bridiman posed the question which sixteen years later would divide England: 'whether he would be for the king or the country'. Significantly, Brangston replied that 'hee had bin asked that question before'. Considering the question, he 'said a while after, hee would be for the king'.[40]

Few people welcomed the beginning of fighting in the summer of 1642; but it can scarcely be said that the outbreak of war went unanticipated in earlier years. With retrospect, it seemed to the godly minister Richard Baxter that 'the Warre was begun in our streets before the King or Parliament had any Armies'.[41] Securing popular allegiance became the prime objective of both King and Parliament over the summer and autumn of 1642. For the King in particular, this sudden interest in popular politics conflicted with his earlier successes in winning over gentry opinion through appeals to patriarchal authoritarianism. In the winter of 1641, Sir Thomas Aston, one of the Crown's most skilful propagandists, had restated the bluntest Latinate clichés of that ideology: 'the *primates*, the *nobiles*, with the *minores nobiles*, the gentry, consult and dispose the rules of government; the plebeians submit to and obey them.'[42] Yet there was a hollow ring to such rhetoric. For in its search for soldiers, the Crown was forced to deal openly with groups of plebeians on something like equal terms. We have already seen how, at the outbreak of fighting, King Charles made an appeal to the Peak Country miners. Over late August and September 1642, the King succeeded in mustering a regiment of Peak miners; but only after protracted negotiations between the divine right monarch and the largely illiterate miners had resulted in the grant of extensive concessions to the latter. The canny miners' Royalist allegiance flowed from the deliberate priority they gave to their local conflicts and solidarities, and reminds us of the importance of contingency as a factor in popular allegiance. For the King was aided in his negotiations by the fact that the main Parliamentarian protagonist within the Peak Country was Colonel Sir John Gell, who for twenty years had led the legal campaign to force the miners to pay a tithe upon their lead production.[43] Elsewhere, popular support for the Royalist cause had deeper cultural and religious roots.

The close connection between puritanism and Parliamentarianism in 1642 helped the Royalists to play upon popular anti-puritanism and to depict themselves as the protectors of the old festive culture of 'the people'. We saw in Chapter 2, Sections I–III how, in the sixteenth century, those who claimed to represent the 'commons' sought to speak on the behalf of a united, collective 'commonality'. Godly religion, for all that it worked within the institutions of village politics, did much to disrupt that older social world. We might understand the formation of puritanism as a war both within and against popular culture, in which the lower-class opponents of puritanism set godly values of sobriety, chastity, diligence and quietude against the rumbustious, inclusive, hedonistic, moderate protestantism of the 'commons' of early Stuart England. In some local contexts, the puritan struggle against church ales, wakes and village festivities might be understood as a cultural offensive against those senses of community that had hitherto legitimated popular politics. The godly had therefore to confront the same forms of resistance as did other 'enemies of the commons': anonymous but corrosive murmuring backed by the vindictive libels; outright statements of verbal hostility; assault, riot and intimidation; carnivalesque mockery and humiliation by merry-makers during traditional holidays.[44] The forms of plebeian anti-puritanism tell us much about the tactical basis of pre-war popular politics; while their logic reveals much about the socio-cultural sources of wartime popular Royalism.

The exclusive nature of puritanism, while it seemed to validate the godly's self-perception as an embattled minority, damned them in the eyes of those who claimed to speak for the 'commonality'. This was especially so in those towns and villages where local institutional power was held by an exclusive group of godly 'chief men' of the 'better sort'. In 1620 in Stratford-upon-Avon (Warwickshire) the composer of one anonymous libel of the 'Chief Rulers in the Synagogue of Stratford' singled out their small number as evidence of their lack of representativeness: they were 'but a few . . . I think they are but seven'. Godly attempts to discipline the poor through discriminatory systems of poor relief were similarly represented by anonymous libellers as breaches of the traditional values of the commonality. A libel addressed 'To all sturdy puritan knaves' was picked up in the streets of Dorchester (Dorset) in 1606. This played upon the hypocrisy, lowly origins and lack of charity that defined the town's godly elite:

> Thy mind is high, thy purse is small
> God knows it to be true
> For were it not for other men's goods
> thy state were of bad hue.

Between around 1580 and 1640, such libels developed into a small, burlesque literary genre. Their anonymous authors typically highlighted certain themes: the bookish piety of the godly, their contempt for the poor, their breach of Christian charity and duty, the lack of legitimacy which underpinned the local rule exercised over godly towns and villages. Anti-puritan libels were often heavily sexualised, and dwelt in lurid terms upon the fevered lust that allegedly simmered within the puritan mind-set. Most importantly, libels countered godly claims to represent the commonwealth of the village:

> You carry your bible God's word to expound
> And yet in all knavery you daily abound . . .
> Yea covetousness, lechery and lying for gain
> Amongst you puritans is not counted vain.

The libels therefore reveal something of the anonymous, semi-secret nature of social critique within many towns and villages in early Stuart England. But they also highlight how the politics of the parish intersected at the outbreak of the English civil wars with the politics of the realm.[45]

Puritanism complicated popular politics. It highlighted the diversity of popular political culture, and has led some historians to conclude that the seventeenth-century conflicts are best understood in terms of 'vertical' solidarities of religion, culture and locality, rather than 'horizontal' ties of class.[46] Similar complications arise from the dabbling of the gentry in popular anti-puritanism. Years before the civil war, conservative gentry in many parts of England had delighted in infuriating godly opinion by allying themselves with the older, residual culture of the 'commonality'. The Crown occasionally aided them in this. In the latter years of James I's reign, and much more so during the Caroline period, the official leadership of the Church of England moved away from the Calvinist emphasis upon sabbatarianism and church discipline. In their place, the increasingly influential Arminians sought to encourage forms of worship that bore similarities to the communal religious culture preferred by lower-class anti-puritans. To the godly, official support for church ales and Sunday games provided further evidence of the growing force of popery within the Church and the Court. And despite the Arminian connection between ecclesiastical and social hierarchy, the attack on puritanism created possibilities for popular Royalism. This was most apparent in those counties such as Herefordshire and Gloucestershire, where the old customs of May Day dancing, whitson ales, rush-bearing and horse-racing received enthusiastic sponsorship from leading anti-puritan gentry and nobility.[47]

Later Royalist gentry allegiance cannot be plotted from attitudes to popular festivals in the 1620s and 1630s. As Ronald Hutton points out, both future Royalists and future Parliamentarians amongst the Somerset magistracy were united in their opposition to church ales in 1633, seeing in them potential focuses for popular rebellion. Nonetheless, as Peter Stallybrass suggests, courtly gentlemen's patronage of whitson revels, rush-bearing rituals and Rogationtide traditions (all objects of godly contempt) strove to create 'a mythical unity of prince, gentry and people' which was important in forming a cultural basis for wartime popular Royalism.[48] While the ideals of social hierarchy which were manufactured in games and festivals represented the people as politically passive and deferential, they also legitimised and disseminated a symbolism which was later used to articulate a popular Royalist culture. It should be no surprise that the maypole became such a powerful symbol of popular Royalism. At Ludlow (Shropshire), cultural war preceded military division when in June 1642 the inhabitants 'set up a maypole and a thing like a head upon it ... and gathered a great many about it and shot at it in derision of Roundheads'.[49]

There was a powerful politics to the social use of alcohol in early modern England; this became especially overwhelming during the

English Revolution. During the 1650s, Quarter Sessions juries were to hear regular complaints against nostalgic Royalists who had been caught giving voice to their old loyalties. But alcohol did more than loosen Royalist tongues; drink and alehouse culture had long been targets of puritanism. In labelling the Royalists as drunken dissolutes, Parliamentarian propagandists formed a new pool of support for the King. Royalists within Hereford seemed to their Parliamentarian opponents to have come from amongst the Sabbath-breakers, 'totally ignorant in the ways of God, and much addicted to drunkenness and other vices, but principally to swearing'.[50] Successful Royalist appeals to 'the commons' therefore connected with that deep vein of burlesque ribaldry that ran through popular political culture.

It is only in recent years that historians have begun to appreciate the strong regional, ethnic and national basis of popular Royalism. Mark Stoyle has suggested that the Cornish conceived of godly preachers as agents of an English linguistic and cultural imperialism. Literate, metropolitan puritanism reciprocated, branding the Cornish as illiterate pagans. Just as the landless poor of southern and East Anglian villages had been socially excluded from the godly's definition of 'the people', so the Cornish were disqualified on cultural and ethnic grounds. For the godly, 'the people' were understood to be both protestant and English; the Welsh and Cornish inhabited that English empire, but just like English catholics and paupers, were only partial members of it.[51] Writing in 1645, John Corbet assumed a cultural geography to Royalism, claiming that 'the common people addicted to the King's service have come out of blind Wales, and other dark corners of the land'. Corbet also plotted popular allegiance according to economics. In those areas dominated by 'powerfull gentry', the 'rabble' were active for the King's party. In contrast, where the dominant class 'consisted chiefly of yeomen, farmers, petty-freeholders, and such as use manufactures', then 'the poore and needy ... observed those men by whom those manufactures were maintained that kept them alive' and turned to support the Parliament.[52] In Corbet's account, therefore, the economic and political interests of their local social superiors drove the political allegiances of the lower orders. Although we shall see in Section III how inaccurate such accounts were, they remain important for the light they shed upon the sources of popular allegiance. In particular, Corbet's account illuminates the willingness of contemporaries to conceive of the English Revolution not only as a religious and a cultural war, but also as a social conflict.

John Corbet's interpretation of economic and cultural geography also determined other Parliamentarian accounts of popular allegiance. Most notably, Richard Baxter emphasised the social basis of popular allegiance in 1642, paying special attention to the strong loyalty shown by the industrious 'middling sort' to the Parliament. For Baxter:

> On the parliament's side were ... the smaller part (as some thought) of the gentry and the greatest part of the tradesmen, and freeholders, and the middle sort of men; especially in those corporations and counties which depend on clothing and such manufactures.[53]

Corbet deduced a similar socio-economic pattern to the formation of parliamentary allegiance. 'Setting aside ... some gleanings of the gentry', Corbet recalled that in 1642 'the yeomen, farmers, cloathiers, and the whole middle ranke of the people' had been the main supporters of the parliamentary cause.[54] Corbet was a godly minister who served during the war as chaplain to the Parliamentarian governor of Gloucester, Colonel Edward Massey. In 1645, he published his instant local history of the English revolution, *An historicall relation of the military government of Gloucester.* Richard Baxter came from a similarly partisan background: the son of a godly yeoman, he was brought up with a strong sense of his family's isolation from the festive, 'popish' culture of the 'vulgar rabble'. Like Corbet, Baxter went on to become a godly minister and, during the civil war, acted as chaplain to the Parliament's forces. His autobiography was written with longer retrospect than Corbet's, and published posthumously in 1696.

Baxter's and Corbet's writings have been used to bolster the Marxist argument that the civil war saw a revolutionary 'middling sort' confronting a Royalist party primarily made up of gentlemen. Both Christopher Hill and Brian Manning have found in Corbet a powerful validation of this 'bourgeois revolution' thesis. But it is Dave Rollison who has developed the subtlest application of Marxist theory to the local history of class conflict in the English Revolution. As he puts it:

> Corbet's account [of the civil war] ... is more than merely compatible with a class-based explanation of what happened and why it happened. Terminology aside, Corbet offers a class analysis and explanation that Marx himself would have been happy to own.[55]

Marxist historical interpretation has rather more life left in it than its critics have supposed, in particular in its organising assumption that politics arises in part from social conflict over access to resources. Yet its most baleful influence upon radical historiography has been its failure to address the roots of popular conservatism. Nowhere has this been more apparent than in Marxist approaches to popular Royalism during the English Revolution. In such accounts, popular Parliamentarianism is interpreted as the political side-product of longer processes of economic and social 'modernisation'. Hence, parliamentary domination of East Anglia and London is presented as a product of the agrarian capitalism of the former and the economic sophistication of the latter. By contrast, the running dog of popular Royalism is dismissed as backward and feudal. As Brian Manning sums up the matter:

> the King's party was essentially a party of gentlemen, who dominated its whole ethos. It was the more deferential and the less independent of the poor and middle sort that followed the king, accepting the lead of their social superiors and contributing little to the royalist cause except perhaps a more virulent hostility towards puritans and puritanism.[56]

Evidence of the powerful support given by the industrious 'middling sort' to the Parliament is not hard to find in the contemporary printed propaganda. But historians need to be cautious about its use. For the term 'middling sort' was not a neutral sociological category, but was rather a heavily politicised label that acquired a new national resonance during the English Revolution. Like the better-known terms 'roundhead' and 'cavalier', the 'middling sort' was a product of the political imagination of the 1640s.[57]

The term 'middling sort' was not an invention of the English Revolution; albeit only very occasionally, historians have found references to the phrase before the 1640s. Its use as a national socio-political category, however, was an enduring innovation of the 1640s. It is perhaps unsurprising that archivally based studies of popular allegiance should find yeomen farmers, wealthy artisans, clothiers and merchants (that is, the wealthier non-gentry groups supposed to comprise the 'middling sort') present on both sides of the civil war divide.[58] Yet Baxter, Corbet and other pro-Parliamentarian writers covered over the diversity of middling sort allegiance. In defining their supporters as the 'middling sort', they were able to resist Royalist accusations that the Parliament's cause led towards popular insurrection. Hence, for one Parliamentarian propagandist, while the 'middle sort of people, and the yeomanry' represented the upholders of English liberty, 'the scum of the people' remained hostile to the parliamentary cause. Parliamentary writers were especially keen to show that they represented neither degenerate aristocrats nor seditious 'peasants'. Hence, in Portsmouth, the Royalists were supposed to be favoured by 'poor mechanic persons', while the Parliament was backed by 'the better sort'. In Bristol,

> the king's cause and party were favoured by the two extremes in that city; the one the wealthy and powerful men, the other of the basest and lowest sort, but disgusted by the middle rank, the true and best citizens.[59]

This presentation of the parliamentary cause was aided by the strong pre-war linkage between godly religion and the 'industrious' values of the 'better sort' of people. Importantly, this linkage provided a prior logic to the Parliament's claim to represent both the 'middling sort' and the sober, diligent, protestant values which were felt to be embodied in that class. In any case, as a loose political label rather an abstract sociological classification, the term 'middling sort' was innately flexible. For Corbet, the 'middle ranke' of Gloucestershire were simply 'such as use manufactures that enrich the country'.[60]

In representing their cause as that of the 'middling sort', the Parliament's propagandists placed themselves in the same contradictory position as that which trapped the Crown: for both, the problem remained of how to capture the support of that 'lower sort' whom their propaganda disparaged. Just as Royalists tried to depict the parliamentary cause as dominated by authoritarian puritanism, so parliamentary propaganda worked on the two fundamental anxieties which defined early Stuart popular politics: fear of popery and of the gentry. 'Would you know why so many of the gentry in most counties throughout the kingdom are so malignant [that is, royalist]?' the godly preacher Jeremiah Burrowes asked his readers. The answer lay in a cunning gentry plot:

> They would fain bring it to be with us as it is in France, that the gentry should be under the nobility and courtiers, and all the country people, the peasants, be under them as slaves, they live in miserable bondage under the gentry there, who generally are cavaliers.

The leading Parliamentarian newspaper *Mercurius Britanicus* similarly discerned a popish plot to raise up a French tyranny over freeborn English commoners, accusing the Royalists of having:

a plot in hand to enslave the whole commons of the kingdom, and therefore cannot endure to hear that the yeomanry should be held of any esteem, or have anything to do in matters of the least public concernment.

That broad basis of English governance that Sir Thomas Smith had sensed back in 1562 should then be broken:

> It was the old court-plot, ever to hoist up the prerogative of the king, to suppress the liberty of the subject; setting before his eyes the absolute power of France as a pattern of emulation, so that in time the ancient and free English title of yeoman should have been changed into peasant or slave.[61]

Once again, John Corbet's political sociology was representative of Parliamentarian logic. The 'powerfull gentry' supported the Crown out of a desire 'to rule over their neighbours like vassals'. The gentry's desire of 'vast dominion' and 'dignity' led them to 'an hatred of the commons and a strong disposition to the ends of tyranny'. This was the language of 1549, turned to the political needs of 1645. Seeking a popular basis for puritanism, Corbet tried to connect the gentry's alleged social conservatism to their 'hatred and fear' of 'reformed religion, which seemed to them a peevish affectation of novelty'. And so for a moment the social classifications of the Commotion Tyme and the English Revolution seem to blur, as an oppressed commons harried by a merciless nobility become transformed into a godly middling sort opposed by popish courtiers. How did all of this relate to the reality of popular politics and social conflict in rural England during the English Revolution? Sections III–V attempt to answer that question.

III   Rural Riot in the English Civil War

We saw in Section II how the language and logic of print propaganda helped to define civil war allegiances. Yet popular politics was not conjured out of the magical discourses of print propaganda. Nor, for many labouring people, was religion the sole source of their wartime political loyalty. Rather, religious identities and hostilities intermingled with and informed other influences upon political allegiance. If a single generalisation can be made about popular responses to the outbreak of war in 1642, it is that such responses were much more autonomous of elite politics than has often been supposed. This should not be taken as proof that popular politics in the civil war were either united or homogeneous. For overlying this relative autonomy, as we saw in the previous section, was a radical diversity. This section will look at how historians have explained the diverse pattern of popular allegiance within rural England, and will scrutinise the rural protest and riot during the first civil war (1642–46).

Even at the height of the English Revolution, it was still possible to find elite contemporaries who were willing to conceive of politics as something removed from the people. Sir Arthur Haselrig, for instance, remained of the opinion that 'the people care not what government they live under, so as they may plough and go to market'.[62] Yet plebeian neutralism was often more aggressive than this remark suggests. In the course of a pro-Royalist rising in Kent in 1643, two blacksmiths led crowd attacks on a Parliamentarian gentleman's house. One of the blacksmiths was overheard to remark 'let us go to Hadlow and Peckham and plunder there, for they are rich rogues, and so we will go away into the woods'. His companion replied 'But we must plunder none but Roundheads'. The blacksmith was reported to have responded: 'We will make every man a Roundhead that hath anything to lose. This is the time we look for.' Whether accurate or not, reports of such speech tended to both confirm gentry suspicions that the lower orders might use the opportunity of the civil wars to impose a levelling tyranny, and to illuminate how civil war popular allegiances were influenced by perceptions of social conflict as well as religion.

Buchanan Sharp has used such evidence to argue that:

> the riots of the civil war period can be regarded as a manifestation of positive political indifference, rather than passive neutrality, a statement that the issues raised by the conflict between King and Parliament were of little or no concern to many ordinary people when weighed in the balance against such pressing local issues as disafforestation and enclosure.

Evidence in support of Sharp's thesis is not hard to find. Thus, for instance, the autumn of 1645 found the estate steward Mr Brunker (whom we last met in Chapter 3, Section IV), watching anxiously as armed clubmen gathered within his locality. Brunker concluded that the intention of that 'clubbe armie' was to 'conteme all superriors whatsoever and doe what they please'.[63] Yet critics of Sharp's thesis might answer that such evidence tells us more about elite fears than about the reality of popular protest in the 1640s. After all, as John Morrill and John Walter remind us, 'land and liberty was not to be the cry of the English Revolution'. As we saw in Chapter 3, Section II widespread rural disorder broke out in many parts of England between 1641 and 1643, and again between 1648 and 1649 (John Morrill has counted some 26 English counties within which enclosure rioting occurred in the years 1640–4). Morrill and Walter observe how rioters directed their attacks against recent large-scale enclosures, especially those on Crown and Church lands, and on the estates of major Royalist nobility and gentry. In partial confirmation of long-established elite fears, labourers and tenants broke into the deserted houses of their lords, pillaged the contents, rifled estate records, laid waste to the formal gardens which demarcated manor houses as gentry space and broke down new enclosures. Yet it was not only on the 'larger estates whose royal, aristocratic and episcopal owners were associated with a discredited regime' that such riots occurred.[64]

In those parts of England that fell under Royalist control, pro-Parliamentarian gentry were also liable to be pillaged by their tenants. An outstanding example concerns the Cranborne (Dorset) estates of the Earl of Salisbury. Salisbury was a Parliamentarian peer, but for much of the first civil war his Dorset estates lay under the control of the Royalist forces. On 8 May 1643 the Royalist army under the command of Prince Maurice passed through Cranborne. Maurice's soldiers sacked Salisbury's residence, threatening 'with fearfull othes to pull down the howse or burne it'. When Prince Maurice threatened 'to hange the first causers of the plundering', the soldiers replied that 'one and all' were responsible. The local tenants then invaded Cranborne House, making for the muniment room. Here they scattered and destroyed the court rolls that contained the records of their copyhold tenures. The inhabitants of the Cranborne estates had shown an increased hostility to seigneurialism prior to the attacks on Cranborne House. In April 1643, the tenants had refused to pay their rents, and by the end of the first civil war the Earl's bailiff at Cranborne reported that throughout the war, 'the poore sorte of people' had 'carried what they pleased out of the wood'. He explained that he and his factor 'durst not oppose [the poor sort] for fear of losing our lives which they did threaten'. Clearly, the disturbed conditions of the civil war created the possibility for the poorer sort to give voice to resentments that, in peacetime, they were more likely to articulate only in the semi-secret surrounds of the alehouse. Lawrence Stone perhaps overstates his case when he sees such evidence as suggestive of 'the class war [which] can be seen in the countryside as law and order broke down'. But Stone's assessment of the politics of the Cranborne tenants is certainly closer to the truth than David Underdown's who, highlighting the perils of ecological determinism, classifies Cranborne as a 'deferential' area on the grounds of its location in the chalk downlands.[65]

There can be little doubt that many labouring people saw the collapse of civil authority during the civil wars as an opportunity to set right local wrongs. But this did not necessarily lead to popular neutralism. In some regions, we might be tempted to interpret popular allegiance according to an 'inverse deference' model, in which the bulk of the lower orders took the opposing side to that of local powerbrokers. We have already seen, for instance, how many miners within the Derbyshire Peak Country were led to support the Crown due to their antagonism to the leading Parliamentarian gentleman Sir John Gell. Similarly, the strong support shown for the Parliamentarian cause by the inhabitants of the Forest of Dean (Gloucestershire), where the many poor cottagers, squatters and miners had been dispossessed of their local rights by the Crown in the 1620s and the 1630s, grew out from their prior animosities to the King. The local leader of the Royalist cause in the Forest of Dean was Sir John Winter, the chief beneficiary of the enclosure of the Forest in the late 1630s and, like his father before him, a leading opponent of the Forest of Dean miners' claim to free mining rights within the jurisdiction. As in Colchester, local conflicts gave a sharp focus to the Parliament's denunciations of national arbitrary tyranny, and forced a connection between the defence of local custom and the defence of the rights of the protestant English. It should therefore be unsurprising that parliamentary newsbooks regarded the commoners and miners of the Forest of Dean as the 'constant friends of the parliament'.[66]

Popular politics in the 1640s was not always so conditional. On 17 September 1642, the gentleman William Davenport of Bramhall in north-east Cheshire was appalled to receive a petition from 24 of his tenants concerning their choice of political allegiance. Although the letter was couched in the language that Davenport might expect from a properly subservient group of tenants, its content and implications were far from deferential. The petitioners commenced with a discussion of how their affection for the Parliamentary cause might influence their future relationship with Davenport:

Wee your Worships tenants ... havinge these manie dayes with sadd spirites weighed not onlie the woffull distractions off our kingdome, but also the present standinge that is betwixt your woorshippe and ourselves, have thought it our dutie, as well for the workeinge upp off a sweete union, as for the takinge away off all jealousies amongst us, to present youre woorshippe with these few lynnes off our humble request.

It was this concern for their relationship with their lord, according to the petitioners, that had led them to compose the petition. War had already come to Cheshire, and Davenport's tenants wished to demonstrate that considerations of plebeian duty to their lord would not influence their allegiance. They therefore requested:

that ethir you would be pleased to bend your intencions that waye which wee maye with upright hartes and saffe consciences cleave to you both in lyffe and death ... or else that your worshippe will not repute us ill affected or false-harted tenants in refusinge to venture our lyves in causses that our harts and consciences doe perswade us are not good or lawfull, nor such as wee dare safelye and with good consciences maintayne and deffend you in. For, howsoever wee would not for the world harbour a disloyall thought against his Majestie, yett wee dare not lifte upp our handes against that honorable assembly of Parliament.

Just as the petitioners wished to preserve the fiction of their loyalty to the Crown, so they also tried to maintain an appearance of deference to established social authority while acting upon their 'consciences' in support of cause which they deemed 'good' and 'lawfull'.[67] In this case, abstract considerations of conscience, law and parliamentary authority held supremacy over local loyalties.

Six days after William Davenport received his tenants' petition, the movement of a Royalist army towards Manchester inspired the ringing of church bells and mustering of pro-Parliamentarian inhabitants in north-east Cheshire. Some of the gentry of the area 'came with their tenants and well-affected neighbours, to assist the town'.[68] On the surface, the cross-class unity shown by the inhabitants of north-east Cheshire appeared to provide confirmation of what historians have called the 'tenant deference' interpretation of popular allegiance, which proposes that commoners passively followed the political lead given to them by their social superiors.[69] Yet, as we have seen, tenants in that corner of north-east Cheshire were well capable of making autonomous political decisions. A similarly autonomous political will seems to have driven the formation of popular allegiances in the clothing districts of the West Riding of Yorkshire upon the outbreak of civil war. Parliamentary print propaganda deliberately targeted the middling ranks of English society in the first few months of war. One such publication proposed that other Parliamentarians should follow the example of the defenders of Manchester:

> O England's yeomen and husbandmen looke to yourselves, for if you stand not to it, as we of Manchester do, but be overcome, look forever to be slaves.

Another proclaimed the belief that the Royalists intended to 'disarm the middle sort of people, who are the body of the kingdome'. Combined with the enthusiastic preaching of militant godly ministers, such propaganda had its effect upon the cloth workers, farmers and rural labourers of the West Riding. Mustering to the cry of 'A Fairfax, A Fairfax', large crowds of 'clubmen' armed themselves to defend their textile villages from the advancing Royalist forces which they believed to be composed of murderous, plundering catholics. Yet in spite of the cry which called the crowds together, initial leadership came not from the Fairfax family (who were the most prominent Parliamentarian supporters within the West Riding) but from local constables and some lesser gentry. One sympathetic account went so far as to suggest that as the Royalist forces approached, the wealthier Parliamentarians fled, leaving 'not a gentleman to command us'.

West Riding Parliamentarianism was swiftly given the label of 'Bradford club-law'. The popular insurrections in the West Riding forced a division in gentry allegiance: faced with a pro-parliamentary rising from below, the parliamentary leaders in the area, Sir Thomas and Lord Ferdinando Fairfax, were forced 'to join with readiness of people'. Yet as both Brian Manning and Andy Hopper have suggested, it was not only Royalist gentry who worried over the implications of Bradford club-law. Parliamentarian gentry also found the image of a militant commons in arms an appalling prospect. The image of 'the necessitous people' rising 'in mighty numbers' and installing their own government 'whosoever they pretend thought that first . . . to the utter ruin of all the nobility and gentry of the kingdom' was sufficient to have impelled the hitherto Parliamentarian Hothams of Hull into the King's camp.[70]

The wide variety of popular allegiances defies easy explanation. Were the lower orders motivated by class-based hostility to the gentry and the nobility, as both modern Marxist historians and many elite contemporaries believed? We have seen that although there is more than a grain of truth in such an argument, this remains far too large and simplistic a generalisation. In particular, this interpretation faces the problem that religious loyalties and anxieties crossed class boundaries in Stuart England; that political allegiances did not follow neat social boundaries; that 'class-based' allegiances were often attributed to plebeians by hostile observers in order to blacken the name of popular politics; and that on both sides, at least at the start of the war, the armies were led, and to a lesser extent officered, by the gentry and nobility. Social conflict heavily coloured political allegiances during the English Revolution, but it did not determine them. Similarly, the supposition that the lower orders simply deferred to their social superiors when choosing sides has been shown to be quite fallacious. Opposing religious identities, given a sharp focus by print propaganda, certainly provided the cutting edge to military and political conflict in the 1640s, but once again are complicated by social and local factors.

This tangle of conflicting influences has led many historians of the subject to avoid any broad explanation of popular allegiances during the first civil war, and to retreat instead into narrowly focused local case studies. Only one recent historian has had the boldness to propose a fresh interpretative framework within which local patterns of popular allegiance can be explained. In his remarkable book *Revel, riot and rebellion*, David Underdown has argued that variations in popular allegiance can be plotted according to local and regional differences in economy, social structure, local culture and ecology. Underdown argues that 'the division in the English body politic which erupted in civil war in 1642 can be traced in part to the earlier emergence of two quite different constellations of social, political and cultural forces, involving diametrically opposite responses to the problems of the time'. On the one side stood:

.

those who put their trust in a traditional conception of the harmonious, vertically-integrated society . . . in which the old bonds of paternalism, deference, and good neighbourliness were expressed in familiar religious and communal rituals.

Such values were most dominant, in Underdown's analysis, in lowland, agrarian England, within which long-established gentry families maintained a strong hold over those beneath them. In contrast, in poorer, more socially polarised, upland England, and especially within:

cloth-making wood-pasture districts...the gentry and middling sort...wished to emphasise the moral and cultural distinctions which marked them off from their poorer, less disciplined neighbours, and to use their power to reform society according to their own principles of order and godliness.

Although 'these two socio-cultural constellations can be observed in all parts of England', they were most clearly expressed in an ecological contrast between different regions, such that:

two alternative societies existed side by side, both increasingly polarised between rich and poor, but one relatively stable and reciprocally paternalistic and deferential, the other more unstable, less harmonious, more individualistic.[71]

Underdown's argument has not gone without criticism. It has been suggested that his idealised typology does not match the real geography of popular allegiance in 1642. Flat, agrarian East Anglia, for instance, remained solid for the Parliament throughout the first civil war, while pastoral-industrial Cornwall and North Wales were constant sources of Royalist support. It may be that in classifying upland, industrial England as a source of social and political disorder, Underdown was merely reiterating contemporary elite prejudices against such 'dark corners of the land'. Moreover, lurking within Underdown's interpretative schema is a powerful determinism: allegiances are presented as the product of long-term economic and social change, and religion and ideology seem to be downgraded, becoming mere expressions of structural differences between regions.[72] And yet, there is much that the social historian of early modern popular politics might learn from Underdown's work. The strength of his argument lies in his willingness to understand the pattern of popular allegiance in 1642 within the deeper context of early modern popular political culture, and in the attention he gives to regional differences and social change. We have seen throughout this book how contemporaneously meaningful were local and regional identities to plebeian political culture. We have also seen how the sudden assertion of a public plebeian presence within national politics at moments such as 1536–7, 1549, and 1641–2 is best understood as a manifestation of an already forceful popular politics hitherto operative within local and regional contexts. Underdown's work helps to clarify the significance of those marked regional contrasts, while also demonstrating how the politics of the parish connected with the politics of the nation during the first civil war. One of the most revealing examples of that connection is to be found in the clubmen movements that emerged towards the end of the first civil war.

IV 'The Peasantry with Arms in their Hands': the Clubmen Movements, 1644–5

The origins of the 'clubmen' movement are to be found in one of the defining terms of the 1640s: 'club law'. The phrase recurs extensively within both archival and printed accounts of rural riot during the English Revolution. We saw in Section III of this chapter how the pro-Parliamentarian popular rising in the West Riding was named 'Bradford club-law'. In the West Country during the early stages of the first civil war, country people were already implementing 'a rough and ready club law' to recover cattle, sheep and cloth stolen by marauding Welsh soldiers. The term was not necessarily suggestive of any clear political allegiance. Rather, as Ronald Hutton has pointed out, 'all irregular troops, whether employed privately or by the opposed factions' were 'indiscriminately' labelled 'clubmen'. But the term referred to more than merely 'their primitive equipment'. The concept of 'club law' referred to collective and autonomous (but not necessarily neutral) political actions on the part of the lower orders. In some contexts, 'club law' carried a still heavier implication: the insinuation that the lower orders were not only asserting an autonomous politics, but that they intended to level the social order.[73]

Hutton is certainly correct to draw attention to the indiscriminate use of the term 'clubman', which became the accepted label for the variety of popular movements that arose in 1645 across disparate parts of England and Wales. These included Shropshire, Worcestershire, Herefordshire, Wiltshire, Dorset, Somerset, Berkshire, Sussex and Hampshire together with parts of South Wales. The clubmen movements varied widely in their political loyalties. Some were avowedly neutralist. Some sided with the King, and others with the Parliament. Nonetheless, all were defined by a common concern to end the war. Arguably, the alliances formed between clubmen and local Royalist or Parliamentarian forces reflected this ambition, as, in their keenness to see the war brought to a conclusion, the clubmen sided with whichever forces seemed most likely to triumph. Even this generalisation is difficult, as in some areas, such as the textile region of Somerset, clubmen's political loyalties seem to have been more than skin-deep. But what remains striking about the various clubmen movements are their similarities. The various movements of 1645–6 were organised in strikingly similar ways, and often deployed the same political language. They provide us, therefore, with a lens on rural popular politics at the end of the first civil war. We shall focus our attention upon the clubmen movements in two regions: the West Country and the border marcher counties.

Since the outbreak of the first civil war (1642–6), small-scale, local hostility to the depredations of both Parliamentary and Royalist soldiers had occurred wherever there were military forces. But it was not until the winter of 1644–5 that large-scale, organised opposition began. The absence of major gentry figures from the leadership of such protest meant that they were soon labelled as 'clubmen'. The first such movements originated in Shropshire in December 1644, when 1200 people rose, led by a parson and some minor local gentry, to resist Royalist plundering. By February 1645, local Royalist leaders were referring to 'seditious people in the county who were mustered three thousand' in a 'rebellion'. By early March 1645, clubmen had also gathered to oppose the movement of Royalist troops in Herefordshire. On 5 March 1645, a large meeting of 'the inhabitants of all the North West part of the County of Worcester', presided over by a local minister, established an inter-parish association to defend themselves against:

> all Popery and Popish superstitions ... to defend the King's Majesty's person ... to preserve and uphold the ancient and just privileges of Parliament and known laws of this kingdom against all arbitrary government ... [and] to retain the property of the subject.

The following day 6 March 1645 saw 'the sufficient and best able men' of the parishes in Broxash Hundred in Herefordshire draw up a declaration to maintain (in similar terms) 'our lives and estates for the true Protestant religion, his Majesty's person, [and] our own estates and privileges' and to defend themselves 'against all papists', excise collectors and the forced impressment of troops. Importantly, the border marcher clubmen not only organised themselves against plunder, but also tried to represent their grievances to the authorities: the Worcestershire clubmen enlisted a local vicar to present their complaints to the Royalist high sheriff.

The immediate cause of trouble within the three border marcher counties was the recent formation, by the Royalist gentry of the region, of an Association of the counties of Worcestershire, Shropshire, Herefordshire and Staffordshire. This Association assumed the power to raise revenue and impress troops. Still more provocatively, the gentry Association included amongst its leadership some well-known catholic recusants. In response, the Worcestershire clubmen emphasised their hostility to popery, and their opposition to 'the execution of any commission intrusted upon any pretence whatsoever in the hands of any Papist'. Similarly, the Herefordshire clubmen refused 'to be led away by papists . . . out of our own country' and stressed their right 'to defend ourselves from all insolencies and violences whatsoever offered us or our estates at home'. The clubmen intended to initiate a dialogue with the dominant Royalist authorities. Ill-disciplined Royalist troopers had already plundered both areas. Prince Maurice, the local commander, had endeavoured to impose order upon his forces, and with this in mind the clubmen declarations cited the Prince's own recent orders. But clubmen attempts to secure aid from the established authorities were soon marginalised as military conflict broke out between the Herefordshire clubmen and local Royalist forces.

On 18 March 1645, a scuffle between Royalist soldiery and the inhabitants of the Herefordshire village of Cowarne led to the activation of the defence league established in the clubmen articles. This developed into a larger confrontation between the Herefordshire clubmen and the Royalists. An armed crowd of perhaps 4–6000 marched on Hereford to confront its unpopular Royalist governor. A later memoir described how 'an armed crowd came up and faced the walls of Hereford, calling out for redress or vengeance'. The 'peasantry . . . with arms in their hands . . . delivered a set of demands in writing', including the withdrawal of garrisons, the return of plundered goods, freedom from plunder, imprisonment and forced impressment, and the return of civilian government to the county. The Parliamentary commander in the region, Edward Massey, who attempted to woo the clubmen to his side, watched these developments with glee. Although negotiations between Massey and the clubmen proved fruitless, the frightened local Royalist commanders persuaded the field army under Prince Rupert to crush the clubmen. On 29 March, Rupert's Royalist forces encountered 2000 clubmen near Ledbury (Worcestershire), most of whom scattered at the sight of the soldiers. A few fired on the Royalists, with the result that Rupert's men captured and hanged three of their number. For the moment, this was the end of the 'agrarian insurrection'. But with the crushing Royalist defeat at Naseby in the summer of 1645, clubmen resurfaced in Shropshire and south Worcestershire. Partly inspired by the threats of the local Royalist commander to 'fire your houses without mercy' and 'hang up your bodies', the Shropshire and south Worcestershire clubmen co-operated with the local Parliamentary forces. In December 1645, the clubmen of north-west Worcestershire also reappeared.[74]

By June 1645, 'club' activity was at its strongest in the West Country counties of Somerset, Dorset and Wiltshire. The plebeian inhabitants of some parts of these counties already possessed a long-established tradition of riotous opposition to high food prices. The region also contained a number of large royal forests and other major estates where enclosure and disafforestation had proved important sources of social friction. Military control of the West Country fluctuated during the first civil war, such that both visiting armies and established garrisons frequently plundered all three counties. Plundering soldiers had already encountered organised village opposition in the area, but on nothing like the scale of the clubmen risings of the spring and summer of 1645. On 25 May 1645, clubmen from Dorset and Wiltshire gathered at Gussage Corner to establish a 'covenant' for a 'peace-keeping Association', intended to protect the inhabitants of both counties from plundering soldiers. In Somerset by early June 1645, a gathering of 5000 inhabitants, many carrying arms, drew up a petition for the attention of the locally dominant Royalist authorities which complained of the excesses of the soldiery. By the end of the month, Somerset's clubmen were mustering at Pensy-Pound on Sedgemoor, where they established a similar organisational model to that of the Wiltshire and Dorset clubmen.

As in the border marcher counties, both Royalist and Parliamentarian leaders in the West Country attempted to influence the clubmen, meeting with varying success. The clubmen from the textile villages around north-east Somerset co-operated with the Parliamentary forces under the command of Oliver Cromwell, while those originating from the Bridgwater area aided Sir Thomas Fairfax's troops during June 1645, helping to push Royalist forces out of their area. Importantly, these areas had been the site of anti-Royalist risings on the outbreak of war in 1642. In contrast, clubmen from Dorset, Wiltshire and east Somerset mustered in support of the local Royalist forces in August 1645, only to be dispersed, following a brief engagement, by Cromwell's New Model Army. Underdown has found in this regional pattern a confirmation of his ecological interpretation of popular allegiance. The contrast in allegiance is striking, although as Underdown admits it is partially to be explained in some areas by the greater propensity of Royalist troopers to plunder. But still more impressive are the similarities between the clubmen movements both of the West Country and of the marcher counties.[75]

The clubmen movements were much more than a 'mechanical reaction to increasing military depredations'.[76] As with other forms of plebeian organisation, it is possible to detect some fundamental organising principles at work within the movements. Most obviously, the clubmen represented parish politics in arms. Leadership came from the established elites of village and small-town society: lesser gentry, wealthier farmers, clothiers and ministers. These were the 'sufficient and best able men' who set their names to the Herefordshire clubmens' declaration. In Dorset and Wiltshire, the clubmen were led by 'the ablest men', who were chosen for their 'wisdom, valour, and estate'. The 'sufficient men' of their villages led those in Somerset. Significantly, the term 'middling sort' did not appear in clubmen articles. Although the clubmen leadership clearly came from the social strata represented by that term, the discriminatory implications and national connotations of the label were inappropriate to the clubmen projection of their movement as the united, common voice of the country.

The forms assumed by clubmen organisation are equally revealing. These were indistinguishable from parish organisation and local government, and followed the characteristic forms of crowd organisation and popular politics. Villagers learned of clubmen articles by their appearance 'in every parish church', and gathered to the sounding of church bells. Like the rebels of 1549 and 1536, clubmen meetings were activated by the dispatch of warrants to associated villages, as though a militia muster was under way. Writing their own job descriptions, the authors of clubmen articles specified that all searches, distraints and assessments were to be made only by 'constables, Tythingmen, and other sworn officers of the county'. As though they were making a parish assessment, or raising a common purse to maintain a collective legal case, they established common funds to provide pensions for wounded clubmen, and for the widows of those killed in defence of their communities.

Like enclosure and food rioters, the clubmen sought to negotiate from a position of strength with established authority. The clubmen were more successful in the pursuit of their limited aims than we might suppose. Hutton points out that in early 1646 the new Royalist commander in the border counties 'found it expedient to take the Clubmen into partnership to restore local order, and in a declaration . . . recognised their right to self-defence'. In Somerset, clubmen support for the New

Model Army helped to drive the undisciplined Royalist forces under Goring out of their region. Afterwards, the Somerset Grand Jury in 1646 issued orders against military plunder. Once again reminding us of enclosure and food rioters, the clubmen exploited the language and declarations of authority in justification of their activities. Thus, the Worcestershire clubmen cited the Royalists' own standing orders in criticism of the indiscipline of their soldiers. The Dorset and Wiltshire clubmen established that their 'constant watch' against soldiers should be maintained 'in pursuance of the Statute in that case provided'. Similarly, they intended to arrest any plundering soldiers and place them before their 'Commander-in-Chief with tender of witnesses to prove the crime', as though they were village constables presenting a criminal to a local magistrate.

Such conduct was expressive of the enduring force of legalism within popular political culture. The leaders of the Herefordshire clubmen reminded their subscribers that there should be 'no confusion amongst us nor disorderly mutinies but a continual union'. The Dorset and Wiltshire clubmen ensured that when their declaration was read to a gathering at Badbury (Dorset), 'Mr. Thomas Young a lawyer' was present. Combining legalism with anti-popery, the Worcestershire clubmen appealed to the Grand Jury of the county to consider the role of papists on the Royalist gentry Association. The Worcestershire clubmen presented the catholic presence amongst the gentry Association as a confirmation of the long-standing fear that papists intended to disturb English liberties and household authority. They therefore highlighted the threat represented to their 'wives and children' by the 'outrageous and violence of the soldiers; threatening to fire our houses; endeavouring to ravish our wives and daughters'.

Clubmen rhetoric was organised around the assumption that adult male householders enjoyed a legitimate right to defend the material and patriarchal basis of their household. Within this, the clubmen discerned a larger principle: by defending themselves against plunder, they intended 'to retain the property of the subject'. Just as the defenders of agrarian custom, when prosecuted before Star Chamber for enclosure riots, had justified the riotous defence of common rights as the necessary defence of their household economy, so the Dorset and Wiltshire clubmen explained how they had been forced to take action due to their fear that 'Destruction, Famine and . . . Desolation will inevitably fall upon us, our wives and children'. Once again, specific complaint against military oppression led the clubmen to a more general analysis: in this case, the suggestion that 'the Great Charter of England and the Petition of Right' had been 'altogether swallowed up in the arbitrary power of the sword'.

In spite of gentry fears to the contrary, social conflict did not lie at the heart of clubmen politics. The idealised community that the authors of the clubmen articles presumed to represent was that of the united rural village, linked to its immediate neighbours, and headed by wealthier farmers and minor gentry. But it is significant that the articles assumed both that the poorest classes within village society would have less interest in the clubmen movement than the 'able and discrete men', and that some of the richest might also be the least enthusiastic about the movement. This was implicitly recognised in the clubmen articles, which stated the element of compulsion that underlay clubmen organisation: thus, the Wiltshire and Dorset clubmen established that:

> all men furnish themselves sufficiently with as many and good arms and ammunition as they can procure; and the rich out of a good conscience to relieve the poor herein, as also in their labours of watching, and other assistance in some proportionable measure.

Rather more harshly, a note of clubmen discussions asked 'Whether the able and rich who will not join with us be not only counted ill-affected but liable to pay for the poor who do their county service?' The funds collected for the maintenance of the organisation were to be spent upon payments to the village poor to encourage them to take part in clubmen gatherings: hence, 'day-labourers' were to 'be paid by general rate once a week by [the] chief of the parish for as many days as they had been on the general employment'. By way of contrast, one of the articles of the clubmen association for the 'Northwest parts' of Worcestershire expressed an open concern over the disinterest of 'poor men' in their movement. The articles established that the poor were to be paid by their masters for their attendance at clubmen meetings, and that if a poor man refused to attend such a meeting, his household was to be denied parish relief.

Clubmen organisation was built upon that vague, indeterminate area beyond the village, but smaller than the county: the 'Country', defined by migration patterns, local gossip, customary knowledge, kinship, credit links and trade networks. This was the spatial nexus within which enclosure and food riots were organised, and which in the mid-1640s provided the locus for clubmen organisation. Thus, it was the 'inhabitants of all the North west parts of the County of Worcester' that met together

on Woodbury Hill to form their clubmen association. Both in the Woodbury area of the county, and in the Malvern Hills, clubmen organisation
followed local geography. The 'Country' basis of clubmen organisation
was most apparent in the warrant of the Wiltshire clubmen which called
on the inhabitants of Dinton to appear at Buxbury, less than four miles
away, 'to confer with your neighbouring parishes about matters concerning your and their defence and safety'. The Worcestershire clubmen
managed to combine two of the defining terms of seventeenth-century
popular political culture in their anxiety that they might be 'led away by
papists...out of our own Country'. Their demand that the Royalist
garrisons in Herefordshire should be kept by their 'native countrimen'
was similarly expressive of this localism. But the localism of clubmen
actions should not be taken as evidence that the clubmen were not
possessed of a larger political vision.

In his enduring analysis of the clubmen movements, John Morrill
finds logic within clubmen ideas.[77] He suggests that far from being 'apa-
thetic' towards the issues raised by the civil wars, and disconnected from
its politics, the clubmen movements were 'very positive, clear-sighted
[and] principled'. For Morrill, the clubmen were 'radical conservatives
...the true champions of a fully developed provincialism and conservatism'. Far from being distant from civil war politics, the clubmen were
excited into rebellion by the prospect of peace negotiations between the
Crown and the Parliament in the winter of 1644–5. In Morrill's analysis,
the breakdown of these negotiations formed 'an important precipitant
of the Club risings'. Rather than being, as John Corbet saw them, 'foolish
neuters', the clubmen 'developed a convincing justification for their
neutralism'. The clubmen thus emerge from Morrill's analysis as possessed
of a real political agency, and moved by an ideological dynamic. Most
importantly, although Morrill recognises the powerful conservatism of
the clubmen agenda, he sees that their politics had important similarities
to that of the post-war radical movements:

> The doctrine of popular sovereignty developed by the Clubmen to
> justify a highly conservative political programme has close affinities
> with the Leveller demand for radical extension of local autonomy and
> liberty.

Wartime clubmen and post-war radicals arrived at quite different political
conclusions. But many of their starting points were the same. Both were
concerned with the defence of established rights against arbitrary

power; both advanced the polity of the village and small town as the best model for the future government of the realm; both articulated their politics through a language of patriarchalism and tradition, yet at the same time were innovative and dynamic in their political organisation. Yet superficially, what is most obvious from a comparison of the two movements was their differences. Whereas the Leveller movement (which we consider in Section VI) sought the fundamental redistribution of formal political authority, and whereas the Diggers wished to see an irreversible shift in the distribution of social power and resources, our examination of clubmen articles suggests that the movements were indeed conservative: suspicious of innovation, hostile to outsiders, defensive of the established place of the united village community within the larger polity. But perhaps such an assessment obscures important aspects of clubmen ideas. As we have seen, the clubmen sought to open negotiations with dominant military authorities, rather than to drive armies out of their region all together. With this in mind, it is scarcely surprising that clubmen articles should be pragmatic, interested more with establishing a workable organisation than with ideology, and where expressive of ideological concerns, concerned to occupy the middle ground in religion and state politics. In any case, our assessment of the clubmen movements remains heavily dependent upon their written declarations. Yet, as we recognised in our earlier discussion of early Tudor rebellions, such documents, written as they were by parish governors, may well fail to reflect ideological heterogeneity. In contrast, in the case of the Digger movement of 1649–50, the voice of the rural poor seems to speak with greater clarity.

V The Politics of the Parish in the English Revolution: the Digger Movement, 1649–50

On the first day of April 1649, a small group of men and women made their way on to common land upon St George's Hill, an area of waste ground that separated the village of Cobham from Walton-upon-Thames (Surrey). Here they established a settlement, and began to cultivate the commons. They were led by Gerrard Winstanley, a Lancashire man who before the wars had been a minor merchant in London, but whose livelihood had been ruined by the wartime disruption of trade. Winstanley had been reduced to the demeaning status of a wage labourer, and had moved into the nearby countryside to make a living by pasturing his neighbours' cows. Like many others in the late 1640s, he was engaged upon a personal and political quest for spiritual salvation. Winstanley combined the radicalising experience of downward social mobility with a politicised search for salvation: working from his prior experience in the radical sects of London, Winstanley developed his own analysis of godliness and of his social world.[78] Back in January 1649, in a printed pamphlet, he had described the moment of revelation that had led him to St George's Hill. The word of God had reached Winstanley while in a trance, enjoining him to 'worke together. Eat bread together; declare this all abroad'. He understood this to mean that 'The poor people by their labours ... have made the buyers and sellers of land, or rich men, to become tyrants and oppressors over them.' Thus, in Winstanley's analysis, the poor had made themselves slaves to the rich. Liberation from such 'oppression' lay in the formation of autonomous communities upon the common land, which the poor would manure, improve and cultivate.[79] The cultivation of the commons was but a means to an end. Since the Diggers laboured upon common land rather than upon private estates, he hoped that the authorities would leave his followers to their work:

> if the rich wil stil hold fast this propriety of *Mine and thine*, let them labour their own Land with their own hands. And let the common-People ... that say the earth is ours, not mine, let them labour together, and eat bread together upon the Commons, Mountains, and Hills. For as the inclosures are called such a man's Land, and such a man's Land; so the Commons and Heath, are called for common-people's, and let the world see who labours the earth in right-eousnesse ... And who can be offended at the poor for doing this? None but covetous, proud, lazy, pamper'd flesh, that would have the poor still to work for that devil (particular interest) to maintain his greatness, that he might live at ease.[80]

Winstanley imagined that his self-sufficient community would became an example to others, and that Digger communities would multiply across the country. In the course of this peaceful social revolution, governed by the 'universall law of equity', a new spirit would rise up:

> in every man and woman, then none shall lay claim to any creature, and say This is mine, and that is yours, This is my work, that is yours; but every one shall put to their hands to till the earth, and bring up

cattle, and the blessing of the earth shall be common to all ... There shall be no buying nor selling, no fairs nor markets, but the whole earth shall be a common treasury for every man, for the earth is the Lords.[81]

The power of 'rich men' proved greater than Winstanley had imagined. Over April and May 1649, the Diggers (or 'True Levellers', as they named themselves) were assaulted by the wealthy farmers who dominated the nearby village of Walton-upon-Thames. Winstanley categorised his local opponents as 'covetous Free-holders, that would have all the Commons to themselves, and that would uphold the Norman Tyranny over us'.[82] Yet it is revealing that the traditional methods of rural protest were deployed against the Diggers. Some of the men who came to attack the colony on St George's Hill were dressed 'in women's apparell' as though they came for a charivari. The Walton inhabitants burnt the Diggers' cottages, as if they were driving indigent paupers beyond the parish bounds, or expelling wage-labourers employed upon the commons by some antagonistic local lord. The Walton tenants combined litigation with crowd action, initiating suits against the Digger cottagers in the local law courts, and complaining to the Council of State. By late August 1649, faced with litigation, intimidation and collective violence in Walton, the Diggers had crossed into the neighbouring parish of Cobham, where they established a new colony upon Little Heath. Once again the Diggers encountered local hostility, but this time from a different source. The manor of Cobham had recently passed into the hands of the rector of West Horsley, John Platt. It was this 'parson Platt' who organised local opposition to the Diggers in Cobham. Whereas Winstanley had held the yeomanry of Walton responsible for driving out the Diggers, in Cobham he described how 'parson Platt' had intimidated the local tenants into taking part in actions against the Diggers: 'the poor tenants ... durst do no other, because their Land-Lords and Lords looked on, for fear they should be turned out of service, or their livings'. The most recent historian of this subject has shown how not only were the 'middling sorts of Cobham ... much more divided in their response to the Diggers than Walton's inhabitants had been', but that 'an important core group of local people' joined with the Diggers. Although most of these Cobham Diggers were 'landless labourers and cottagers', they included at least one of the established farmers of the village.[83]

Most historical attention has focused upon the actions and ideology of the Digger movement in Walton and Cobham. Yet the contrasting receptions afforded to the Diggers in the two Surrey villages also reveal much about popular politics in rural England during the English Revolution. In his forensic examination of the subject, John Gurney has argued that whereas Walton was 'a parish with a long tradition of hostility towards outsiders', the neighbouring parish of Cobham had a quite different recent history. Cobham lacked a regular minister after 1644, at the same time as the nearby town of Kingston became a base of Anabaptist influence. There was, therefore, a prior context to the development of radical religious ideas within the area. Moreover, Gurney argues that 'Local support for the Diggers may also have been connected with Cobham's marked traditions of social conflict.' From the late sixteenth century, the tenants of Cobham had taken action against the local lords in defence of popular rights to timber and to low copyhold fines and rents. Finally, the area had been hit by high wartime taxation, which exacerbated existent conflicts. Hence, 'the Diggers were by no means alone in Surrey in resorting to direct action to meet subsistence needs'. Rioters in Windsor Forest in the 1640s allegedly threatened to 'breake downe the gates pales and hedges' of the park and 'to lay all to comon'. Like many other parts of the country, the 'poorer sort' of Surrey were coming in crowds to enclosed woods and cutting down trees 'for they wanted wood, and would have it, as long as it was to be had'. The Diggers had intended to 'take those Common Woods [on St George's Hill] to sell them, now at first to be a stock for our selves, and our children after as, to plant and manure the Common land withall'. We cannot say whether the rioters in the rest of Surrey would have followed the Diggers in claiming a fundamental entitlement to timber 'in the name of the Commons of England, and of all the Nations of the world, it being the righteous freedom of the Creation'. But the theft of wood in Surrey provides a sharp reminder of how long-running streams within the implicit, semi-public politics of the parish might flow into the great issues involved in the English Revolution.[84]

By April 1650, the Diggers had been driven out of Cobham. Winstanley had spent much of the previous year in ploughing and publishing. The printed pamphlets and declarations that he wrote in justification of the Diggers' utopian project have formed the main historical source about the movement. But Digger politics was not born fully formed out of the printing press. Rather, the movement represented a development upon long-established traditions, forms and anxieties within early modern popular politics. Nonetheless, it remains significant that the Diggers chose to articulate their political agenda through the printing press. We shall assess the relationship between print and popular radicalism in Section VI of this chapter. Like all radical movements during the English Revolution, the Diggers exaggerated the geographical extent and numerical basis of their support. One London newsbook reported how, echoing the traditional cry of enclosure and food rioters that 'thousands will assist us', the Diggers invited 'all to come in and help them, and promised them meat, drink and clothes...They give out, they will be four or five thousand within ten days'.[85] Printed Digger broadsides provide lists of places where Digger colonies had been established. These included Cox Hall (Kent), Barnet and Enfield (Middlesex), Dunstable and Iver (Buckinghamshire), Wellingborough and Bosworth (Northamptonshire) and some unnamed places in Gloucestershire and Nottinghamshire. Digger settlements tended to be established in places that had experienced recent conflict over enclosure and customary entitlements. Enfield was the site of large-scale enclosure riots in 1649, for instance.[86] Religious radicalism provided a second important network for the extension of the Digger project. Digger agents, dispatched from the community at Cobham on a circuit around the Home Counties, were apprehended at Wellingborough in 1650. Their travels had taken them past the Chiltern village of Caddington, the site of protracted enclosure riots in the 1630s. The names of three of the Caddington rioters of 1630s were to appear again in *The Husbandmen's Plea Against Tithes* in 1647, a printed pamphlet which denounced 'tithe mongers' in Hertfordshire, Bedfordshire and Buckinghamshire. Extrapolating from the suggestive coincidence, Steve Hindle has therefore discerned 'a localised relationship between the popular protest of the 1630s and the political radicalism of the 1640s and 1650s'.[87]

We shall now focus in particular upon two printed declarations produced by Digger communities beyond the south-east: Iver and Wellingborough. These declarations illuminate how the 'poor commons' whom the Diggers claimed to represent had grown in number during the civil wars. Analysis of the social background of the ten signatories to the Digger broadside from Iver suggests that 'The majority were copyholders [of Iver], well versed in the ways of the manorial courts against which they protested.' Many poorer landholders had been scarred by recent wartime experiences and, at least in those villages where the Digger alternative was presented to them, were willing to identify themselves within a social collectivity that also included the established poor. Keith Thomas has suggested that 'the whole Digger movement can be plausibly regarded as the culmination of a century of unauthorised encroachment upon the forests and wastes by squatters and local commoners'.[88] There is much to commend such a view. But the Digger movement also represented the articulate expression of one of the enduring social alliances upon which early modern popular politics could be built: the coalition of poorer landed villagers (typically small farmers and artisans) with their landless neighbours.[89] We have seen both in Cobham and in Iver how some Digger colonists came from the poorer landholders within the village. Such men and women had been badly hit by wartime taxation and economic depression, and were often reduced to making a living from waged labour, or had even become dependent upon parish poor relief. As we saw in Chapter 3, Section II contribution to parish poor rates was a critical indicator of status, and was especially insisted upon by the poorest ratepayers, whether landed or not. For such people, engagement with the Digger movement presented an opportunity to express both their anger at their reduced social position (finding themselves suddenly in the demeaning position of receiving, rather than contributing to, parish relief), and their longer-established hostilities to the manorial system. Two defining themes in both declarations are therefore a developed critique of manorialism and an anxiety about the powerlessness of the parochial poor.

A closer sense of how Digger ideas worked within established plebeian political language is given in the Iver Diggers' suggestion that the 'great ones' of their village intended to get:

> a custome to dyet the Markets, and make dearth in time of plenty ... we must be starved ... and why? Because the rich will have it so, no other reason can be rendered.

The terminology might as well come from the dearth years of the 1590s. Henry Danyell, a labourer of the Kentish village of Ash, had spoken in the same terms back in 1598, when he expressed his hope that war would:

> afflicte the rich men of this countrye to requite their hardnes of hart towards the poore ... he had a hundred, and a hundred that would take his parte, to pluck out such as the constable [of Ash] was, and take their corne from them, which they did kepe to the hurt of such as he was:

That constant concern of Tudor popular politics, the belief that the rich intended to starve the poor through a combination of the enclosure and high food prices, continued to structure the Iver Diggers' perception of their social world. But what came next in the Iver Diggers' analysis of their intense parish politics had no precedent in earlier decades:

> Therefore you of the poorer sort, understand this, that nothing but the manuring of the common Land, will reduce you into a comfortable condition.

The Wellingborough Diggers also spoke in the common dialect of early modern popular politics. Building from the feeling that the rich had unjustly denied charity to the poor, they worked upon the old cliché that it was better to hang for theft than to starve:

> rich men's hearts are hardened, they will not give us if we beg at their doors; if we steal, the Law will end our lives, divers of the poor are starved to death already, and it were better for us that are living to dye by the Sword than by the Famine.

Yet again, we are reminded of the seditious voices of the sixteenth century: in this case, that of the Colchester weaver Edward Whyte, who in 1566 stood accused of saying that:

> Wee can gett noe worke nor we have noe monye and yf we sholde steale, we shoulde bee hanged, and yf we sholde aske, noe man wolde gyve us.

The Wellingborough Diggers therefore shared Edward Whyte's analysis of the political economy of dearth in early modern England. But they differed as to how the 'oppression' of the 'rich men' should be lifted. Whereas Whyte threatened that:

> we wyll have remedye one of these dayes or ells wee wyll lose all, for the commons wyll ryse . . . for yee shall see the whottest harvest that ever was in Englonde

the Wellingborough Diggers, like their comrades in Iver, leapt from a reiteration of Tudor plebeian complaint into the radical millenarianism of Gerrard Winstanley:

> And now we consider that the Earth is our Mother, and that God hath given it to the children of men, and that the common and waste

Grounds belong to the poor, and that we have a right to the common ground both from the Law of the Land, Reason and Scriptures.

There was no equivalent to such an analysis in the record of seditious speech in the sixteenth century. Digger ideology, while drawing upon the deep linguistic resources of early modern popular political culture, was defined by a bitter, imaginative eloquence that seems highly original.[90]

The Digger movement spoke in a language of class that was simultaneously local and panoramic. An appreciation of the intensely parochial character of English social conflict ran through Digger rhetoric: the Iver Diggers spoke of how 'idle persons, [with] slow bellies . . . raigne and ride over the common people in every Parrish, as Gods and Kings'. Those who were 'in Authority in our Parrish' intended to make the poor 'absolute slaves and vassals to their wills'. The Diggers of Wellingborough were equally concerned with the unequal distribution of power and wealth within the parish. Articulating the patriarchal sense of responsibility for the plebeian household that was so often built into early modern popular politics, they worried that:

> we have spent all we have, our trading is decayed, our wives and children cry for bread, our lives are a burden to us, divers of us having 5.6.7. 8.9. in Family, and we cannot get bread for one of them by our labour.[91]

Yet, like Gerrard Winstanley, the authors of the Iver and Wellingborough declarations moved with ease from an assessment of the micro-politics of the parish into a macro-analysis of English social relations. In their discussion of the 'bondage' of the seigneurial system which had lasted for the '600 yeares' since the Norman Conquest, the Iver Diggers concluded that 'Cain is still alive in all the great Landlords, and such like Earthmongers who are continually crucifying their poor Brethren by oppression, cheating and robbery'. They saw hope in 'a promise in Scripture' to liberate the poor and to 'restore the whole of Creation into the glorious liberty of the Sonnes of God' where there should be no property, but only 'the quality, community and fellowship with our own kind; for the first shall be last, and the last shall be first, and he that sitteth as he that serveth'.[92]

The Iver Diggers' angry lyricism illuminates both what was radically new about Digger ideas, and something of how they placed themselves within the politics of the parish. The sense that inequalities of wealth and power had locked the poor into 'bondage', coupled with the belief that equality was a godly condition, remain suggestive of the radical potential latent within early modern plebeian political language. They also remind us that gentry fears of the 'levelling' instincts of the lower orders were not always just paranoid fantasies. But there is another side to the Wellingborough and Iver declarations, one that has typically escaped the attentions of historians of the Digger movement. Throughout this book, we have seen how early modern popular politics sought simultaneously to threaten and to intimidate rulers, while also cajoling and encouraging its opponents into ameliorative action, putting right the limited local wrongs which protest had been designed to illuminate. Hence, enclosure rioters often symbolically broke down sections of newly built enclosing walls, but took no action against older enclosures. Similarly, food rioters sought to impose a 'just price' for grain, rather than to redistribute food and wholesale. We see a similar logic at work within the Wellingborough declaration, cutting across and contradicting the authors' more obvious class analysis. The Wellingborough Diggers cited 'the truth of our necessity' to justify their cultivation of the commons. A statement of their desperate condition, and criticism of the local rich for refusing them charity followed this. But the Wellingborough Diggers went on to praise:

> some of those rich men amongst us, that have had the greatest profit upon the Common, [who] have freely given us their share in it, as one Mr John Freeman, Thomas Nottingam and John Clendon, and divers others; and the Country Farmers have proffered divers of them to give us Seed to sow it, and so we find that God is perswading Japheth to dwell in the tents of Shem: and truly those that we find most against us are such as have been constant enemies to the Parliaments Cause from first to last.

Once again, the Wellingborough Diggers moved easily from the specific to the general: Freeman, Nottingam and Clendon, the kind 'rich men' of Wellingborough, were to be numbered amongst that 'small number of those that considers the poor and needy', whom 'the Lord may deliver . . . in the time of their troubles'. God would favour the charitable rich, just as he would cast down the tyrants: 'We Find in the Scriptures . . . That in the last days the oppressor and proud man shall cease'. Rich men who placed the values of the moral economy before those of the market would receive the praise of the poor:

> blessing shall be upon the heads of those Rulers that sell Corn, and that will let the poor labor upon the Earth to get them Corn, and our

lines shall blesse them, so shall good men stand by them, and evil men shall be afraid of them, and they shall be counted the Repairers of our Breaches, and the Restorers of our Paths to dwell in.[93]

The Wellingborough Diggers' qualification of their analysis of class society provides the clearest justification for a social interpretation of Digger ideology and language. We have seen that there was much that was new in the Digger movement: the reimagination of the commons as the space within which a new society would arise; the clarity of their critique of seigneurialism and of social inequality; the abolition of private property. Some of this agenda represented a development upon earlier strains within early modern popular politics; some of it was wholly new. In part, the Digger movement stemmed from the traumatic experience of war, revolution and regicide. The Diggers understood the civil war in brutal class terms: for Winstanley, the execution of Charles I had significantly weakened the power of rich men. The Wellingborough Diggers attempted to identify their greatest oppressors amongst the local rich men as cavaliers; from a different standpoint, and suggestive of a class-based neutralism, the Iver Diggers proposed that in future, 'the rich' should be left to 'fight all the battels that are to be fought'.[94] But the Diggers also drew upon older forms and ideas. While the characteristic early Stuart enclosure rioter would have been appalled by the prospect of a community of goods (crowd actions in defence of common rights, we should bear in mind, were frequently justified on the grounds that enclosure would be damaging to the material interests of the patriarchal household, and that enclosure represented a form of theft), Digger hostility to the gentry and to manorialism finds muffled echoes in the earlier period. The defenders of the custom of tenant right in the northern border counties who staged a play at Kendal (Westmorland) in 1619 in which ravens drove 'poore sheep in[to] hell wch ravens were compared to greedy landlords & the sheepe to their poore ten[a]nts whoe oppressed them & fed upon their carkesses', like the Warwickshire rebels of 1607 (whom, it will be remembered, also took the name of Diggers) who denounced the 'incroaching Tirants' who 'would grinde our flesh upon the whetstone of poverty', might have found themselves in sympathy with much of Winstanley's writings.[95]

The Digger movement, then, continues to command our attention because it gave a clear and public voice, in print, to one recurrent aspect of early modern popular political culture. But perhaps what is most important about the movement is the light it sheds upon the lack of common interest between the rural poor and wealthy farming elites. By the mid-seventeenth century, the latter had come to dominate many parishes. In the hard circumstances of post-war England, battered by cold winters, the dearth of food, and the imminence of political crisis, the charity of 'rich men' was thin indeed. The Diggers had sought to represent the voice of the 'poor commons' and 'lower sort', whom they cast in conflict with the inheritors of the Norman Yoke: kings, priests, lords and rich farmers. For Winstanley, the ' Lords of Mannors... were William the Conqueror's colonels and Favourites, and he gave a large circuit of Land to everyone, called A Lord-ship'. Wealthy farmers represented the footsoldiers of the Norman conquest: 'covetous Free-holders that would have all the Commons to themselves, and that would uphold the Norman Tyranny over us'.[96] In Winstanley's interpretation, a combination of gentry and middling sort farmers held the poor commons in subordination. This alliance maintained their tyranny through their ownership of land and their domination of the parish and thereby of the state. Gerrard Winstanley's sharp analysis of mid-seventeenth-century English society illuminated an acute dilemma for the political grouping with which his 'True Levellers' were most often compared. It is to the politics of that movement that we now turn.

VI The Levellers and the 'Poor and Middling Sort of People'

In naming itself as the protector of 'the people' from a reactionary seigneurialism during the first civil war, the Parliamentary cause had invoked a full-blooded popular politics. In so doing, it had undercut its own carefully manufactured claim to represent an orderly and godly middling sort against the baying Royalism of the 'vulgar'. The contradictions of the parliamentary populism of 1642–6 anticipated the radical movements of the later 1640s. The Levellers were the most prominent of those post-war radical movements, and cohered around the dynamic leadership and journalism of John Lilburne, Richard Overton, John Wildman and William Walwyn. Originating in 1645, the movement's main concerns included the abolition of church tithes, trade monopolies and arbitrary government; the stiffer prosecution of the Parliamentarian war effort; the closure of negotiations with the Crown; official sanction for 'liberty of conscience' (that is, toleration of protestant dissent); legal reform; and the reorganisation of central and local government. Initially based upon the Baptist Gathered Churches of London and the south-east, and growing out of prior agitation within London City and company government over democratic rights, by 1647 the movement had acquired a significant following amongst the junior officers and soldiery of the New Model Army.[97] Later in its life, the Levellers began to establish footholds within other urban centres, and within some isolated pockets of rural England. In the autumn and winter of 1649, as the Commonwealth regime moved against the unlicensed press and open political organisation, the Leveller movement dissipated. Yet despite its short life, like the Diggers, the history of the Leveller movement illuminates some important aspects of popular politics in the English Revolution.

The collapse of the movement stemmed in part from the new regime's grant of important concessions to the Gathered Churches and the purge of militants within the New Model Army. But it also grew from contradictions within the Leveller programme and the lack of a real unity of interest amongst its supporters. This section probes the logic of Leveller populism, focusing in particular upon the significance of social division within the movement. As we shall see, these turned on the contradictions implicit in the Leveller appeal to a united 'poor and middling sort of people'. The section also addresses the impact of print upon popular politics during the English Revolution and the differing characteristics of urban and rural popular politics.

Gathering around a populist critique of the soon-to-be victorious Parliamentary regime in 1645, at first the new London-based radical movement was labelled the 'Lilburnists'. It was not until the summer of 1647 that the movement gained the name of 'Levellers'. The term was an insult, intended to blacken the urban radicals with the allegation that they intended the abolition of property and the levelling of social distinction. Most obviously, the word 'Leveller' recalled the hostile labels given to enclosure rioters, especially those poor labourers caught up in the Midland Rising of 1607. The Leveller movement had carried that stigma since its inception. Thus, one early critic of the London radicals argued that Lilburne's supporters amongst the 'rabble Rout ... have a purpose to put downe all the Nobility and Gentry in the Kingdome'. In spite of such calumny, the fundamentals of John Lilburne's 'teachings' were represented accurately enough: Freeborn John 'hath plainly taught his disciples, that the power now resides in the Parliament, is inherent to the people ... that the power is the people's birth-right'. This led the radicals' critics to the well-worn argument that such 'popularitie' would prove destructive of both public and private authority, such that 'every servant [will] become a master and mistress, and cast off the yoke of obedience to their superiors, whether parents, masters or governors'.[98]

A variety of collective self-descriptions emerged within Lilburne's radical movement. In their printed declarations, the Leveller leadership called their followers 'Honest men', 'the well-affected', or (after the Whalebone tavern in which the leadership met), 'the Whaleboneers'. Alternatively, the movement identified itself as 'The free people of England', or (after one of its later policy formulations), 'The subscribers and approvers of the petition of the 11 September 1648'. The Leveller colour was sea-green, and so in some publications the title 'The sea-green order' was deployed. But these other labels proved ephemeral as, in spite of its implications, the term 'Leveller' was adopted within the movement itself. The most radical of its regular journals, the short-lived *Mercurius Militaris*, used the term with ease; and H. N. Brailsford has suggested that the Leveller 'rank and file' may not have 'disliked the name quite as much as their leaders professed to do'.[99] The deliberate populism of the Levellers, in particular their claim to represent 'the people', 'the well-affected' or 'the lower and middle sort', has concentrated historiographical attention.

The Levellers are best remembered for their constitutional proposals, which their leaders gathered together in printed Agreements of the People (October 1647, amended in December 1648 and again in May 1649). These laid down a new system for post-war government, based upon the sovereignty of the House of Commons, the extension of the parliamentary franchise, the redistribution of parliamentary seats, the establishment of regular parliaments, the toleration of diversity in protestant religion and the reform of the law.[100] Yet this focus upon constitutionalism has obscured the diversity of Leveller politics. The initial basis of the movement in London was apparent in the constant concern over the democratisation of City government. Strong support for artisanal and mercantile independence was shown in the demands for an equivalent democratisation of London companies and guilds and for the removal of state monopolies over trade. Radical London weavers, for instance, applied the Leveller critique of the central state to their local conditions. They argued that the 'Egyptian taskmasters' who dominated their company should be displaced on the grounds that since 'all men being equall to other and all Jurisdictive power over them is invested in one or more persons who represent the whole', so there should be a democratic franchise within the Weaver's Company.

Leveller proposals for legal reform grew from demands for the destruction of arbitrary prerogative courts, the use of English in legal proceedings and the redistribution of power into the localities.[101] Religion was central to the Leveller political project. The close relationship between the Baptist Gathered Churches and the Levellers generated strong support for the abolition of tithes, the toleration of protestant religious diversity and the reorganisation of the established Church.[102] Throughout, Leveller proposals assumed that an active, industrious 'people' would defend and articulate their 'liberties' through a reformed, responsive legal system and a new system of local and national political representation.

Aside from their supporters within army garrisons, the Levellers were a primarily urban movement. Working within the pre-existent forms of urban popular politics discussed in Chapter 4, Section IV, the Levellers were adept at combining print propaganda with street politics.[103] Between 1645 and 1649, they kept up a steady stream of printed petitions, pamphlets and declarations which helped to define them as a political movement, and which focused crowd politics. Leveller petitions to Parliament, like those of godly citizens in the agitation of 1641–2, were signed by thousands of London citizens and presented to Parliament by large crowds. Taken together with the events of 1641–2, we might see in the Leveller movement a deeper metropolitanisation of political culture, in which the capital and its ruling institutions became an increasingly vital forum for the articulation and demonstration of popular complaint from across the country.

Leveller demonstrations took the form of elaborate processions in which printed declarations and the Leveller colour of sea-green were prominent. The funeral of Robert Lockyer, a Leveller common soldier who had been executed for his role in an army mutiny, formed the centrepiece to one such demonstration. Lockyer's coffin was paraded through the streets of London:

> accompanied with many thousand citizens... about 1000 went before the Corps[e], by five or six on file together, the Corps[e] then came, with six trumpets sounding a souldiers knell... the Troopers Horse advanced in the rear of this regiment, clothed all over and led by a footman... some thousands succeeded these in rank and file, and the women brought up the reer... most of this great number that thus attended the Corps[e] had Sea-Green and black ribbons in their hats, or pinned to their black ribbons on their breasts.[104]

The Leveller leadership enjoyed the largely consistent support of one London newsbook, *The Moderate*, and at other times enjoyed sympathetic coverage in some of the other weekly newsbooks that flourished in the absence of effective print censorship between 1641 and 1649.[105] In the last two years of their existence, the Levellers broadened the geography of their civilian support, securing the support of inhabitants within smaller towns scattered across England. Yet the Leveller leadership made little attempt to engage with rural popular politics, and the movement appears to have enjoyed little support amongst rural labourers.

This lack of rural, lower-class support had much to do both with the division of material interest between 'middle' and 'lower' sorts of people in mid-seventeenth-century England, and with the way in which popular politics was represented in Leveller propaganda. In a sharply focused discussion of radical ideology, Brian Manning has suggested that, although Leveller propaganda occasionally sought to appeal to a united 'lower and middle sort of people', those two social groups had very little in common.[106] This connects with the argument made in Chapter 1, Section IV, Chapter 2, Section IV and Chapter 3, Section II, in which we saw how, over the course of the sixteenth century, richer farmers had gradually distanced themselves from popular protest and had become increasingly antagonistic to the interests of their poorer neighbours. Far from being 'ahead of their time', the language of the Leveller movement actually helped to focus this fundamental conflict within early modern popular politics.

Christopher Hill has remarked perceptively that 'The Levellers were never a united, disciplined party or movement, as historians find to their cost when they try to define their doctrines with any precision.'[107] John Lilburne's own speeches and journalism reproduced this heterogeneity. At one moment, he echoed the clichés of early modern popular politics, speaking of plots afoot by rich men to starve the poor, while in the next breath Lilburne worked upon elite prejudices and anxieties. Trying to press his reform agenda upon the parliamentary and army leadership during the dearth year of 1649, he conjured up one of the gentry's recurrent nightmares: 'the poor peoples rising up to cut the throats of the rich men'. Richard Overton, usually the most radical of the three leaders, was similarly contradictory in his attitude to crowd politics, seeing in the power of the 'Rude Multitude' a force for religious and political conservatism.[108] Yet in spite of this, the Levellers defined themselves as an avowedly populist force, the leading representatives of 'the people'.

More than any other concept, the meaning of 'the people' was critical to Leveller political discourse. When pushed by their critics in the Putney debates of October 1647 as to how widely they wished to redistribute the franchise amongst 'the people', Leveller representatives contradicted one another. It seemed self-evident to the hot-blooded Colonel Rainsborough that 'the poorest man in England is not at all bound in a strict sense to that government that he hath not had a voice to put himself under'. Full of bitterness, the common trooper Edward Sexby echoed the Colonel's words. For Sexby, it had been 'the poor and mean' who had 'preserved this kingdom':

> There are many thousands of us soldiers that have ventured our lives; we have had little propriety in the kingdom as to our estates, yet we have had a birthright. But it seems now [by the arguments made by the Levellers' critics] except a man hath a fixed estate in this kingdom, he hath no right in this kingdom. I wonder we were so much deceived.

But other Leveller representatives at Putney developed colder, more conformist assessments of popular politics. The London Leveller Maximilian Petty made it clear that he had been sent to represent the view that, while the franchise should be extended, qualifications on the grounds of wealth and social standing should remain: specifically, women, children, apprentices, servants and wage-labourers were to remain exempt from the franchise.[109] The point was made with greater clarity in the second version of the Agreement of the People (December 1648). The first clause of the Agreement limited the proposed electorate to those not:

> receiving Alms, but such as are assessed ordinarily towards the relief of the poor; not servants to, or receiving wages from any particular person . . . they shall be men of one and twenty yeers old, or upwards, and Housekeepers.[110]

The Levellers claimed to speak in 'the common voice of the people'. Certainly, some of the favoured clichés of early modern popular political discourse were faithfully reproduced within Leveller propaganda. Hence, John Wildman set into print the classical rhetoric of the enclosure rioter with his assurance to agitators within the New Model Army that they should 'be confident, that 1000s and tens of 1000s are ready and ripe to assist you'. Similarly, an editorial in *The Moderate* for March 1649 warned of how 'Hunger breaks stone walls and famine cryes out with a loud voice.'[111] Yet the dominant Leveller voice was that of the literate, office-holding, propertied, godly, urban man. Of course, that was not the only voice to be heard within the movement. The Leveller women's petition of spring 1649 drawn up by the Baptist Katherine Chidley, for instance, observed that:

> we are assured of our Creation in the image of God, and of an interest in Christ, equal unto men, as also of a proportionable share in the freedoms of this Commonwealth.

As with crowds of women who had gathered outside Parliament during the crisis months of 1641, Leveller women presented their published petitions to the House of Commons in 'multitudes'. Ann Hughes has argued that the women's petitions should be seen not as a form of proto-feminism, but rather as an aspect of a Leveller rhetoric that stressed the damage done to the 'honest household' by war, arbitrary government, and the absence of a political settlement. In this respect, the Leveller women presented themselves as having been forced into action by the threat posed to their households by political instability. The point is well made, and reminds us of the contested place occupied by women within early modern public politics. Nonetheless, the Leveller women's petitioning and organisation shows that the movement comprised more than 'honest men' alone. In taking open political action as authors, petitioners and demonstrators, women demonstrated that they had 'an equal interest with the men of this nation'.[112] Similarly, and despite the assurances of the Levellers' petition of 11 September 1648 that any representative parliament would be prevented 'from abolishing propriety, levelling Men's Estats, or making all things common', there were others within the movement who took a perverse delight in the name of Leveller.[113] But that ideological diversity was spoken over by the dominant voice of the masculine urban middling sort.

One source of Leveller politics, ironically, grew from middling sort anxiety about the new political agency held by the lower orders. In March 1649, an editorial in *The Moderate* passed favourable comment upon parliamentary debates concerning the need to set the poor to work. The editorial went on to encourage legislators 'Either take some care to ease and relieve [the poor] else their necessities will enforce them to be rich, and level what they never intended.' Much of Leveller social policy was driven by a combination of fear of the poor and Christian sympathy for them. Rather than granting political agency to the poor, moderate Leveller proposals were intended to calm social tensions and to return the poor to subordination.

Learning from their prior experience of administering local systems of poor relief, the radicalised middling sort proposed to apply the politics of the parish to the traumatised post-war nation. In the Leveller programme, the social order was to be tinkered with. The participation of the middling sort in political institutions would be both legitimated and extended, but the poor were to remain effectively powerless. Thus, the 'well-affected' of Leicestershire demanded the removal of tithes, the payment of the army, the removal of free quarter (all characteristic regional Leveller demands), and the improvement of fens and forests in order to 'set the poor to work'. Motivated by the desire that the poor 'may not starve in these times', this agenda nonetheless represented a denial of popular agency. In a letter published in *The Moderate* in October 1648, the mayor and aldermen of Newcastle distinguished between a politically active 'people', whom the Parliament was supposed to represent, and a naive but potentially dangerous 'commons':

> The Lord direct us for his glory, and the good of the poor commons of England, who are like to be bought and fed because they are ignorant of their owne freedoms and birth-rights, which they are willing to sell for a mess of pottage.[114]

Within mainstream Leveller ideas, the 'commons' could qualify for membership of 'the freeborn people', but only on the terms set by that 'freeborn people'. Hence, when the tin-miners of Cornwall petitioned for the removal of the Crown's monopoly over the county's mining industry, the Levellers contextualised that Cornish demand within their own metropolitan experiences. Much as Lilburne sought to set 'thousands of poor people' to work 'at Cloth-working, Dying and the like useful professions' through the restoration of 'Marchandizing...to its true and proper freedome', so it seemed to the authors of *The Moderate* that the Cornish tinners sought:

> to attain...the comon interest and privilege of other subjects, of selling their own goods, digged, and obtained with the hazard of their lives, for their best advantage, paying all ancient and legall dues, and that they may not be left at last under perpetuall bondage and worse condicion than they were [before the wars], they believing themselves a part of the freeborn people of England.[115]

If the Levellers had a key constituency, it was those hitherto relatively affluent householders who had been hit by wartime depredations: high taxes, plunder, increased poor rates. The traditional terminology of plebeian social complaint was mobilised on the behalf of that social fraction: 'Most of the people of England sell their clothes and pawne their estates to pay taxes.' Riots against the collection of taxes, especially the excise which 'layes the burden heavily upon the poore, and men of middle quality' had therefore to be represented as the actions 'not [of] the scum and Mallignants . . . but such as have faithfully served the parliament'.[116] More than any other issue, the excise was represented within Leveller propaganda as the critical issue that united the 'poor and middle sort of people'. Hence, to John Wildman, 'that unmercifull taxation of EXCISE . . . eateth the flesh and sucketh the blood of the poor and middling sort'. John Lilburne linked the excise with tithes, depicting these joint evils as 'Those secret thieves, Drainers and Robbers of the poor and middle sort of people'.[117] Yet elsewhere, as we have seen, Leveller social policy sought to exclude the poorer element within that imagined social alliance.

The emptiness of the Levellers' claim to represent a united 'poorer and middling sort' reminds us that politics is about more than language and representation. Beyond the populist discourse of the Leveller movement lay the grim reality of parish politics in the mid-seventeenth century. The closed parish vestry, the enclosed farm and the stinted common pasture were the local manifestations of an agrarian capitalism that had long set 'middling sort' and 'lower sort' in conflict. The rhetoric of urban radicals, however impassioned, was insufficient to bridge that gap. Writing in 1647, the Leveller Lawrence Clarkson demanded of his readers 'Who are the oppressors but the nobility and gentry; and who are oppressed if not the yeoman, the farmer, the tradesman, and the like?'[118] The tragedy of Leveller politics was neatly encapsulated in Clarkson's antique political sociology, which at the time of its publication was perhaps one hundred years out of date. Things may have seemed like that to the united commonality of 1549. The reality of the mid-seventeenth century English village was rather different.

VII   The Formation of a Public Sphere? Speech, Print and Popular Politics, c. 1660–95

In May 1660, the Stuart dynasty was restored within England. Over the next six years, Parliament passed a body of legislation that was intended to prevent any repetition of the English Revolution. In particular, the legislation sought to close down popular politics. Both post-Cromwellian political dissidents and supporters of the Restoration regime would therefore have been amazed to find that the recent historiography of later Stuart politics has been so preoccupied with the formation of a 'public sphere' defined by legal, open political debate. Historians have lifted the concept of the 'public sphere' from the work of the Marxian sociologist Jürgen Habermas, who argued that later seventeenth-century England witnessed a 'political confrontation' over rights of political organisation and communication which was 'peculiar and without historical precedent'. Central to this confrontation was the 'fiction' that 'bourgeois private persons' constituted a united, single 'public'. In Habermas's model, the construction of this fictional public forced the English state 'to legitimate itself before public opinion' in new ways. Most importantly, the state was gradually forced to withdraw from its regulation of political debate and communication. Bourgeois values predominated within this lightly regulated public sphere. Especially important were the new norms that regulated public discourse: the notion of cultural superiority, or 'politeness', which lifted this broad, educated elite above the *plebs*; and the claim that this elite embodied a rational spirit of critical inquiry. According to Habermas, this new 'public sphere that functioned in the political realm arose first in Great Britain at the turn of the eighteenth century'. In his account of the origins of the public sphere in England, Habermas attaches special importance to the failure of attempts by the state to regulate the political environment of coffee houses in the 1670s, and to the 'elimination of the institution of censorship' which he locates in 1695 with the end of the Licensing Act.[119]

This penultimate section assesses the significance of changes in later Stuart popular politics in the light of Habermas's formulation. In particular, it addresses the following issues: the significance of continuing limits upon public political speech; the failure of government attempts to suppress political debate in the coffee houses during the 1670s; the extent to which the Exclusion Crisis constituted a discontinuity in urban popular politics; the enduring influence of earlier forms of popular political culture in the later seventeenth century; the importance of print propaganda and crowd organisation to factional and party politics after 1678. Throughout, we shall see that there was no simple, unitary transition towards a more democratic 'public sphere' of political debate.

It should not surprise us to find that legal rights to a free press, open assembly and political discussion remained contested throughout the later Stuart period. We have already seen in Chapter 1 how elite anxieties about public politics helped to define the Tudor and early Stuart central state. What is remarkable about the *c.* 1660–1715 period is not that privy councillors and legislators attempted to restrict political participation, but that, despite major political crises, the state gradually backed away from confronting forms of political organisation and communication which in earlier decades had been deemed illegal. This uneven process represented a major shift in the nature of state ideology and structures of power in early modern society. Although the patriarchal ideology of earlier years still helped to define the public image of the later Stuart polity, other more inclusive official ideologies were beginning to evolve.

In part, changes in the self-definition of the later Stuart state reflected a broadening in public political participation. That ambivalent social strata whose shifting loyalties and identities have been so important to this book, and who in the middle years of the seventeenth century started to be labelled the 'middling sort of people', secured a permanent, public place within the later Stuart polity in the last years of the seventeenth century. And yet, as we shall see in the conclusion to this book, the broadened polity of those years was defined not only by a relative internal openness of political debate, but also by the exclusion of the large bulk of the population. The 'polite', commercial values which urban middling sorts claimed to personify not only justified their inclusion within the polity; their powerful normative force also delegitimised the political culture of the 'vulgar' and less 'rational' poorer sort.

In May 1660, to scenes of mass rejoicing in London, Charles II returned to take up his English throne. Elections in the following March and April returned a parliament (the so-called 'Cavalier Parliament') committed to a legislative programme which would prevent any repetition of the events of 1640–2. A failed rebellion by political radicals in January 1661 (Venner's Rebellion) only heightened parliamentary commitment to the repression of political dissent. Prior to the election of the Cavalier Parliament, the Convention Parliament of 1660 had attempted to draw a line under civil war divisions. Under the Act of Indemnity and Oblivion, all former supporters of the Republic (with the exception of regicides) were pardoned, and it was made an offence to discuss any other person's political conduct during the preceding twenty years. By way of contrast, the Treason Act of 1661 extended the definition of treason to include those who declared the King to be a papist, or who attempted to maintain the authority of the Long Parliament. Another Act of the same year criminalised the submission of petitions to the Crown Parliament by more than ten persons. In an attempt to break the historic relationship between godly religion and urban authority, the Corporation Act passed in November 1661 excluded from urban government all those who would not take the Anglican sacrament and swear an oath of allegiance to the Crown. The passage of the Uniformity Act in May 1662 hardened the legislative commitment to religious uniformity, requiring all religious ministers to swear loyalty to the Crown and to accept the *Book of Common Prayer*. The Act for Regulating Select Vestries of 1663 established similar requirements for membership of parish vestries. In 1664, the passage of the Conventicle Act forbade meetings 'under colour or pretence of any exercise of religion' of five or more persons. The following year saw the passage of the Five Mile Act, which prevented former ministers who had lost their livings as a consequence of the Uniformity Act from coming within five miles of a parish where they had been incumbent, or of any town or city.

This body of legislation tells us much about the nature of the Restoration regime. Whereas the legislation enacted by the Convention Parliament had attempted to erase the memory of the civil war from collective memory, the repressive legislation passed by the Cavalier Parliament was defined by a preoccupation with the events of 1640–2. England had fallen into civil war, the King's advisors believed, because pre-war governors had been insufficiently attentive to the deep roots of the English Revolution. Godly enthusiasm, popular petitioning, open political debate, and crowd organisation were felt to have combined within the urban environment (and especially within London) to generate a popular politics which had eventually overwhelmed the early Stuart state. In contrast, the restored monarchy would build itself upon the closure of public politics and the re-establishment of social hierarchy. Whereas county government could be influenced by Privy Councillors through the appointment of justices to the Commission of the Peace, the loyalty of urban and parochial governors was considered to be much more insecure. In attempting to prescribe the religious and political views of towns and parish officers, the Cavalier Parliament therefore provided explicit recognition of the place of town and parish government within the national polity. In particular, the legislation revealed a defining anxiety concerning urban politics. The attempt to prevent dissident preachers from visiting towns, coupled with the restriction of the franchise to richer urban householders through the remodelling of town charters, highlighted long-standing elite concerns about the volatility and social breadth of urban politics. Such concerns seemed validated when, from the late 1660s, urban opposition to the central government began to re-emerge, especially over religion.[120]

Governmental anxiety concerning urban popular politics connected to worries over the communication of political news and ideas, whether written, printed or spoken. The radical political movements that had burst into life at the end of the first civil war had been crushed after the regicide. Thereafter, the fortunes of the uncensored press seesawed in motion with the ebb and flow of central state power. With the return of political instability upon the death of Oliver Cromwell in 1658, restrictions upon printing became increasingly inefficient and the press returned to its role as an important medium for the communication of news and the definition of political identities. Successful Royalist journalism helped to ensure the restoration of Charles II, whose Cavalier Parliament in 1662 passed an Act that required the registration of printing presses and re-established pre-publication censorship. Known as the Licensing Act, this legislation was preceded by the establishment of the office of licenser of the press, responsible for enforcing orders in council against seditious tracts. In August 1663, that office passed to Sir Roger L'Estrange, who remained the Crown's censor until the Glorious Revolution; yet censorship was never fully effective. Seditious printed material found its way into England from across the Channel; meanwhile, despite the attentions of L'Estrange, secret presses continued to operate in London. L'Estrange was also responsible for the suppression of hand-written seditious documents, which he regarded as still more dangerous than printed seditious material.[121] The censorship of written communication was complemented by the Treason Act, which sought to regulate verbal dissidence. This continuing concern with seditious speech and hand-written libels reminds us that the authorities remained well aware that the communication of political ideas did not depend upon the printing press alone.

The censorship of writing, print and speech has provided historians with a rich archive concerning popular political opinion in Restoration England. The surviving records of county Quarter Sessions and Assize circuits, coupled with the state papers for the 1660s and 1670s, provide innumerable examples of men and women being prosecuted for articulating their hostility to the Restoration regime. Such material illuminates how far the English Revolution had restructured popular political language. Memories of the still-recent civil wars ran deep: the Yorkshire yeomen James Parker stood indicted in November 1663 for his recollection of how:

> I served Oliver [Cromwell] seaven yeares as a souldier, and if any one will put up the finger on the accompt that Oliver did ingage, I will doe as much as I have done. As for the Kinge I am not beholdinge to him. I care not a fart for him.

The old antagonisms that had led into civil war remained. Thomas Gibson saw in the Stuart restoration the re-establishment of popery:

> the Kinge and Queene are now both come into England, and . . . wee should [have] notheinge but Popery, as formally hath beene, and that the Queene hath broughte a Pope with her from beyond sea.

Still older rhetorical forms helped to structure the verbalisation of popular political opinion. Echoing the sanguine fantasies of plebeian social critique in the sixteenth century and the characteristic threat of food or enclosure rioters to 'bring thousands to assist' in the rectification of grievances, the Londoner Thomas Fauster was charged in 1663 with saying 'I hope ere long to trample in Kings and Bishops blood and I know five or six thousand men will join with mee in pulling downe the Bishops.' The Yorkshire miller Christopher Maud was accused of saying in November 1665 that 'There will bee blood spilt before all the assessments [for recent taxes] be payd.' Maud went on to demonstrate the same appreciation of the early modern calendar of revolt as the grain rioters, who saw 'the dead time of the year' as the appropriate moment for rebellion: 'the assessments . . . were soe great now, that people had the best time [for rebellion] in respect that they had sowen downe their seed'. But it is important that in spite of all the discontinuities of the 1640s and 1650s, Maud conceived of rebellion in similar terms to the rebels of 1381, 1536 and 1549. He intended that:

> it was their best course to relieve themselves from the great burden of assessments that lay soe heavy upon them, to take clubs and pitch-forkes, and such weapons as they could gett, and goe to the Kinge.

For Maud at least, insurrection formed a means by which popular complaint could be represented to the monarch.[122]

Running into these older linguistic structures were the new religious and political languages of the English Revolution. Tim Harris provides an account of how in 1664, a Quaker had entered a meeting of his fellow Friends in London 'with his hair cropped and wearing nothing but a loin-cloth, exclaiming God "will put the locks of the head, and shave the Crowne ... Woe to [King] Charles and [Prince] James, destruction draweth Nye"'. Readership of such lurid reports induced a deep gloom in officers of the central state. One report in the state papers of 1661 described 'a generall defection in point of affection in the middle sort of people in City and Country from the King's interest and virulent opposition to the Prelacy'.[123] But we ought to be cautious before validating such assessments. The representatives of the recently restored Stuart regime felt insecure, and reports to the Privy Council tended to exaggerate the extent and depth of popular hostility to the Crown.[124] Moreover, it is difficult to read collective political attitudes off from individual allegations of seditious speech.

Throughout this chapter, we have stressed the diversity of popular politics, both on a regional basis and in terms of individual political allegiance. For every example of resentful hostility to the Restoration regime brought before criminal courts in the 1660s and 1670s, an equivalent case of popular royalist sedition might be produced from the 1650s. Ironically, the terms of the Restoration Settlement made it possible for extreme supporters of the Stuart regime to fall foul of the law. John Hague of Aston (Derbyshire) discovered this to his cost in 1661 when he:

> tooke uppon him to speake of the act of oblivion, & said the Kinge was a foole & and knave if he made it not voyde, & Hanged not upp all the Roundeheads.

After all, legal records of seditious speech only survive as a result of neighbours' willingness to denounce one another to the authorities: those in John Hague's company 'reprehended him', 'telling him of the dangerous consequences of these words'.[125] One possible motive for denunciation was fear of implication in such conversation; another may well have been loyalty to the authorities. Finally, such records present us with an artificially frozen sense of popular political allegiance. Those accused of speaking seditious words are characteristically presented as both emphatic in their verbal violence and as consistent in their politics. The reality (especially given that so many seditious

accusations originated out of alehouse conversation) was probably
rather more blurred.

However we choose to interpret the content of seditious words allegations of the later Stuart period, the fact of their existence reveals the
limits imposed by the state upon the communication of political ideas
and news. New treason legislation appeared on the statute books during
the reigns of William and Mary and of William III, and remained in
operation throughout and beyond our period.[126] If a 'public sphere' of
rational political conversation did indeed emerge in English towns
during the later seventeenth century, then it did so in opposition to the
continuing force of that legislation. For, as in the Tudor period, the
treason laws introduced a powerful element of self-censorship into political communication. In the course of a monologue concerning the rituals of the established Church in 1679 William Mandeville of Rotherham
(Yorkshire) commented that 'I dare not whistle treason, but I know what
I thinke.' In Mandeville's case, his attempt at self-censorship broke
down, and he ended up facing an indictment for seditious speech.

Treason and sedition legislation sought to censor the articulation of
personal political beliefs and to regulate the flow of news. Mary Daly, a
'poore widdow' of North Shields (County Durham), explained how false
news of the death of James II spread amongst her neighbours in February 1685. Margaret Atking asked her 'Neighbour, did not you heare the
post of last night?' Daly answered 'Yes, I heard and saw it, but what is the
newes, neighbour?', to which Atking replied 'Very badd newes, for our
new King James is dead.' Daly described how the news had passed from
house to house, until Mrs Hebden had said 'I heare noe such newes, and
God forbid it should be true, and I advise you to speake noe more of it.'
Mary Daly followed Mrs Hebden's advice, until she was persuaded to
give information to the court. Two other women then abused her,
saying that 'shee is fitt to be whipped through the towne for informing
against her neighbours'. Mary Daly's story tells us something about the
perils of public political communication in later seventeenth-century
England. Her account of Mrs Hebden's speech suggests how individuals
controlled their own political speech, and how neighbours watched out
for one another. Finally, the threats made against Mary Daly imply how
communal constraints limited the willingness of individuals to inform
against one another. Although her testimony suggests that, far from
taking part in a 'public sphere' of open political conversation, the women
of North Shields consciously controlled their own speech, it also hints at
one fundamental weakness within the early modern state: the inability

of state structures to penetrate, with any permanency, a popular political culture which was often defined by silence as much as by speech.[127]
    In Restoration London, the story was rather different. Here, the
mid-1670s saw the government retreat from an initial attempt to silence
public political debate within the novel commercial arena of the coffee
house. Since the 1650s, Londoners had developed a taste for coffee,
which they drank within the specialist coffee houses. By the 1670s, 'all
the neighbourhood' were said to 'swarm [to the coffee houses] like bees,
and buzz there like them too'. The buzz of the coffee house came not
only from excess of caffeine; it also emanated from political conversation, as coffee houses became centres for the exchange of political
news, gossip and opinion. The first coffee houses had been tolerated by
the Republican regime. After the Restoration, despite official hostility,
coffee houses retained their reputation as centres for the exchange of
news. So ingrained was the connection between coffee and news that one
coffee house master trained his parrot to squawk 'Where's the news?' at
potential customers. There was a commercial logic to the association
between news and coffee; Londoners came to coffee houses both to
drink and to talk. During periods of weak press censorship, printed
propaganda could be read and bought at coffee houses, further concen-
trating the association between commerce and politics within the capital.
Even in conditions of full press censorship, hand-written libels and
letters containing political news were circulated through the coffee
houses.
    During the 1660s, government ministers were careful to ensure that
the coffee house environment was monitored and observed by their
agents. The first proposals for the suppression of the coffee houses were
made during that decade, and were repeated in 1672, but it was not
until December 1675 that the Privy Council issued a proclamation for
their suppression. This was echoed by an order of the common council
of the City of London in the same month. Both orders were inspired by
growing extra-parliamentary condemnation of the government's close
relationship with France, which as the leading European catholic power
seemed the outstanding example of 'popish tyranny'. Much of this
criticism was voiced within the coffee house environment. Yet within less
than a fortnight the declaration was rescinded. In its place, the government attempted to regulate the political culture of the coffee house by
requiring coffee house masters to swear oaths to prevent 'all scandalous
Papers Books or Libells concerning the Government' from being
brought into or read within the coffee house, and to silence anyone

'declaring uttering or divulging ... false and scandalous Reports of the Government'.[128] A small matter in itself, the government's failure to suppress the coffee houses appears with retrospect to anticipate a longer-term transformation of politics, the origins of which have been located within the Exclusion Crisis of 1678–81.

From the early 1670s, growing hostility to 'arbitrary' government and to the government's pro-French foreign policy found expression in two overlapping discourses: a 'Country' critique of courtly corruption; and a fear of 'popery'. In the autumn of 1678, these anxieties were given new life in the rumour that English catholics, with the support of the French, connived at a 'Popish Plot'. It was imagined that in this plot, thousands of English protestants would be slaughtered, including the King, in order to ensure the succession of his catholic brother James, Duke of York. The Popish Plot set the tone for political debate over the next three years, which revolved around courtly corruption, hostility to arbitrary government and to catholicism, and the relationship between the established Church and dissenting protestants. Faced with a crisis of confidence in his regime, Charles II dissolved the Cavalier Parliament in January 1679, leading to the first general election since 1661; a second general election followed later in the year, and a third in 1681.

For three years, high politics was dominated by what historians have labelled the Exclusion Crisis: the attempt to exclude by legislation, on the grounds of his catholicism, the Duke of York from succeeding to the throne. The crisis was not confined to the question of the succession, but also focused longer-running fears of popery and arbitrary government. Recent historiography has emphasised how both pro- and anti-Exclusionists employed printed propaganda in order to engage with an increasingly news-conscious and politically involved reading public. Pro-Exclusionists attempted to secure popular support for their cause through printed petitions to the Parliament. Urged to 'beat the ring-leaders of sedition at their own weapon of popularity', anti-Exclusionists sought to represent the loyal opinion of 'the people' through addresses to the Crown. Urban corporations and enfranchised freeholders in the countryside were involved in the crisis in their capacity as voters in parliamentary elections and as signatories to petitions and addresses. A still wider body of people was included in the debate as spectators or as participants in crowd demonstrations and riots and through their readership of propaganda.[129]

As in 1640–2, the printing press helped to crystallise political division. The Exclusion Crisis saw the first use of the party identities that were to define political division in later years: 'Whig' for the proponents of exclusion, and 'Tory' for Cavalier loyalists. The new vitality of print propaganda was facilitated by the lapse of pre-publication press censorship in 1679, thanks to the failure of the new Parliament to renew the Licensing Act, coupled with the passage of the Habeas Corpus Act. Despite this, both many local magistrates and Sir Roger L'Estrange continued to prosecute publishers under the law of seditious libel. In her remarkable recent book, Paula McDowell has shown how the poor street hawkers who sold printed political material were also subjected to constant legal harassment by urban magistrates. Yet the political crisis continued to be fuelled by the semi-illicit press. Ironically, much of the printed propaganda produced during the crisis stemmed from the anti-Exclusion camp. Sir Roger L'Estrange, while attempting to restrain the 'outrageous liberty of the press', himself contributed to the increase in print propaganda. Concluding that 'Tis the press that is made 'um Mad, and the Press must Set 'um Right again', L'Estrange became one of the leading proponents of the Tory case against Exclusion. In so doing, like the Royalist journalism of the 1640s, L'Estrange personified the contradictions implicit in the conservative appeal to the people. On the one hand, he appeared as the enemy of the new 'public sphere' defined by print; on the other, in attempting to form a populist loyalism via the printing press, L'Estrange helped to broaden and diversify politics. In his own words, L'Estrange sought to mould the political opinions of 'the common people ... who are much more capable of being ... wrought upon, by ... a pamphlet, then by ... any other, and more sober form whatsoever.' He concluded that printed propaganda aimed at 'the multitude' might be beneficial to the state, since it might 'redeem the vulgar from their former mistakes, and delusions'.[130]

By 1681, the intensity of the Exclusion Crisis had abated. This had much to do with the success of Tory attempts to engage positively, via print propaganda and crowd demonstrations, with popular politics. The anti-Exclusionist press worked to great effect upon repetitive themes: the peril of a new civil war; the horrors of the 1640s and of the 'godly' Republic; and the ideological descent of the Exclusionists from the Cromwellian tyrants of the 1650s. As we have seen, memories of the civil wars remained intense amongst the English population. For a minority, the Restoration represented the re-establishment of a decadent court and an ungodly episcopacy. But for many, the civil wars were remembered as a disaster. The pro-Exclusionist petitioning campaign of 1679–80 played directly into their opponents' hands: the campaign immediately evoked memories of the petitioning movements of 1641–2. L'Estrange reminded his readers that 'popular commotions are the most criminal and dangerous of all sorts of oppressions'. Fear of a 'Presbyterian Plot' persuaded some to take direct action against the Whigs. London apprentices, led by one 'Captain Tom', intended to mount a demonstration against the '2 Horrid Plots' which had recently threatened the nation: 'the one by the Papists, and the other by the Presbyterians; that of the Papists is pretty well over, but the Presbyterians is not'. The apprentices intended to gather on 29 May 1680, the anniversary of the Restoration, to burn an effigy of Oliver Cromwell and to pull down dissenting meetinghouses and bawdy houses in London. Once again, then, we see older types of crowd organisation (the apprentices' long habit of tearing down bawdy houses) providing a format for new forms of collective politics. The 29th May remained lodged within the political calendar throughout the seventeenth and eighteenth centuries as a day given over to ostentatious collective demonstrations of loyalty to the Stuarts. In 1682, for instance, bonfires were lit around the City and Westminster on 29 May, into which Whig declarations were flung 'by vote of the vast multitude', while loyal healths were drunk to the royal family. The effigy of 'Jack Presbyter', the personification of po-faced presbyterianism, was incinerated in bonfires on 5 November 1681, as Tory crowds gave a twist to the anti-catholic calendar. In combination with the success of print propaganda, the Tory appeals to crowd politics had by 1681 regained control of London's streets and open spaces.[131]

Both Whigs and Tories therefore appealed to a public politics which lay beyond Westminster and the court. Both sides sought to control public space in London, Westminster and other towns through crowd demonstrations, and the physical harassment of their opponents. Both sides employed a populist journalism to define their own political programmes and to stereotype their opponents. Both sides exploited the coffee house environment as a means of disseminating their propaganda. And both Whig and Tory publishers tried to generate a popular political readership. One Whig publisher explained how his regular invective against popery was printed on a single sheet, so that the 'vulgar' might afford it. The rhetorical and pictorial forms of such publications were designed 'for the Rabble, and drunken, sottish Clubs, in Ballad Doggerel, with witty Picture affixed'. Again, we are reminded of how much popular political forms of the later seventeenth century owed to their ancestors: in this case, to the hand-written libels which had so worried the judges in Star Chamber. Similarly, print woodcut imagery that adorned such publications was sometimes based upon the same inversive, charivaric imagery as rural Skimmington riots. And, like the hand-written libels which had criticised the Duke of Buckingham in 1620s, or which had called apprentices together to attack the Archbishop of Canterbury's residence at Lambeth Palace in 1640, seditious printed tracts were found 'scattered' and 'dropt' around the streets of London.[132]

But although the print propaganda of 1678–81 connected with earlier forms, in other respects the Exclusion Crisis represented an important discontinuity in the history of political communication and organisation in early modern England. This was less than apparent at the time. An extreme legal judgment of Judge Jeffreys that 'No person whatsoever could expose to the public knowledge anything that concerned the affairs of the public, without licence from the King' provided substantial legal backing for the suppression of dissident publishers. By November 1682, the government had banned the publication of all regular news sheets save for its own *London Gazette*, and the *Observator*, published by L'Estrange.

In 1685, upon the accession of James II, pre-publication censorship was re-established. Yet the heavy hand of state censorship did not preclude royal government from sponsoring its own interventions into popular political opinion. Pro-government newspapers continued to circulate, and during the spring of 1688 were distributed for free in London's streets. The autumn of the previous year had seen James II's agents placing pro-Stuart 'books and papers in coffee houses and houses of public entertainment'. The invasion of England by William of Orange's army was preceded by the invasion of public opinion by his printed propaganda. In particular, his *Declaration ... of the reasons inducing him to appear in arms in the kingdom of England for preserving of the Protestant religion and for restoring the laws and liberties of England, Scotland and Ireland*, which James II's advisors warned him would 'gain the people's affections', enjoyed a wide readership. Allies of William received copies of the declaration to distribute, and bundles of free copies were sent to booksellers to sell at their own profit. The Glorious Revolution therefore represented not only a foreign invasion, but also a further intervention into popular political opinion. Nonetheless, the new regime demonstrated a similar attitude to the press as that which it had displaced. Between October 1689 and April 1695, some 17 trials for unlicensed printing were mounted. Yet in 1695, Parliament failed to renew the Licensing Act, and pre-publication censorship vanished. The expiry of the Licensing Act led to a huge expansion in printed propaganda. By 1705, there were 12 newspapers appearing regularly in London, and by the end of Queen Anne's reign many of the major provincial towns had their own newspaper. Thereafter, state-sponsored attempts to stifle critical publishers were forced to rely upon the laws of seditious libel alone. Governments continued to view the press as a potentially destabilising force. With this in mind, regardless of their political colour, successive regimes continued to sponsor news-papers and publishers whom they deemed supportive, and to harass those whom they saw as critics.[133]

To what extent might these shifts in the relationship between the state, political conflict, the printing press and popular politics be under-stood in terms of the formation of a public sphere of open political activity? We will recall that, according to Habermas's formulation, the structure of the English state underwent fundamental alteration at the beginning of the eighteenth century, allowing a larger freedom to public political organisation and debate, and thereby redefining the basis of its own legitimation. Quibbling with Habermas's periodisation, Steve Pincus has located the origins of a public sphere in the government's failure to suppress the coffee houses in 1675. For Pincus, this demonstrates that 'The centre of English political opinion had apparently shifted in favour of the public sphere'. The attempt at suppression generated a print debate over the coffee houses, in which the coffee house was defended because it provided an arena for reasoned debate. Whereas those uphold-ing the government line saw coffee houses as 'seminaries of sedition', others argued that such establishments contributed to the stability of the realm. In this analysis, far from engendering further religious division, 'the vain pratings' of religious enthusiasts in coffee houses were 'over-balanced by the sage and solid reasonings' of 'experienced gentlemen, judicious lawyers, able physicians, ingenious merchants, and under-standing citizens'. This 'most intelligent society' was formed within the coffee house, which became an agent to 'civilise our manners, enlarge our understandings, refine our language, teach us a generous confidence and handsome mode of address'. Thus, far from being a seminary of sedition, 'The coffee house is the citizens Academy.' Moreover, although the coffee houses were especially numerous within the metropolis, they proliferated into 'a variety of larger English towns'. Following recent his-torians of gender relations in the long eighteenth century, Pincus argues that women's conversation was enabled within this 'polite' public sphere, and that 'There is little warrant for the claim that women were excluded from coffee houses.' Pincus concludes that 'Coffee houses provided the social and cultural locus for an early modern English public sphere.' The coffee house thus emerges as a key site within later seventeenth-century political culture, providing a modernising forum in which conversation, print propaganda, rumour and rationality were mixed into a destabilising concoction, breaking down old hierarchies such that 'each man seems a Leveller, and ranks and files himself as he lists, without regard to degree or order'.[134]

The debate over the coffee houses anticipated later confrontations over print censorship, the validity of party organisation and formal rights to speech, petition, representation and assembly. With the benefit of long hindsight, it is possible to see the partial resolution of these confrontations in favour of broadened political participation as amounting to a process akin to that which Habermas described. During the last years of the seventeenth century, the English state stepped away from some confrontations over the public sphere – most importantly, the coffee houses and pre-publication censorship – while in other areas it granted important liberties. The passage of the Triennial Act in 1694, for instance, extended opportunities for formal participation in parliamentary politics, at a time at which it has been estimated that perhaps one in four adult males possessed the right to vote in parliamentary elections.[135] Changes in the attitudes of legislators to the reporting of their deliberations also helped to widen popular knowledge of parliamentary activities. Throughout the early modern period, authority had been closely bound up with secrecy. This was as true of the politics of the parish, as it was of the Parliament. Before the civil wars, and immediately after the Restoration, Parliament had attempted to keep its deliberations secret. Similarly, parish vestrymen were liable to agree that their resolutions should be 'kept secret and not to be revayled further than [the] company'. The decision of the House of Commons to publish its votes in October 1680 'to render them publick to the people', therefore represented another important step towards the formal recognition that Parliament operated within a broad polity. One member of the House of Commons observed that there was 'scarce a parish but one or more bought them [the printed votes of the House] and lent them to their neighbours, by which most of them knew what was done'. The visibly dynamic relationship between representatives and electors fed back into changing conceptions of the relationship between ruler and ruled: another member argued that 'I think it not natural, nor rational that the People who sent us hither, should not be informed of our actions.'[136]

This freer flow of political information was both stimulated and enabled by the printing press. Although the lapse of pre-publication censorship in 1695 was partly accidental, the death of the Licensing Act therefore has something of a symbolic quality to it.

But this argument requires qualification. First, as we saw in Chapter 1, the Tudor and early Stuart polity had been much wider than the ideal envisaged within classic patriarchal theory. If such a 'public sphere' did indeed emerge after the 1670s, this represented a public recognition of the broad basis of the early modern polity, rather than a fundamental readjustment of the social basis of government. Secondly, the cool 'rationality' of this later Stuart 'public sphere' should not be overstated, for it was formed within a maelstrom of religious and party conflict. Participants were not so much attempting to define a socially capacious public sphere within which their differing ideologies could be rationally debated, so much as finding new ways of conducting long-established religious and ideological conflicts. Lastly, any 'public sphere' that emerged in the late seventeenth and early eighteenth centuries was more visibly defined by its exclusions than it was by its inclusions. We shall venture beyond those exclusions in our conclusion.

CODA

BEYOND THE PUBLIC SPHERE: THE POLITICS OF THE POORER SORT IN EARLY EIGHTEENTH-CENTURY ENGLAND

The Whig order that dominated early Georgian England defined itself as the embodiment of the rights of the 'Freeborn Englishman'. According to the Whig version of history, in 1688 a corrupt, popish, arbitrary regime had been toppled. In its place, the Glorious Revolution had restored the 'rights of the people' to liberty, property, protestantism and parliamentary representation. And yet, in contrast to such libertarian rhetoric, the majority of the English people remained excluded from formal participation within that broadened polity. Given the significance of parliamentary representation to Whig ideology, it is revealing that the distribution of the franchise remained deliberately restricted. It was certainly the case, as we have seen, that within some boroughs the right to vote was widely distributed. But in many other urban seats, and all the more so within the countryside, the parliamentary franchise remained firmly lodged within the hands of the propertied classes. Rather like early seventeenth-century puritans, when Whig theorists used the term 'the people', or 'free men', they therefore referred to a restricted group, defined by age, religion, gender and class. In this definition, adult, protestant men who held sufficient property to be economically independent constituted 'the people'. One Whig writer spelt this out in 1701:

It is owned, that all governments are made by man, and ought to be made by those men who are owners of the territory over which the

187

government extends. It must likewise be confessed, that the FREE-
HOLDERS of England are owners of the English territory, and therefore have a natural right to erect what government they please.[1]

The social distribution of literacy, coupled with the organisation of the
public sphere, helped to maintain the exclusivity of the Whig regime.
Participation within print politics was, if not wholly restricted to the literate,
certainly biased in their favour. Of course, literacy rates were increasing
in the later seventeenth and early eighteenth centuries. But it remains
the case that the majority of the population possessed little or no literate
skills. The national proportion of adult men able to sign their own name
had increased from about 30 per cent in 1641 to about 45 per cent by
1714. Women's literacy was much lower: about 10 per cent of women
could sign their own name in the mid-seventeenth century, rising to about
25 per cent by the early eighteenth century. As in earlier periods, the
rich were more likely to be able to read and to write than the poor, and
urban inhabitants were similarly privileged above rural inhabitants.[2]

Class, geography and gender therefore structured the distribution of
literacy. The same is true of the organisation of the 'public sphere', which
was most visibly constituted within privileged urban sites. In particular,
the coffee house, the Walk and the Assembly Rooms of the Georgian
town were established as locations for 'polite' and rational conversation.
The relocation of public politics into such sites was connected to physical
and cultural changes within the town. The period c. 1660–1730 has been
identified as one of 'urban renaissance' in which a classicised vision was
projected on to the urban environment. Like their rural counterparts,
the urban poor were unwelcome within the ordered spaces that constituted the public sphere of middling sort discourse.[3] In spatial, social and
political terms, therefore, the Whig order was defined by a set of dominating exclusions.

It is one of the finest ironies in the history of early modern popular
politics that it was the Tories, supposedly committed to the defence
of the old values of social authoritarianism and patriarchalism, who
developed the clearest critique of the social foundations of the Whig
regime. Just as the Tory proto-feminist Mary Astell dissected the logic by
which Whig men maintained domestic authority while claiming to
champion liberty, so Tory journalists and polemicists tore apart the
Whig claim to speak for 'the people'.[4] The Tory deconstruction of Whig
ideology had commenced during the Exclusion Crisis. Sir Roger
L'Estrange accused the Whigs of acting 'in the Name of the People, with-

out the People's Commission'. Anti-Exclusionist opinion concurred, condemning Whig propaganda as 'the contrivances of a very few ... meerly imposed upon the People by artifice and surprize'. At times, the Tories of the 1680s could sound almost like Levellers of the 1640s. One Tory tract published in 1680 argued that Parliament was not representative of the people, since the House of Commons derived its authority from less than:

> a third part of the Nation ... none have votes in Elections, but Freeholders of at least forty shillings a Year, and Citizens and Burgesses ... the whole number of Labourers, Servants, Artificers and Tradesmen, not residing in, or at least free of cities and Boroughs are totally excluded.

Another Tory observed how 'the members of Parliament are chosen by the men of money, the freeholders'. Analysing the logic of the Tory critique, Mark Knights comments that 'This strain of thought sat very uneasily with a conservative strand within loyalist opinion which argued that voting was not natural right.' But it was precisely within such ideological inconsistencies that populist Toryism thrived. Tory organisation reflected this populism. Whereas the Whig petitioning movement of 1679–80 had been directed primarily towards enfranchised voters, the Tory 'Loyal Addresses' of 1681 reached deeper into English society, providing a political voice for the 'inhabitants' rather than simply for the voting population. Like those parliamentarians of the 1640s who had denounced the royalist appeal to the 'vulgar rabble', some of the first Whigs recognised popular Toryism, and denounced the Loyal Addresses as articulating the opinions of 'the scum'.[5]

Although many Tory writers of the early eighteenth century held the politics of the 'vulgar mob' in deliberate contempt, Tory paternalism struck a deep vein within popular culture. The demonstrators who gathered on Restoration Day to burn effigies of 'Jack Presbyter' were ritually renewing the old festive culture of popular Royalism. This had always cast itself in opposition to the perceived individualism and hypocrisy of the 'godly' and in defence of an ersatz communalism. The subversive potential of such seemingly conservative values was most apparent when the Tories were out of national office. The appeal to 'High Church' values by anti-Whig protesters during the War of Spanish Succession, for instance, was about more than religious doctrine alone. In his study of popular protest in early eighteenth-century London, Nicholas Rogers has observed how hostility towards the Whigs focused upon the poverty caused by their war policy, and the Whigs' association with the puritanical campaign for the reformation of manners launched by dissenting churches.[6]

In its own inversive way, Jacobitism could provide an especially cutting critique of the dominant order. One London weaver who expressed the opinion in 1690 that King William was a 'Dutch dogg and an Usurper' also felt that:

> the nobility was a parcel of Rogues and all of them lived as high as Kings. And that the nobility did not vote in King William for the good of the Commonwealth nor for religion but to preserve their riches and honours.[7]

Once again, it scarcely mattered to lower-class Jacobites that the official ideology of Jacobitism emphasised hierarchy and authoritarianism. Jacobitism touched on the most sensitive nerve within the Hanoverian body politic: the apprehension that the Glorious Revolution had fractured the proper succession to the throne. A Stepney labourer articulated that view in September 1715: 'King George has no right to the Crown No by God King George has no right to the Crown.' The rumours concerning the new King's household arrangements further impaired his popular standing: 'The King is a Blockhead & a Cuckold', opined Andrew Roberts in 1718. Popular criticism of the new monarchy often took mocking, charivaric forms. Anti-Hanoverian crowds regularly burnt George I in effigy with horns on his head, in vivid depiction of his cuckolded status.[8] Coupled with King George's perceived corruption, his diminished patriarchal status damned him in the eyes of many. One man was alleged to have grumbled in 1716 that:

> Wee have a King and as soone as he comes he asks a maintenance for his children It's like a person coming into Towne with a Coach and six horses and then flinging himselfe of the parish It's not to be borne, Wee will not have such as Cuckoldy King.

Popular hostility to the monarch was summed up in the profane brevity of one Middlesex cordwainer: 'King George, King Turd'.

Nicholas Rogers has argued that there was a levelling logic to Hanoverian Jacobitism. He calls it 'a script to defy the law', and argues that Jacobitism could represent a deliberate form of transgression, consciously designed to infuriate and offend representatives of the Whig order. Within Jacobitism, labouring people found 'a libertarian critique of monarchy' which contradicted the Jacobite polemicists' emphasis upon hereditary right, but which confirmed 'the illegality of the Revolution settlement'. This analysis was summed up in the alleged seditious speech of George Cleeve in 1716, who warned that 'King George must have a care what he did otherwise he would lose his head as King Charles had done.' Following Edward Thompson, Rogers sees popular Jacobitism as a manifestation of a defiant, occasionally violent, plebeian culture which prized independence above all else. Thus the 'idiom of defiance' articulated within popular Jacobitism showed that the labouring classes of early Georgian England could do what 'they bloody well pleased'.[9]

The riotous politics of the poor therefore battered at the doors of the 'polite' public sphere. The burlesque forms taken by popular political protest in early Hanoverian England should not blind us to its seriousness. Coupled with an expanded military, the 1715 Riot Act represented a major extension of the state's ability to crush crowd protest. Similarly, the continuing force of sedition and treason legislation meant that articulating anti-Hanoverian sentiment could be dangerous. And yet, despite the increased repressive capacities of the post-1715 Whig state, what is impressive about the pattern of crowd protest in early eighteenth-century England is the consistency of its dogged, bloody-minded spirit.

This was as true of the politics of the parish as it was of the politics of the realm. Throughout this book, we have seen how the micro-politics of social relations and parish affairs connected and conflicted with the dominating discourses and administrative structures of the central state. One recurrent theme has concerned the changing loyalties of the 'better sort', or the 'middling sort of people' as they were becoming known in the later seventeenth century. We have seen how that social fraction came to exercise institutional authority within the parish, through their control of closed vestries, local office and parish funds. In many cases, that political agency was deployed against the unruly culture of the village poor. Steve Hindle has recently shown how post-Restoration parish elites attempted to reimpose order upon their local subjects through such parish vestries. In particular, he has identified an 'extraordinary sensitivity' on the part of 'parish elites to the threat of popularity in the wake of the [English] Revolution'. The 'late unhappy wilfulness and disorder in this kingdom' had, parish governors believed, provoked 'irregularity in the management . . . of affairs relating to the good of the parish'. 'The meaner sort of people who have least interest and little judgment' had acquired undue authority during the English Revolution, while those of 'far better rank and condition' had been displaced from their proper place of authority: 'carried tumultuously rather by number than by worth'. Precisely the same terminology was used to justify the exclusion of the poor from participation within the national polity of Augustan England.[10]

It has been a defining argument of this book that early modern villages had a politics of their own. That politics was deeply concerned with the ownership and control of material resources: hence, our heavy emphasis upon food and land. Village politics was also concerned with agency and authority. The periodic capacity of labouring people to organise collectively and in public has therefore been presented as a political achievement in its own right. Similarly, the capacity of elites (whether local or national) to break such organisation has been conceived of as highly political. Throughout, we have seen how the shifting contours of community were shaped and re-shaped through the exercise of social power. Over the course of the early modern period, we have charted an uneven, contested, messy process by which the legitimising language of community and the institutional apparatus of parochial organisation passed into the hands of parish elites. That process was most apparent at the moment at which the term 'the parish' became synonymous with the parochial elite. But we have also seen how local resistance to the exercise of social power helped to form collective plebeian identities within individual villages, 'countries' and regions. Social memory had a special force in the formation of such localised identities: lost rights were bitterly recalled; customs and liberties that had been successfully protected in earlier generations were jealously defended in the present. The social organisation of memory could therefore provide the rural poor with the political will to rebuild a sense of community, apart from that of the rulers of their village.

For the poor inhabitants of Wheatley (Oxfordshire), community was recalled as something that had been fractured by the wholesale enclosure of the nearby woods.[11] Giving evidence to the Court of Exchequer court in 1687, old Joan Battin remembered how the forest of Shottover had once had deer in it:

and that then the Towne of Wheatley rich & poore had common for all cattel to feed in the said forrest . . . without any difference between poore & rich & without stint.

After the Restoration, enclosure commissioners had apportioned some 20 acres of land to the village poor as compensation for the extinction of their common rights within the forest. The freeholders had received a further 60 acres, and a proportion of the old forest land. In their evidence to the Court of Exchequer in 1687, Joan Battin and her neighbours recalled the enclosure of the forest in terms of expulsion, dispossession and the spatial reordering of property and social power. In the articulate analysis of her neighbour Richard Darling, 'the landholders .... shutt the Cottagers quite out of all their commons'. Yet the poor cottagers insisted that they remained a part of the fiscal community of the village, pointing out that 29 of the 92 cottager households contributed to the parish poor rate. Such payments, under custom, implied rights that Joan Battin felt she had never lost:

> Shee is an inhabitant in Whateley parish and saies if shee had a cow to put in the Common she has as good right as other of the now Inhabitants of Whateley have there.

Her poor neighbours agreed and sought to prove their case by presenting the Court of Exchequer with verbal accounts of local history that sustained their claims. It was explained how, before 1687, the cottager John Powell had resisted his exclusion from the freeholders' 60 acres, and 'did putt in his cattell' upon the land. The freeholders had then impounded Powell's cattle. Yet the Wheatley cottagers learnt that in the neighbouring village of Horspath, the village poor had successfully sued their wealthier neighbours at the Court of Exchequer over an identical matter. Emboldened by the example of the poor of Horspath, the Wheatley cottagers also lodged a complaint at Exchequer, thereby initiating the legal process in which their stories of local history were transcribed and preserved within the court's archives. Out of these conflicts, a different kind of community was being born in the villages which bordered on the old forest of Shottover: one nourished by memories of lost customs, illuminated by claims to living rights and moved by a dogged, litigious, bloody-minded spirit.

The Exchequer action of 1687 did not conclude the confrontation between landed and near-landless in Wheatley. Conflict continued over the enclosed woods into the eighteenth century. Further Exchequer action commenced in 1725, in the course of which the oldest inhabitants of Wheatley again provided evidence concerning the past use of the forest. Joseph Fiddes, a 73-year-old gentleman, provided some guilty memories of the hard winter of 1677, which he remembered as 'the time of the great frost'. In those days, he had been employed on a Wheatley freeholder's farm, possibly as an overseer. The farm occupied the grounds of the old forest. Fiddes explained how, during the winter of 1677, 'Several of Whately poor' came on to the enclosed land:

> and began to cut branches. He made them stop thinking it belonged to [his employer] and threatened to fire and presented a gun.

In their evidence to the Court of Exchequer, the poor cottagers of post-Restoration Wheatley invoked two communities: one live, the other dead; the one born from the death of the other. One community, that of the open forest where rich and poor had been 'togeather', where 'there was noe difference in the usage of the Comons betweene the Cottagers & Landholders', died at the end of a gun in the winter cold of 1677. And another was stirring into life. This community was formed from the political agency of poor but assertive cottagers, convinced of their 'rights' upon the land, touchy over infringements of what remained of custom, conscious of their status as ratepayers, householders and independent people; a community and a local culture inundated with bitter memories.

NOTES

Introduction   Interpreting Popular Politics in Early Modern England

1 See H. Ellis (ed.), *Holinshed's chronicles*, 6 vols (1577 and 1587; new edn, London, 1807–8). For a useful introduction to the *Chronicles*, see A. Patterson, *Reading Holinshed's chronicles* (Chicago, 1994). For Shakespeare's use of Holinshed, see E. M. W. Tillyard, *Shakespeare's history plays* (London, 1944), 56–60.

2 I. M. W. Harvey, *Jack Cade's rebellion of 1450* (Oxford, 1991).

3 For that speech, see J. Samaha, 'Gleanings from local criminal-court records: sedition amongst the "inarticulate" in Elizabethan Essex', *Journal of Social History*, 8 (1975), 61–79; J. A. Sharpe, 'Social strain and social dislocation, 1585–1603', in J. Guy (ed.), *The reign of Elizabeth I: court and culture in the last decade* (Cambridge, 1995); J. Walter '"A rising of the people"? The Oxfordshire rising of 1596' *P&P*, 107 (1985), 90–143.

4 See preceding reference. For my own attempt, see A. Wood, 'Poore men woll speke one daye': plebeian languages of deference and defiance in England, *c.* 1520–1640', in T. Harris (ed.), *The politics of the excluded, c. 1500–1850*. (Basingstoke, 2001), 67–98.

5 For an evocative account of proverbial culture, see D. Rollison, *The local origins of modern society: Gloucestershire 1500–1800* (London, 1992), ch. 3.

6 *Henry VI Part II*, 4.7.39–43; 4.2.12; 4.2.19–20; 4.8.19–23.

7 *Henry VI Part II*, 4.2.62–5.

8 *Henry VI Part II*, 4.2.37–41; 4.2.126–8; 4.2.171–9.

9 *Henry VI Part II*, 4.8. 25–7.

10 *Henry VI Part II*, 4.2.73–104; 4.7.1–17; 4.4.7–8; Ellis (ed.), *Holinshed's chronicles*, III, 222–4.

11 Tillyard, *Shakespeare's history plays*, 70–6, 179–94.

12 M. Hattaway, 'Rebellion, class consciousness, and Shakespeare's *2 Henry VI*', *Cahiers Elisabethans*, 33 (1988), 13–22; T. Cartelli, 'Jack Cade in the garden: class consciousness and class conflict in *2 Henry VI*', in R. Burt and J. M. Archer (eds), *Enclosure Acts: sexuality, property and culture in early modern England* (Ithaca, 1994), 48–67; A. Patterson, *Shakespeare and the popular voice* (Oxford, 1989), chs 1–3.

13 On these subjects see, respectively, J. A. Sharpe, *Crime in seventeenth-century England: a county study* (Cambridge, 1983); P. Clark and P. Slack (eds), *Crisis and order in English towns, 1500–1700* (London, 1972); P. Slack, *The impact of plague in*

Tudor and Stuart England (London, 1985); D. Cressy, *Literacy and the social order: reading and writing in Tudor and Stuart England* (Cambridge, 1980); E. A. Wrigley and R. S. Schofield, *The population history of England and Wales, 1541–1871: a reconstruction* (1981; 2nd edn, Cambridge, 1989); K. E. Wrightson and D. Levine, *Poverty and piety in an English village: Terling, 1525–1700* (1979; 2nd edn, Cambridge, 1995); D. Levine, *Reproducing families: the political economy of English population history* (Cambridge, 1987). For especially important syntheses, see K. E. Wrightson, *English society 1580–1680* (London, 1982); J. A. Sharpe, *Early modern England: a social history, 1550–1760* (1987; 2nd edn, London, 1997).

14 For a summary, see R. C. Richardson *The debate on the English revolution* (1977; 3rd edn, Manchester, 1999).

15 An important exception was always John Morrill's work. Partly because of his local emphasis, Morrill always had more time for those below the county gentry. See his reissued *Revolt in the provinces: the people of England and the tragedies of war, 1630–1648* (1976; 2nd edn, Harlow, 1999).

16 For liberal political science, see for instance D. D. Raphael, *Problems of political philosophy* (1970; 2nd edn, Basingstoke, 1990), esp. ch. 2. For traditional political history, see for instance G. R. Elton, *Political history: principles and practice* (London, 1970); C. Russell, *The crisis of parliaments: English history, 1509–1660* (Oxford 1971).

17 For that assumption, see for instance M. A. Kishlansky, *Parliamentary selection: social and political choice in early modern England* (Cambridge, 1986), preface and chs 1–2; J. C. Davis, 'Radicalism in a traditional society: the evolution of radical thought in the English commonwealth, 1649–60', *History of Political Thought*, 3 (1982), 193–213.

18 R. B. Manning, *Village revolts: social protest and popular disturbance in England, 1509–1640* (Oxford, 1988), 1–6. For the concept of 'pre-politics', see E. J. Hobsbawm, *Primitive rebels: studies in archaic forms of social movements in the nineteenth and twentieth centuries* (New York, 1965), 2–3.

19 See especially R. Cust and A. Hughes (eds), *Conflict in early Stuart England: studies in religion and politics* (London, 1989); A. Hughes, *The causes of the English civil war* (1991; 2nd edn, Basingstoke, 1999).

20 Arguments over the popular impact of the Reformation had always made religious historians sensitive to the social context of politics. See for instance E. Duffy, *The stripping of the altars: traditional religion in England, 1400–1580* (New Haven, 1992). For changing views of the Tudor polity, see the encouraging signs in S. Alford, 'Politics and political history in the Tudor century', *HJ*, 42, 2 (1999), 535–48.

21 P. Collinson, *Elizabethan essays* (London, 1994), 11.

22 T. Harris, *London crowds in the reign of Charles II: propaganda and politics from the Restoration until the Exclusion Crisis* (Cambridge, 1987).

23 See especially G. Rude, *The crowd in history, 1730–1848* (London, 1964); E. P. Thompson *Customs in Common* (London, 1991). For popular politics, see for instance N. Rogers, *Whigs and cities: popular politics in the age of Walpole and Pitt* (Oxford, 1990); D. Hay and N. Rogers, *Eighteenth-century English society: shuttles and swords* (Oxford, 1997). For a very different view of Hanoverian England, see J. C. D. Clark. *English society, 1688–1832: ideology, social structure and political practice during the ancien regime* (Cambridge, 1985).

24 Most importantly in *A freeborn people: politics and the nation in seventeenth century England* (Oxford, 1996); but the argument is implicit in his seminal *Revel, riot and rebellion: popular politics and culture in England, 1603–1660* (Oxford, 1985).

25 Alan Everitt, quoted in A. Hughes, 'Local history and the origins of the civil war', in Cust and Hughes (eds), *Conflict in early Stuart England*, 225.
26 For that scepticism, see especially, Harris, *London crowds*, ch. 1.
27 Underdown, *A freeborn people*, 10–12, 30, 49, 59–60.
28 F. McGlynn and A. Tuden, 'Introduction', in F. McGlynn and A. Tuden (eds), *Anthropological approaches to political behaviour* (Pittsburgh, Pennsylvania, 1991), 3, 17, 24–5.
29 A. Leftwich, *Redefining politics: people, resources and power* (London, 1983), 11.
30 C. Geertz, *The interpretation of cultures* (London, 1975), esp. ch. 1.
31 Scott, *Weapons of the weak: everyday forms of peasant resistance* (New Haven, Connecticut, 1985).
32 M. A. Ackelsberg and M. L. Shanley, 'Privacy, publicity and power: a feminist rethinking of the public-private distinction', in N. J. Hirschmann and C. Di Stefano (eds), *Revisioning the political: feminist reconstructions of traditional concepts in western political theory* (Oxford, 1996), 213, 220. For three outstanding works of feminist historiography, all of which pay close attention to the public/private distinction, see L. Roper, *The holy household: women and morals in Reformation Augsburg* (Oxford, 1989); L. Davidoff and C. Hall, *Family Fortunes: men and women of the English middle class 1780–1850* (London, 1987); L. Gowing, *Domestic dangers: women, words and sex in early modern London* (Oxford, 1996).
33 K. E. Wrightson, 'The politics of the parish in early modern England', in P. Griffiths, A. Fox and S. Hindle (eds), *The experience of authority in early modern England* (London, 1996), 10–46.
34 For a critique of the growing particularism within early modern social history, see K. E. Wrightson, 'The enclosure of English social history', in A. Wilson (ed.), *Rethinking social history: English society, 1570–1920 and its interpretation* (Manchester, 1993), 59–77.
35 See especially Gowing, *Domestic dangers*; G. M. Walker, 'Crime, gender and the social order in early modern Cheshire', University of Liverpool, Ph.D., 1994.
36 A. Fox, 'Rumour, news and popular political opinion in Elizabethan and early Stuart England', *HJ*, 40, 3 (1997), 597–620; Fox, 'Ballads, libels and popular ridicule in Jacobean England', *P&P*, 145 (1994), 47–83; Wood, 'Poore men woll speke one daye'.
37 P. D. Griffiths, 'Secrecy and authority in late sixteenth- and seventeenth-century London', *HJ*, 40, 4 (1997), 925–51.
38 A. Wood, 'The place of custom in plebeian political culture: England, 1550–1800', *Social History*, 22, 1 (1997), 46–60.
39 On the middling sort, see especially K. E. Wrightson: 'Estates, degrees and sorts: changing perceptions of society in Tudor and Stuart England' in P. Corfield (ed.), *Language, history and class* (Oxford, 1991), 30–52; Wrightson, 'Sorts of people in Tudor and Stuart England', in J. Barry (ed.), *The middling sort of people: culture, society and politics in England, 1550–1800* (Basingstoke, 1994), 28–51. On parish vestries, see especially S. Hindle, *The state and social change in early modern England, c. 1550–1640* (Basingstoke, 2000), chs 6–9; Hindle, 'Power, poor relief and social relations in Holland fen, c. 1600–1800', *HJ*, 41, 1 (1998), 67–96.
40 Most recently in T. Harris, 'Problematising popular culture', in T. Harris (ed.), *Popular culture in England, 1500–1850* (Basingstoke, 1995), 1–27.
41 For book-length studies, see Rollison, *Local origins of modern society*; A. Wood, *The politics of social conflict: the Peak Country, 1520–1770* (Cambridge, 1999).

42   J. W. Scott, *Gender and the politics of history* (New York, 1988), 41.

43   S. Hindle, 'The shaming of Margaret Knowsley: gossip, gender and the experi-
     ence of authority in early modern England', *Continuity and Change*, 9 (1994),
     391–419; M. Gaskill, 'Witchcraft and power in early modern England: the case of
     Margaret Moore', in J. Kermode and G. Walker (eds), *Women, crime and the courts
     in early modern England* (London, 1994), 125–45.

44   J. Simons, *Foucault and the political* (London, 1995), 82–3.

45   'Introduction', in P. Griffiths, A. Fox and S. Hindle (eds), *The experience of authority
     in early modern England* (Basingstoke, 1996), 1–9.

46   As in, for instance, the accounts of ritual offered in M. E. James, *Society, politics and
     culture; studies in early modern England* (Cambridge, 1986), ch. 1; and C. Phythian
     Adams, 'Ceremony and the citizen: the communal year at Coventry, 1450–1550',
     in Clark and Slack (eds), *Crisis and order*, 57–85.

47   K. Sharpe, *Criticism and compliment: the politics of literature in the England of Charles I*
     (Cambridge, 1987), 205–7.

48   A. Wood, 'Custom, identity and resistance: English free miners and their law,
     c. 1550–1800', in Griffiths, Fox and Hindle (eds), *The experience of authority*, 249–85.

49   Wrightson, 'Politics of the parish', 31–7.

50   J. C. Scott, *Domination and the arts of resistance: hidden transcripts* (New Haven,
     1990), 21–2, xi, 15, 16, 20.

51   Thompson, *Customs in common*, 56–7.

52   Thompson, *Customs in common*, 7–12, 78, 83–7.

53   Thompson's interpretation owes much to D. Hay, 'Property, authority and the
     criminal law', in D. Hay *et al.* (eds), *Albion's fatal tree: crime and society in eighteenth-
     century England* (London, 1975), 17–63.

54   For an accessible discussion, see R. Simon, *Gramsci's political thought: an introduction*
     (London, 1982).

55   Q. Hoare and G. Nowell Smith (eds), *Selections from the prison notebooks of Antonio
     Gramsci* (London, 1971), 244.

56   C. Ginzburg, *The Cheese and the worms: the cosmos of a sixteenth-century miller* (1976;
     Eng. trans., London, 1980); E. D. Genovese, *Roll, Jordan, roll: the world the slaves
     made* (London, 1975) and *In red and black: Marxian explorations of southern and Afro-
     American history* (New York, 1971); P. Joyce, *Work, society and politics: the culture of
     the factory in later Victorian England* (London, 1980).

57   Thompson, *Customs in common*, 87.

58   Hindle, *State and social change*, 230, 223, 226.

1   Authority, the Law and the State

1   A. J. P. Taylor, *Essays in English history*, (London, 1975), 127. I am grateful to John
     Charmley for locating this reference.

2   HMC, *Salisbury*, IV, 5. For similar contemporary worries about the 'small begin-
     nings' of rebellion, see W. P. Baildon (ed.), *Les reportes del cases in Camera Stellata,
     1593 to 1609* (London, 1894), 368–9.

3   T. Elyot, *The book named the governor* (1531; London, 1962); T. Smith, *De Republica
     Anglorum* (1583; Cambridge, 1982); E. Dudley, *The tree of the commonwealth* (1509;
     Cambridge, 1948).

4 Elyot, *The book named the governor*, 1–14.

5 Dudley, *The tree of the commonwealth*, 45–6; Harris, *London crowds*, 16.

6 J. Walter, *Understanding popular violence in the English revolution: the Colchester plunderers* (Cambridge, 1999), 16–20; B. Manning, *The English People and the English Revolution* (1976; 2nd. edn, London, 1991), 102–30, 319–25; A. S. P. Woodhouse (ed.), *Puritanism and liberty: being the army debates (1647–9) from the Clarke manuscripts, with supplementary documents* (London, 1938), 53–5, 57–8; Harris, *London crowds*, 133–44.

7 Walter, *Understanding popular violence*, 42–3; M. Knights, *Politics and opinion in crisis, 1678–81* (Cambridge, 1994), 222.

8 On the body language of class, see A. Bryson, 'The rhetoric of status: gesture, demeanour and the image of the gentleman in sixteenth- and seventeenth-century England', in L. Gent and N. Llewellyn (eds), *Renaissance bodies: the human figure in English culture, c. 1540–1660* (London, 1990), 136–53.

9 Quoted in J. Thirsk (ed.), *The Restoration* (London, 1976), 32, 156–8, 170–1, 184.

10 W. Hunt, *The puritan moment: the coming of revolution in an English county* (Cambridge, Massachusetts, 1983), 22.

11 Smith, *De Republica Anglorum*, 64–5.

12 *Ibid.*, 65.

13 *Ibid.*, 75–7.

14 Collinson, *Elizabethan essays*, 11, 14–27.

15 For the Swallowfield articles, see S. Hindle, 'Hierarchy and community in the Elizabethan parish: the Swallowfield articles of 1596', *HJ*, 42, 3 (1999), 835–51.

16 Collinson, *Elizabethan essays*, 23–5.

17 *Ibid.*, 26.

18 *Ibid.*, 11.

19 See for instance R. Schlatter (ed.), *Hobbes' Thucydides* (New Brunswick, New Jersey, 1975). For important studies of fear in the early modern period, see W. J. Bouwsma, 'Anxiety and the formation of early modern culture', in B. C. Malament (ed.), *After the Reformation: essays in honour of J.H. Hexter* (Manchester, 1980), 215–46; W. G. Naphy and P. Roberts (eds), *Fear in early modern society* (Manchester, 1997).

20 James, *Society, politics and culture*, 262–5; C. Hill, 'The many-headed monster' in his *Change and continuity in seventeenth-century England* (London, 1974), 181–204.

21 The indictments are reproduced in F. W. Russell, *Kett's rebellion in Norfolk* (London, 1859), 220–6.

22 S. Justice, *Writing and rebellion: England in 1381* (Berkeley, California, 1994), 259.

23 Quoted in M. Beloff, *Public order and popular disturbances, 1660–1714* (Oxford, 1938), 129.

24 J. Bellamy, *The Tudor law of treason: an introduction* (London, 1979), 11.

25 Bellamy, *Tudor law of treason*, chs 1 and 2; R. B. Manning, 'The origins of the doctrine of sedition', *JBS*, 12, 2 (1980), 99–121.

26 See for instance G. R. Elton, *Policy and police: the enforcement of the Reformation in the age of Thomas Cromwell* (Cambridge, 1972); S. L. Jansen, *Dangerous talk and strange behaviour: women and popular resistance to the reforms of Henry VIII* (Basingstoke, 1996).

27 *Statutes of the realm*, 11 vols (London, 1810–24), IV (I), 240–1.

28 *Statutes*, III, 894–7.

29   F. Bacon, *Essays, civil and moral* (London, 1892), 21–5.

30   Fox, 'Rumour', 599.

31   *Statutes*, IV, 211–14.

32   For examples of the punishment of libels, see Paley (ed.), *Les reportes*, 161–3, 189, 222–30, 326. On the control of printing, see W. S. Siebert, *Freedom of the press in England, 1476–1776* (Urbana, Illinois, 1952), chs 1–7.

33   J. S. Cockburn (ed.), *Calendar of assize records: Sussex indictments, Elizabeth I* (London, 1975), case 1887.

34   A. Fletcher and D. MacCulloch, *Tudor Rebellions* (1968; 4th edn, London, 1997), esp. chs 1–2, 10; P. Zagorin, *Rebels and rulers 1500–1660. Vol I. Society, states and early modern revolution. Agrarian and urban rebellions* (Cambridge, 1982), chs 1–6; C. S. L. Davies, 'Peasant revolt in France and England: a comparison', *Agricultural History Review*, 21 (1973), 122–34.

35   Bacon, *Essays*, 22–3; Walter, 'Oxfordshire rising', 133.

36   For an isolated, but nonetheless significant, exception, see J. D. Walter 'Grain riots and popular attitudes to the law: Maldon and the crisis of 1629' in J. Brewer and J. Styles (eds), *An ungovernable people: the English and their law in the seventeenth and eighteenth centuries* (London, 1980), 47–84.

37   *Statutes*, IV (I), 104–8, 211–14, 377. A very useful general discussion is provided in Manning, *Village revolts*, 55–7.

38   Although see Manning, *Village revolts*, 234 n. 30 for an important qualification.

39   D. Pickering (ed.), *The statutes at large*, 23 vols (London, 1762–78), XIII, 142–6.

40   On the use of martial law during large-scale rebellion, see for instance S. M. Harrison, *The Pilgrimage of Grace in the Lake counties, 1536–7* (London, 1981), 125; B. L. Beer, *Rebellion and riot: popular disorder in England during the reign of Edward VI* (Kent, Ohio, 1982), 174–5.

41   C. Hill, *Economic problems of the church: from Archbishop Whitgift to the Long Parliament* (Oxford, 1956), 55.

42   For a clear discussion of changes in tenancies, see K. E. Wrightson, *Earthly necessities: economic lives in early modern Britain* (New Haven, 2000), 70–5, 134–5, 183–4, 280–4; for custom, see *ibid.*, 76–7, 152–3, 212–14.

43   The large literature on this subject is now synthesised into a powerful argument in Hindle, *State and social change*, esp. chs 1–2, 6–9.

44   For a useful introduction to the operation of the English criminal law, see J. A. Sharpe, *Crime in early modern England, 1550–1750* (1984; 2nd edn, London, 1999), chs 2–4.

45   Hindle, *State and social change*, ch. 3 provides an overview.

46   *Statutes of the realm*, II, 509–10.

47   Paley (ed.), *Les reportes*, 6.

2   Rebellion in Sixteenth-Century England

1   Compare two 'standard' textbooks on the sixteenth century: one old, the other new. G. R. Elton, *England under the Tudors* (London, 1955), chs 6–9 (quoting page 259); M. Nicholls, *A history of the modern British isles, 1529–1603: the two kingdoms* (Oxford, 1999), chs 3 and 7.

2   On the 1489 and 1497 rebellions, see M. A. Hicks, 'The Yorkshire rebellion of 1489 reconsidered', *Northern History*, 22, (1986), 39–62; I. Arthurson, 'The rising of 1497: a revolt of the peasantry', in J. Rosenthal and C. Richmond (eds), *People, politics and community in the later middle ages* (London, 1987), 1–18.

3   G. W. Bernard, *War, taxation and rebellion in early Tudor England: Henry VIII, Wolsey and the Amicable Grant of 1525* (Brighton, 1986), ch. 5.

4   S. J. Gunn, 'Peers, commons and gentry in the Lincolnshire Revolt of 1536', *P&P*, 123 (1989), 54, 67–9. But see also James, *Society, politics and culture*, ch. 6.

5   M. L. Bush, *The Pilgrimage of Grace: a study of the rebel armies of October 1536* (Manchester, 1996), 375–6. This should be read alongside the still valuable M. H. Dodds and R. Dodds, *The Pilgrimage of Grace and the Exeter conspiracy* (Cambridge, 1915), and M. L. Bush and D. Downes, *The defeat of the Pilgrimage of Grace* (Hull, 1999). For other perspectives, see especially C. S. L. Davies, 'The Pilgrimage of Grace reconsidered', *P&P*, 41 (1968), 54–76; Harrison, *Pilgrimage of Grace in the Lake counties*; G. R. Elton, 'Politics and the Pilgrimage of Grace', in his *Studies in Tudor and Stuart politics and government*, 4 vols (Cambridge, 1974–92), III, 183–215. Richard Hoyle's *The Pilgrimage of Grace and the Politics of the 1530s* (Oxford, 2001) appeared too late to be included in this survey, but is full of valuable new material.

6   Fletcher and MacCulloch, *Tudor rebellions*, 46.

7   Harrison, *Pilgrimage of Grace in the Lake counties*, 123; Bush and Downes, *Defeat of the Pilgrimage of Grace*, 268–80.

8   Quoted by Harrison, *Pilgrimage of Grace in the Lake counties*, 123–4.

9   Fletcher and MacCulloch, *Tudor rebellions*, 25.

10 Bush, *Pilgrimage of Grace*, 404, 415, 298, 322, 283–4, 110, 129; Bush and Downes, *Defeat of the Pilgrimage of Grace*, 150; M. L. Bush, 'Captain Poverty and the Pilgrimage of Grace', *Historical Research* 156 (1992), 17–36.

11 See for instance the disagreement between Dickens and Elton on the causes of the 1536 rebellion: A. G. Dickens, 'Secular and religious motivation in the Pilgrimage of Grace', in G. J. Cuming (ed.), *Studies in Church History*, 4 (1967), 39–64; Elton, 'Politics and the Pilgrimage of Grace'. But see C. S. L. Davies' intelligent critique in his 'Popular religion and the Pilgrimage of Grace' in Fletcher and Stevenson, *Order and disorder*, 58–91. For a two-volume study of rebellion which is predicated upon the formal separation of different 'typologies' of rebellion, see P. Zagorin, *Rebels and rulers 1500–1660*, 2 vols (Cambridge, 1982).

12 Harrison, *Pilgrimage of Grace in the Lake counties*, 72.

13 S. Brigden, 'Popular disturbance and the fall of Thomas Cromwell and the reformers, 1539–1540', *HJ*, 24, 2 (1981), 257–78.

14 For a reassessment of Somerset, see M. L. Bush, *The government policy of Protector Somerset* (Montreal, 1975).

15 For a useful summary, see D. MacCulloch, *The later reformation in England, 1547–1603* (Basingstoke, 1990), ch. 2.

16 The Western Rebellion lacks a serious modern study, although R. Whiting, *The blind devotion of the people: popular religion and the English Reformation* (Cambridge, 1989) contains some new detail. Beer, *Rebellion and riot*, ch. 3, remains heavily dependent upon F. Rose-Troup, *The Western Rebellion of 1549* (London, 1913). J. Cornwall, *Revolt of the peasantry, 1549* (London, 1977), chs 2–8, reiterates the well-known published sources. But see also J. Youings, 'The south-western

202

Notes

rebellion of 1549', *Southern History*, 1 (1979), 99–122. On the role of the gentry, see especially H. Speight, 'Local government and the south-western rebellion of 1549', *Southern History*, 18 (1996), 1–23. On traditions of rebellion in Cornwall, see M. Stoyle, 'The dissidence of despair: rebellion and identity in early modern Cornwall', *JBS*, 38 (1999), 423–44.

17 The articles are reproduced in Fletcher and MacCulloch, *Tudor rebellions*, 139–41 and in Beer, *Rebellion and riot*, 64–5.
18 Holinshed, *Chronicles*, III, 951–2.
19 Beer, *Rebellion and riot*, 50, 69–70; Speight, 'Local government', 12.
20 Holinshed, *Chronicles*, III, 942.
21 Bush, *Pilgrimage of Grace*, 201, 84, 282; Gunn, 'Peers, commons', 55. On the meaning of the Church in popular culture, see especially Duffy, *Stripping of the altars*, chs 1–8.
22 See for instance, R. Whiting, *Local responses to the English Reformation* (Basingstoke, 1992).
23 Bush, *Pilgrimage of Grace*, 175. For more on religious loyalties in Colchester at this time, see M. Byford, 'The birth of a protestant town: the process of reformation in Tudor Colchester, 1530–80', in P. Collinson and J. Craig (eds), *The Reformation in English towns, 1500–1640* (Basingstoke, 1998), 23–47.
24 Reprinted in Fletcher and MacCulloch, *Tudor rebellions*, 144–6; Beer, *Rebellion and riot*, 105–7.
25 A. Wood, *Insurrection and popular political culture in Tudor England: the rebellions of 1549* (Cambridge, forthcoming), ch. 7. On the reformation in Norwich, see M. C. McClendon, *The quiet reformation: magistrates and the emergence of protestantism in Tudor Norwich* (Stanford, 1999). For a preliminary sense of post-rebellion popular complaint in Norwich, see the partial transcriptions in W. Rye (ed.), *Depositions taken before the mayor and aldermen of Norwich, 1549–1567: extracts from the court books of the City of Norwich, 1666–1668* (Norwich, 1905).
26 The best current account of the 1548–9 disorders outside East Anglia and the West Country is Beer, *Rebellion and riot*, chs 6–7. This is likely to be superseded by Amanda Jones' forthcoming University of Warwick doctoral dissertation. See also Wood, *Insurrection*, ch. 4. There is much of interest in D. MacCulloch, *Thomas Cranmer: a life* (New Haven, 1996), 429–46 and P. Clark, *English provincial society from the Reformation to the Revolution: religion, politics and society in Kent, 1500–1640* (Hassocks, 1977), 78–81.
27 Compare J. Strype, *Ecclesiastical memorials: relating chiefly to religion and the reformation of it*, 3 vols (Oxford, 1822), II (I), 259 with Holinshed, *Chronicles*, III, 963.
28 Bush, *Government policy*, 40–83.
29 E. Lamond (ed.), *A discourse on the commonweal of this Realm of England* (Cambridge, 1929), lviii.
30 C. S. Knighton (ed.), *Calendar of the state papers domestic series of the reign of Edward VI, 1547–1553* (London, 1992), (hereafter *CSPD, Edward VI*) no. 273; Bush, *Government Policy*, 75.
31 HMC, *Rutland*, I, 36.
32 D. MacCulloch, 'Kett's rebellion in context', *P&P*, 84 (1979), 37.
33 Wood, *Insurrection*, ch. 4.
34 On memories of the 1549 rebellion, see Wood, *Insurrection*, ch. 12.

35 The most influential account of Kett's rebellion remains Russell, *Kett's rebellion*. This should be read alongside S. T. Bindoff, *Ket's Rebellion, 1549* (London, 1949), MacCulloch, 'Kett's rebellion' and Wood, *Insurrection*, chs 4–5. The accounts in J. Cornwall, *Revolt of the peasantry, 1549* (London, 1977), chs 7, 9 and 12; S. K. Land, *Kett's Rebellion: the Norfolk Rising of 1549* (London, 1977); and Beer, *Rebellion and riot*, chs 4–5 are all derivative of Russell's work of 1859 and of the contemporary printed histories.

36 R. Woods, *Norfolke furies, and their foyle. Under Kett, their accursed Captaine* (1615; 2nd edn, London, 1623), sig. B3.

37 Holinshed, *Chronicles*, III, 964.

38 Woods, *Norfolke furies*, sig. B4.

39 An example is reproduced in Holinshed, *Chronicles*, III, 966.

40 MacCulloch, 'Kett's rebellion', 40.

41 *Ibid.*, 50–3; Fletcher and MacCulloch, *Tudor rebellions*, 75.

42 For transcriptions of the Mousehold articles, see Fletcher and MacCulloch, *Tudor rebellions*, 144–6; Beer, *Rebellion and riot*, 105–7.

43 E. Shagan, 'Protector Somerset and the 1549 rebellions: new sources and new perspectives', *English Historical Review*, 114, 455 (1999), 36–7, 50, 56–7, 41–3, 48. See also Beer, *Rebellion and riot*, 118–19. For a rather unedifying squabble over Shagan's reinterpretation, see contributions from M. L. Bush, G. W. Bernard and E. Shagan in *English Historical Review*, 115, 460 (2000), 103–33.

44 MacCulloch, 'Kett's Rebellion', 49.

45 *Ibid.*, 47.

46 Knighton (ed.), *CSPD, Edward VI*, no. 301.

47 A. Vere Woodman, 'The Buckinghamshire and Oxfordshire rising of 1549', *Oxoniensia*, 22 (1957), 12.

48 Woods, *Norfolke furies*, sigs I1–2.

49 Holinshed, *Chronicles*, III, 981; Woods, *Norfolke furies*, sigs K1–3.

50 For a more detailed discussion of the repression, see Wood, *Insurrection*, ch. 6.

51 Woods, *Norfolke furies*, sig. L.

52 Shagan, 'Protector Somerset and the 1549 rebellions', 51–3.

53 Beer, *Rebellion and riot*, ch. 8; Wood, 'Poore men woll speke', 86–8.

54 D. MacCulloch, *Suffolk and the Tudors: politics and religion in an English county, 1500–1600* (Oxford, 1986), 309–10; R. W. Hoyle, 'Agrarian agitation in mid-sixteenth century Norfolk: a petition of 1553', *HJ*, 44, 1 (2001), 223–38; R. Tittler and S. L. Battley, 'The local community and the crown in 1553: the accession of Mary Tudor revisited', *Bulletin of the Institute of Historical Research*, 57, 136, (1984), 131–9; Wood, *Insurrection*, ch. 5.

55 Quoted in Zagorin, *Rebels and rulers*, I, 85.

56 Knighton, *CSPD, Edward VI*, nos 187–8.

57 C. Sharp, *Memorials of the rebellion of 1569* (London, 1840), 41–3. The 1569 rebellion lacks a modern study. For a clear summary, see *ibid.*, 94–110, which should be read alongside R. R. Reid, 'The rebellion of the northern Earls', *TRHS*, 1st ser., 20 (1906).

58 Sharp, *Memorials*, 163, 173, 121; Smith, *De Republica Anglorum*, 77.

59 Sharp, *Memorials*, 8–9, 54, 44–5, 49, 56; James, *Society, politics and culture*, 294.

60 James, *Society, politics and culture*, chs 4 and 7; L. Stone, *The crisis of the aristocracy, 1558–1641* (Oxford, 1965), 250–7.

61 James, *Society, politics and culture*, 274–6.

62 Following Wrightson, *Earthly necessities*, ch. 3.

63 Sharp, *Memorials*, 47.

64 James, *Society, politics and culture*, 297, 285–6.

65 Hay, 'Property, authority and the criminal law'; J. A. Sharpe, 'The people and the law', in B. Reay (ed.), *Popular culture in seventeenth-century England* (London, 1985), 244–70; Wood, 'Custom, identity and resistance'.

66 Hindle, *State and social change*, esp. 231–8.

67 Harrison, *The Pilgrimage of Grace in the Lake counties*, 56, 53.

68 S. J. Watts, *From border to middle shire: Northumberland, 1586–1625* (Leicester, 1975), 31.

69 R. W. Hoyle, 'Lords, tenants and tenant right in the sixteenth century: four studies', *Northern History*, 20 (1984), 46, 42, 50; Hoyle, 'An ancient and laudable custom: the definition and development of tenant right in north-western England in the sixteenth century', *P&P*, 116 (1987), 49.

70 Stone, *Crisis*, 251; James, *Society, politics and culture*, 291–2.

71 Bush, *Pilgrimage of Grace*, 190; Stone, *Crisis*, 252; Walter, *Understanding popular violence*, 123; R. Clifton, *The last popular rebellion: the western rising of 1685* (London, 1984), 159.

72 P. Collinson, *The birthpangs of protestant England: religious and cultural change in the sixteenth and seventeenth centuries* (Basingstoke, 1988) has had a special significance. For an important collection, see C. Haigh (ed.), *The English Reformation revised* (Cambridge, 1987).

73 P. Lake, 'Anti-popery: the structure of a prejudice', in Cust and Hughes (eds), *Conflict in early Stuart England*, 72–106.

74 For a radically different assessment of the significance of the nobility in the politics of the seventeenth century, see J. Adamson, 'The baronial context of the English civil war', *TRHS*, 5th ser., 40 (1990).

3   Riot and Popular Politics in Early Modern England

1 For the complexities of its early modern history, see especially Wrightson, *Earthly necessities*, 102–4, 136–7, 162–3, 209–12, 234, 274, 283, 326.

2 S. Hindle, 'Persuasion and protest in the Caddington common enclosure dispute, 1635–1639', *P&P*, 158 (1998), 45; B. Sharp, 'Common rights, charities and the disorderly poor', in G. Eley and W. Hunt (eds), *Reviving the English Revolution: reflections and elaborations on the work of Christopher Hill* (London, 1988), 107–38.

3 There is a massive literature on the significance of custom in eighteenth-century popular culture. For especially important studies, see J. M. Neeson, *Commoners: common right, enclosure and social change in England, 1700–1820* (Cambridge, 1993); P. E. Searle, 'Custom, class conflict and agrarian capitalism: the Cumbrian customary economy in the eighteenth century', *P&P*, 110 (1986), 106–33; Bushaway, *By rite*; Thompson, *Customs in common*, ch. 3; Thompson, *Whigs and hunters: the origin of the Black Act* (London, 1975).

4 Manning, *Village Revolts*, esp. chs 1–4.

5 A. Charlesworth, *An atlas of rural protest in Britain, 1548–1900* (London, 1983).

6 Manning, *Village revolts*, 31–107, 322–7.

7   Manning, *Village revolts*, 84.

8   For the classic statement of these issues, see J. Thirsk 'Industries in the country-side' in F. J. Fisher (ed.) *Essays in the Economic and Social History of Tudor and Stuart England* (Cambridge, 1961), 70–88. For an important case study, see V. Skipp, *Crisis and development: an ecological case study of the forest of Arden, 1570–1674* (Cambridge, 1978).

9   D. Levine and K. E. Wrightson, *The making of an industrial society: Whickham, 1560–1765* (Oxford, 1991), 274–344; Wood, *Politics of social conflict*, chs 2–5, 9–13.

10 For an influential case study, see Wrightson and Levine, *Poverty and piety*. For its fuller implications, see Wrightson, *English society*, chs 1, 2, 5–7.

11 Hindle, *State and social change*, chs 1, 2, 6–9; J. R. Kent, 'The rural "middling sort" in early modern England, *c*. 1640–1740: some economic, political and socio-cultural characteristics', *Rural History*, 10, 1 (1999), 19–54.

12 M. Zell, *Industry in the countryside: Wealden society in the sixteenth century* (Cambridge, 1994); S. Hipkin, '"Sitting on his penny rent": conflict and right of common in Faversham Blean, 1595–1610', *Rural History*, 11, 1 (2000), 1–35.

13 For a simplistic assessment of the changing geography of resistance in early modern England, see Wood, 'Poore men woll speke one daye', 88–92.

14 Charlesworth, *An atlas of rural protest*, 72.

15 R. Hoyle (ed.), *The estates of the English crown, 1558–1640* (Cambridge, 1992); R. Manning, *Hunters and poachers: a cultural and social history of unlawful hunting in England, 1485–1640* (Oxford, 1993).

16 Stone, *Crisis*, chs 6–7; Wrightson, *Earthly necessities*, 182–90, 274–88; Hindle, *State and social change*, 44.

17 K. Lindley, *Fenland riots and the English Revolution* (London, 1982); Wood, *Politics of social conflict*, chs 10–11; B. Sharp, *In contempt of all authority: rural artisans and riot in the west of England 1586–1660* (Berkeley, California, 1980), 4–8.

18 Manning, *Village revolts*, 242–4; but for a local exception, see J. E. Martin, *Feudalism to capitalism: peasant and landlord in English agrarian development*, (London, 1983), 168–72.

19 J. S. Morrill and J. D. Walter 'Order and disorder in the English Revolution' in Fletcher and Stevenson (eds), *Order and disorder*, 139.

20 E. Kerridge, *Agrarian problems in the sixteenth century and later* (London, 1969); J. O. Appleby, *Economic thought and ideology in seventeenth century England* (Princeton, New Jersey, 1978); J. Thirsk, 'Agricultural policy: public debate and legislation', in J. Thirsk (ed.), *The agrarian history of England and Wales, V (II). 1640–1750: agrarian change* (Cambridge, 1985), 298–388.

21 For an example, see M. McClain, 'The Wentwood forest riot: property rights and political culture in Restoration England', in S. D. Amussen and M. A. Kishlansky (eds), *Political culture and cultural politics in early modern England* (Manchester, 1995), 123–4.

22 M. Johnson, *An archaeology of capitalism* (Oxford, 1996), esp. ch. 3; Appleby, *Economic thought*, 151–5.

23 For a revealing study, see L. Merricks, '"Without violence and by controlling the poorer sort": the enclosure of Ashdown Forest, 1640–1693', *Sussex Archaeological Collections*, 132 (1994), 115–28.

24 Wood, *Politics of social conflict*, 234, 272, 299.

25 R. W. Bushaway, 'Rite, legitimation and community in southern England, 1700–
    1850: the ideology of custom', in B. Stapleton (ed.), *Conflict and community in south-
    ern England: essays in the social history of rural and urban labour from medieval to modern
    times* (New York, 1992), 110–34; B. Sharp, 'Common rights'; Beloff, *Public order*,
    ch. 4; Wood, 'Custom, identity and resistance'; C. Holmes, 'Drainers and fenmen:
    the problem of popular political consciousness in the seventeenth century' in
    Fletcher and Stevenson (eds), *Order and disorder*, 166–95.
26 Manning, *Village revolts*, 27, 55; Charlesworth, *An atlas of rural protest*, 44.
27 Neeson, *Commoners*; C. Fisher, *Custom, work and market capitalism: the Forest of Dean
    colliers, 1788–1888* (London, 1981); Thompson, *Customs in common*, 117; Beloff,
    Public order, 78–80.
28 For the influence of Thompson's views on studies of eighteenth-century riots, see
    A. Randall and A. Charlesworth (eds), *Markets, market culture and popular protest
    in eighteenth-century Britain and Ireland* (Liverpool, 1996); R. W. Malcolmson '"A
    set of ungovernable people": the Kingswood colliers in the eighteenth century'
    in Brewer and Styles (eds), *An ungovernable people*, 85–127; A. Randall, *Before
    the Luddites: custom, community and machinery in the English woollen industry, 1776–
    1809* (Cambridge, 1991), ch. 3; for Thompson's influence on sixteenth- and
    seventeenth-century studies, see especially J. D. Walter and K. E. Wrightson
    'Dearth and the social order in early modern England', *P&P*, 71 (1976), 22–42;
    Walter 'Grain riots'; P. Clark 'Popular protest and disturbance in Kent, 1558–1640'
    Economic History Review 2nd ser., 29 (1976), 365–82; Sharp, *In contempt*, chs 2–3.
29 Thompson, *Customs in common*, 188, 224. For dissenting views, see especially
    J. Stevenson, 'The "moral economy" of the English crowd: myth and reality' in
    Fletcher and Stevenson (eds), *Order and disorder*, 218–38; J. Bohstedt, 'The moral
    economy and the discipline of historical context', *Journal of Social History*, 26, 2
    (1992), 265–84; D. E. Williams, 'Morals, markets and the English crowd in 1766'
    P&P, 104 (1985), 56–73. Many of these pieces miss their target. Often presenting
    themselves as searching critiques of Thompson's argument, on closer reading
    they provide mere amendments or local qualifications. For Thompson's charac-
    teristically sharp response to his critics, see his *Customs in common*, 259–351.
30 HMC, 12th Report, Appx IX, Gloucester MSS, 458; PRO, SP12/263/86.
31 P. Slack, 'Social policy and the constraints of government, 1547–58', in J. Loach
    and R. Tittler (eds), *The mid-Tudor polity, c. 1540–1560* (Basingstoke, 1980), 105–8.
32 Sharp, *In contempt*, 10–19, 31–2, 38–42. The most accessible introduction to state
    regulation of food supplies in conditions of dearth is R. B. Outhwaite, *Dearth,
    public policy and social disturbance in England, 1550–1800* (Cambridge, 1991).
33 Outhwaite, *Dearth*, 32.
34 Walter and Wrightson, 'Dearth and the social order', 33.
35 *Ibid.*, 26; Charlesworth, *An atlas of rural protest*, 63–118; J. Bohstedt, 'The prag-
    matic economy, the politics of provisions and the "invention" of the food riot
    tradition in 1740', in A. Randall and A. Charlesworth (eds), *Moral economy and
    popular protest: crowds, conflict and authority* (Basingstoke, 2000), 56.
36 On the value of gleaning, see especially P. King, 'Customary rights and women's
    earnings: the importance of gleaning to the rural labouring poor', *Economic
    History Review*, 2nd ser., 44, 3 (1991), 461–76.
37 Bohstedt acknowledges a heavy debt to John Walter's brilliant essay: 'The social
    economy of dearth in early modern England', in J. Walter and R. Schofield (eds),

Famine, disease and the social order in early modern society (Cambridge, 1989), 75–128.

38   For Bohstedt's earlier work on late Georgian food riots, see especially his *Riots and community politics in England and Wales, 1790–1810* (Cambridge, Mass., 1983).

39   On these developments, see especially K. D. M. Snell, *Annals of the labouring poor: social change and agrarian England, 1660–1900* (Cambridge, 1985), chs 1, 2, 5; P. King, 'Gleaners, farmers and the failure of legal sanctions in England, 1750–1850', *P&P*, 125 (1989), 116–50.

40   The preceding summary rests on Bohstedt, 'Pragmatic economy', 57–60.

41   *Ibid.*, 62–3, 77–81.

42   PRO, STAC8/42/11.5.

43   Underdown, *Revel, riot and rebellion*, 44–7, 63–8.

44   PRO, STAC8/98/7.

45   On the social meaning of Rogationtide perambulations, see Justice, *Writing and rebellion*, 165. On the hostility of puritans to Rogationtide, see Thomas, *Religion and the decline of magic: studies in popular beliefs in sixteenth and seventeenth century England* (London, 1971), 71–5. For a detailed example of a Rogationtide enclosure riot, see Walter, *Understanding violence*, 101–2.

46   Stone, *Crisis*, 562: an oft-cited quotation that is hard to resist.

47   John Rylands Library, Nicolas MS, 74/10, 'Accusations against John Phillipps'.

48   John Rylands Library, Nicolas MS, 72/2, Thomas Brunker to Lady Magdalen Bruce, 29 April 1643.

49   For three influential studies, see P. Burke, *Popular culture in early modern Europe* (London, 1978), ch. 7; N. Z. Davis, *Society and culture in early modern France* (Stanford, California, 1975), chs 4 and 5; Thompson, *Customs in common*, ch. 8. For an essential survey of the subject, see E. Muir, *Ritual in early modern Europe* (Cambridge, 1997), esp. chs 3, 5–7.

50   P. Burke, 'Popular culture in seventeenth-century London', in B. Reay (ed.), *Popular culture in seventeenth century England* (London, 1985), 35.

51   Thompson, *Customs in common*, 478–9.

52   J. R. Kent, '"Folk justice" and royal justice in early seventeenth-century England: a "charivari" in the Midlands', *Midland History*, 8 (1983), 70–85. Mrs Joan Yates of East End, Oxfordshire, tells me that 'rough music' persisted in her village until just after the Second World War.

53   A. Howkins and L. Merricks, '"Wee be black as Hell": ritual, disguise and rebellion', *Rural History*, 4, 1 (1993), 45, 46.

54   B. Howard Cunnington (ed.), *Records of the county of the Wiltshire, being extracts from the Quarter Sessions great rolls of the seventeenth century* (Devizes, 1932), 64–6.

55   W. Lambard, *Eirenarcha, or of the office of the Justices of peace* (London, 1581), 179; PRO, STAC8/184/24; R. Houlbrooke, 'Women's social life and common action in England from the fifteenth century to the eve of the civil war', *Continuity and change*, 1, 2 (1986), 171–89.

56   For two detailed reconstructions of such incidents, see D. Rollison, 'Property, ideology and popular culture in a Gloucestershire Village 1660–1740', *P&P*, 43 (1981), 70–97; S. Hindle, 'Custom, festival and protest in early modern England: the Little Budworth Wakes of St Peter's Day, 1596', *Rural History*, 6, 2 (1995), 155–78.

57   Bushaway, *By rite*, 81–3.

58   PRO, STAC8/34/4.42; PRO, STAC8/34/4.44; PRO, STAC8/219/23.13.
59   For two revealing examples, see J. Pearson, 'Threshing out the common in
     continuity: the Great Tey riot of 1727', *Rural History*, 9, 1 (1998), 43–56; Hindle,
     'Persuasion and protest', 37–78.
60   On Gillingham Forest, see E. Kerridge, 'The revolts in Wiltshire against Charles
     I', *Wiltshire Archaeological Magazine*, 57 (1958–60), 64–75; D. G. C. Allan, 'The
     rising in the west, 1628–1631', *Economic History Review*, 2nd ser., 5, 1 (1952),
     76–85; Sharp, *In contempt*, 86–9, 224–37, 247–8; Underdown, *Revel, riot and
     rebellion*, 108–10, 161–2.
61   John Rylands Library, Nicholas Mss 72/8, 'A noat of further passages'.
62   *Ibid.*, 73/4, 'From Meare the 24th of April 1643'.
63   PRO, STAC8/5/21.17, 22–3.
64   PRO, STAC8/144/24.3; J. O. Halliwell (ed.), *The marriage of Wit and Wisdom : an
     ancient interlude* (London, 1846), 140–1.
65   Sharp, 'Common rights'.
66   Walter, 'Social economy of dearth', 106–9, 92, 111; Thompson, *Customs in com-
     mon*, 45; J. S. Cockburn (ed.), *Calendar of Assize records: Kent indictments, Elizabeth I*
     (London, 1979), case 2573. Proverbs, 28: 27; Wood, 'Place of custom', 54–5. On
     the beggar's curse, see Hunt, *Puritan moment*, 57; K. Thomas, *Religion and the
     decline of magic: studies in popular beliefs in sixteenth- and seventeenth-century England*
     (London, 1971), 506.
67   Thomas, *Religion and the decline of magic*, 662–78; A. Macfarlane, *Witchcraft in
     Tudor and Stuart England: a regional and comparative study* (London, 1970), ch. 11.
68   Hindle, *State and social change*, ch. 8; Wood, *Insurrection*, ch. 11.

4   Popular Politics in Stuart England

1   I have made my unhappiness with this conceptualisation clear elsewhere: see
    Wood, *Politics of social conflict*, ch. 1. But, rather weakly, I continue to use the term
    'early modern' because I cannot think of anything better to call the period.
2   Lodged at the heart of much of the urban and economic history of the early
    modern period, this connection between urbanisation and modernity is spelt out
    most clearly in E. A. Wrigley, *People, cities and wealth* (Oxford, 1987), chs 3, 6 and 7.
3   See for instance Harris, *London crowds*, 27; Burke, 'Popular culture in seven-
    teenth-century London', 259–70; Harris, *Popular culture*, 259–70.
4   S. Reynolds, *Kingdoms and communities in western Europe, 900–1300* (Oxford, 1984),
    ch. 6.
5   For a useful introduction to town government, see S. M. Jack, *Towns in Tudor and
    Stuart Britain* (Basingstoke, 1996), ch. 5.
6   J. T. Evans, *Seventeenth-century Norwich: politics, religion and government, 1620–1690*
    (Oxford, 1979), 10–13; T. Harris, *Politics under the later Stuarts: party conflict in a
    divided society, 1660–1715* (London, 1993), 18.
7   What follows depends upon Walter, *Understanding popular violence*, ch. 3.
8   For a very lively recent collection of essays which has a special interest in the
    organisation of urban space, see P. D. Griffiths and M. S. R. Jenner (eds), *Londinop-
    olis: essays in the cultural and social history of early modern London*, (Manchester, 2000).
9   Fox, 'Rumour', 603–5.

10 See the suggestive remarks in J. Barry, 'Popular culture in seventeenth-century Bristol', in Reay (ed.), *Popular culture*, 69.

11 PRO, STAC8/159/6; PRO, STAC8/10/18.

12 Wood, *Politics of social conflict*, 237.

13 Fox, 'Rumour', 618.

14 Norfolk RO, NCR20A/10, fol. 44v.

15 H. Stocks (ed.), *Records of the borough of Leicester: being a series of extracts from the archives of the Corporation of Leicester, 1603–1688* (Cambridge, 1923), 59–65.

16 Evans, *Seventeenth-century Norwich*, 128–9; Harris, *London crowds*, 102.

17 K. Lindley, 'Riot prevention and control in early Stuart London', *TRHS*, 5th ser., 33 (1983), 109–10; T. Harris, 'The Bawdy House riots of 1668', *HJ*, 29 (1986), 537–56.

18 Harris, *London crowds*, 38; P. Kleber Monod, *Jacobitism and the English people, 1688–1788* (Cambridge, 1989), 64–6, 203–4.

19 K. Lindley, *Popular politics and religion in civil war London* (Aldershot, 1997), 47, 215, 49.

20 The ensuing discussion is dependent upon Harris, *London crowds*, 39, 45, 103–6; Knights, *Politics and opinion*, 220, 110.

21 Wrightson, 'Sorts of people', 44–50. On the social composition of protesting crowds in 1641–2, see Lindley, *Popular politics and religion*, 26–35.

22 Lindley, *Popular politics and religion*, 101–2, 110, 154.

23 V. Pearl, 'Change and stability in seventeenth-century London', *London Journal*, 5 (1979), 3–34; I. Archer, *The pursuit of stability: social relations in Elizabethan London* (Cambridge, 1991); Hindle, *State and social change*, 209.

24 Lindley, *Popular politics and religion*, 55–91, 158–65; N. Carlin, 'Liberty and fraternities in the English Revolution: the politics of the London artisans' protests, 1635–1659', *International Review of Social History*, 39 (1994), 223–54.

25 Walter, *Understanding popular violence*, 118–19.

26 See especially D. Hirst, *The representative of the people? voters and voting in England under the early Stuarts* (Cambridge, 1975); J. H. Plumb, 'The growth of the electorate in England from 1600 to 1715', *P&P*, 45 (1969), 90–116.

27 Kishlansky, *Parliamentary selection*, chs 1–5, quoting p. ix.

28 Hughes, *Causes*, 62.

29 For a succinct summary of this, see F. Heal and C. Holmes, *The gentry in England and Wales, 1500–1700* (Basingstoke, 1994).

30 R. Cust, 'Politics and the electorate in the 1620s', in Cust and Hughes (eds), *Conflict in early Stuart England*, 147–8, 156.

31 For the King's negotiations with the Peak miners in August 1642, see A. Wood, 'Beyond post-revisionism? The civil war allegiances of the miners of the Derbyshire "Peak Country"', *HJ*, 40 (1997), 23–40. The best account of the infamous Colchester attacks, is Walter, *Understanding popular violence*, chs 1–2. For an overview of the descent into war, see A. Fletcher, *The outbreak of the English civil war* (London, 1981).

32 HMC, 12th Rept., IX, Southwell MSS, 552; Manning, *English people*, 138.

33 Accounts of these events are legion. For two very different versions, see Manning, *English people*, ch. 4; Fletcher, *Outbreak*, ch. 5.

34 *Eikon Basilike*, 16–21; Lindley, *Popular politics and religion*, 32; Manning, *English people*, 321.

35   For Holt, see Cheshire RO, EDC5 (1638) 81, Holt. For the regional context, see
     R. C. Richardson, *Puritanism in north-west England: a regional study of the diocese of
     Chester to 1642* (Manchester, 1972); J. S. Morrill, *Cheshire, 1630–1660: county
     government and society during the English Revolution* (Oxford, 1974).

36   Most importantly, see J. S. Morrill, *The nature of the English Revolution* (London,
     1993), ch. 3.

37   Hunt, *Puritan moment*, esp. chs 4–6, 10–12; Underdown, *Revel, riot and rebellion*,
     chs 2–5; Wrightson, *English society*, ch. 7; Wrightson and Levine, *Poverty and piety*,
     chs 5–7. For an older work which produces a similar interpretation, see C. Hill,
     Society and puritanism in pre-revolutionary England (London, 1964). For Baxter, see
     Manning, *English people*, 89–90.

38   C. Hill, *The collected essays of Christopher Hill: volume three. People and ideas in seven-
     teenth-century England* (Hassocks, 1986). ch. 12.

39   J. L. Malcolm, *Caesar's due: loyalty and King Charles, 1642–6* (London, 1983), 108.

40   Fox, 'Rumour', 616–17; PRO, SP16/39/40–1.

41   R. MacGillivray, *Restoration historians and the English Civil War* (The Hague, 1974), 155.

42   T. Aston, *A remonstrance against presbytery* (London, 1641), sig. I 4v. For a useful
     survey of the logic of royalist propaganda, see R. M. Smuts, *Culture and power in
     England, 1585–1685* (Basingstoke, 1999), 106–22.

43   Wood, 'Beyond post-revisionism'.

44   Hindle, 'Custom, festival and protest'; Hindle, *State and social change*, 188–203;
     P. Collinson, 'Elizabethan and Jacobean puritanism as forms of popular religious
     culture', in C. Durston and J. Eales (eds), *The culture of English puritanism, 1560–
     1700* (Basingstoke, 1996), 32–57. For an overview of this cultural conflict, see
     especially Collinson, *Birthpangs of protestant England*, 127–55.

45   Collinson, 'Elizabethan and Jacobean puritanism', 43; D. E. Underdown, *Fire
     from heaven: life in an English town in the seventeenth century* (London, 1992), 27–9.
     For a general study of libels in early seventeenth century England, see A. Fox,
     'Ballads, libels and popular ridicule in Jacobean England', *P&P*, 145 (1994), 47–83.

46   Underdown tussles with this question in 'Community and class: theories of local
     politics in the English Revolution', in Malament (ed.), *After the Reformation*, 147–65.

47   Collinson, 'Elizabethan and Jacobean puritanism', 37–42; R. Hutton, *The rise and
     fall of merry England: the ritual year, 1400–1700* (Oxford, 1994), ch. 5.

48   Hutton, *Rise and fall*, 203–5; P. Stallybrass, '"We feaste in our defence": patrician
     carnival in early modern England and Robert Herrick's "Hespides"', *English
     Literary Renaissance*, 16 (1986), 234–52.

49   J. Eales, *Puritans and roundheads: the Harleys of Brampton Bryan and the outbreak of civil
     war* (Cambridge, 1990), 143. On royalism and popular culture, see Underdown,
     Rebel, riot and rebellion, 63–9, 179–81, 200–7; M. J. Stoyle, *Loyalty and locality: popular
     allegiances in Devon during the English Civil War* (Exeter, 1994), 55–74, 231–55.

50   Stoyle, *Loyalty and locality*, 242.

51   M. J. Stoyle, 'Pagans or paragons: images of the Cornish during the English civil
     war', *English Historical Review*, 111 (1996), 299–323; Stoyle, 'The dissidence of
     despair: rebellion and identity in early modern Cornwall', *JBS*, 38 (1999), 423–44;
     Stoyle, *Loyalty and locality*, 232–41.

52   J. Corbet, *An historicall relation of the military government of Gloucester* (London.
     1645), 8–10.

53   M. Sylvester (ed.), *Reliquiae Baxterianae* (London, 1696), 30, 89.

54 Corbet, *Historicall relation*, 16.
55 Rollison, *Local origins*, 158.
56 Manning, *English people*, 28.
57 The contingent, political circumstances within which new social categories often emerge is brought out well in D. Wahrman, *Imagining the middle class: the political representation of class in Britain, c. 1780–1840* (Cambridge, 1995).
58 See for instance Stoyle, *Loyalty and locality*, chs 2–5; Underdown, *Revel, riot and rebellion*, chs 6–7. For an important critique of the 'Manning thesis' (that the middling sort was strongly parliamentarian), see Morrill, *The nature of the English Revolution*, ch. 10.
59 B. Manning, *Aristocrats, plebeians and revolution in England, 1640–1660* (London, 1996), 69; Manning, *English people*, 333–5.
60 Corbet, *Historicall relation*, 17.
61 Manning, *Aristocrats*, 69–70; Underdown, *Revel, riot and rebellion*, 164.
62 D. E. Underdown, 'The problem of popular allegiance in the English civil war', *TRHS*, 5th ser., 31 (1981), 69.
63 B. Sharp, *In contempt*, 8–9, 248–9.
64 Morrill and Walter, 'Order and disorder in the English Revolution', 140; Morrill, *Revolt in the provinces*, 51.
65 On tenant riots in the first civil war, see C. O'Riordan, 'Popular exploitation of enemy estates in the English Revolution', *History*, 78, 253 (1993), 183–200; on the Cranborne riots, see L. Stone, *Family and fortune: studies in aristocratic finance in the sixteenth and seventeenth centuries* (Oxford, 1973), 148–9; Underdown, *Revel, riot and rebellion*, 23, 197; HMC, Salisbury XII, 374–5, 386.
66 D. E. Underdown, 'The chalk and the cheese: contrasts among the English clubmen', *P&P*, 85 (1979), 38. On the Winters' earlier conflicts with the inhabitants of the Forest of Dean, see Sharp, *In contempt*, chs 7–8.
67 HMC, 12th report, appx. pt. IX, Southwell MSS, 550–1.
68 Manning, *English people*, 294.
69 P. Laslett, *The world we have lost – further explored* (London, 1983), chs 2, 8–9, esp. 224–5.
70 Manning, *English people*, 298–305; A. J. Hopper, 'The clubman of the West Riding of Yorkshire during the first civil war: "Bradford club-law"', *Northern History*, 36, 1 (2000), 59–72.
71 Underdown, *Revel, riot and rebellion*, 40–1.
72 For an incisive critique of Underdown's interpretation of allegiance, see Morrill, *The nature of the English Revolution*, ch. 11; for a critique of the model in general, see N. Davie, 'Chalk and cheese? "Fielden" and "forest" communities in early modern England', *Journal of Historical Sociology*, 4, 1 (1991), 1–31.
73 Morrill, *Revolt in the provinces*, 139; R. Hutton, *The royalist war effort, 1642–1646* (1982; 2nd edn, London, 1999), 189.
74 On the clubmen movements in the border marcher counties, see Hutton, *Royalist war effort*, 155–65, 170–2, 178, 180–2, 189–90, 193; Hutton, 'The Worcestershire clubmen in the English civil war', *Midland History*, 5 (1979–80), 39–49; P. Gladwish, 'The Herefordshire clubmen: a reassessment', *Midland History*, 10 (1985), 62–71; I. J. Atherton (ed.), *Sir Barnabas Scudamore's defence against the imputations of treachery and negligence in the loss of the city of Hereford in 1645* (Akron, Ohio, 1992), 10–16; J. Webb (ed.), *Military memoir of Colonel John Birch*, Camden

Soc., 2nd ser., 7 (1873), 111–13. For copies of clubmen articles, see R. N. Dore (ed.), *The letter books of Sir William Brereton: vol 1, January 31st–May 29th, 1645*, Lancashire and Cheshire Record Society, 73 (Gloucester, 1984), 62–3; J. W. Bund (ed.), *Diary of Henry Townshend of Elmley Lovett, 1640–1663: part III. 1645–1663*, Worcestershire Historical Society, 36 (1917), 221–3.

75 On the West Country clubmen, see D. E. Underdown, *Somerset in the civil war and Interregnum*, (Newton Abbot, 1973), 90–1, 98–108, 112–17, 118–19, 135; Underdown, *Revel, riot and rebellion*, 148, 152, 156–9, 166–8, 207, 276–7; Underdown, 'The chalk and the cheese'; Stoyle, *Loyalty and locality*, ch. 6. For an example of West Country clubmen articles, see A. R. Bayley, *The great civil war in Dorset, 1642–1660* (Taunton, 1910), 472–9.

76 Hutton, *Royalist war effort*, 162.

77 Morrill, *Revolt in the provinces*, 132–51.

78 J. D. Alsop, 'Ethics in the marketplace: Gerrard Winstanley's London bankruptcy, 1643', *JBS*, 28, 2 (1989), 97–119; C. Hill, *The religion of Gerrard Winstanley*, Past and Present supplements, 3 (Oxford, 1978).

79 G. H. Sabine (ed.), *The works of Gerrard Winstanley: with an appendix of documents relating to the Digger movement* (Ithaca, New York, 1941), 190.

80 *Ibid.*, 195–6.

81 *Ibid.*, 184.

82 *Ibid.*, 282.

83 *Ibid.*, 367–8; J. Gurney, 'Gerrard Winstanley and the Digger movement in Walton and Cobham', *HJ*, 37 (1994), 775–88.

84 Gurney, 'Gerrard Winstanley', 788–802.

85 C. Hill, *The world turned upside down: radical ideas during the English Revolution* (London, 1972), 110.

86 K. Thomas, 'Another Digger broadside', *P&P*, 42 (1969), 59, 65; D. O. Pam, *The fight for common rights in Enfield and Edmonton, 1400–1600*, Edmonton Hundred Historical Society, occasional papers, new series, 27 (Edmonton, 1974).

87 Hindle, 'Persuasion and protest', 42, 76–7.

88 Thomas, 'Another Digger broadside', 60–1, 58.

89 For pre-war examples of such alliances, see Sharp, *In contempt*, ch. 5; Wood, *Politics of social conflict*, 66–71.

90 Thomas, 'Another Digger broadside', 62; J. S. Cockburn (ed.), *Calendar of Assize records: Essex indictments, Elizabeth I* (London, 1978), no. 290; Cockburn (ed.), *Calendar of Assize records: Kent*, no. 2589; Sabine, *Works*, 650.

91 Thomas, 'Another Digger broadside', 63; Sabine, *Works*, 650.

92 Thomas, 'Another Digger broadside', 64, 61, 62; see also C. Hill, 'The Norman Yoke', in his *Puritanism and revolution: studies in interpretation of the English Revolution of the seventeenth century* (London, 1958), 58–125.

93 Sabine, *Works*, 649–51.

94 Thomas, 'Another Digger broadside', 66; Sabine, *Works*, 356, 650.

95 PRO, STAC8/34/4.20; Haliwell, *Marriage of wit and wisdom*, 140–1.

96 Sabine, *Works*, 359, 282.

97 The best general account of the Leveller movement remains J. Frank, *The Levellers: a history of the writings of three seventeenth-century social democrats: John Lilburne, Richard Overton, William Walwyn* (Cambridge, Massachusetts, 1955). But see also H. N. Brailsford, *The Levellers and the English revolution* (London, 1961).

98 *A just defence of John Bastwick . . . against the calumnies of John Lilburne* (1645), 24, 29, 30, 33.

99 Brailsford, *The Levellers*, 309–10. For uses of the term 'Leveller', see for instance *The Moderate*, no. 43, 1–8 May 1649, BL, TT E.554 (15); *The Moderate*, no. 46, 22–9 May 1649, BL, TT E.556 (31); *Mercurius Militaris*, no. 3, BL, TT E.554 (13); Anon., *Sea green and blue* (1649), BL, TT, E.559 (1). One of the few attempts to conceptualise Leveller self-definitions is A. Hughes, 'Gender and politics in Leveller literature', in Amussen and Kishlansky (eds), *Political culture and cultural politics*, 162–88.   ·

100 D. M. Wolfe (ed.), *Leveller manifestos of the Puritan revolution* (New York, 1944), 223–34; 291–303, 397–410.

101 On London companies and the Levellers, see Carlin, 'Liberty and fraternities'; C. Blagden, *The Stationers' Company: a history, 1403–1959* (London, 1960), ch. 8; G. Unwin, *Industrial organisation in the sixteenth and seventeenth centuries*, (1904, repr. London, 1963), 205–8. On law reform, see S. E. Prall, *The agitation for law reform during the Puritan revolution, 1640–1660* (The Hague, 1966) and A. Cromartie 'The rule of law', in J. S. Morrill (ed.), *Revolution and restoration: England in the 1650s* (London, 1992), 55–69. On monopolies and trade, see M. James, *Social problems and policy during the Puritan Revolution: 1640–1660* (London, 1930), chs 4 and 5.

102 J. C. Davis, 'The Levellers and Christianity' in B. Manning (ed.), *Politics, religion and the English Civil War* (London, 1973), 225–50; M. Tolmie, *The triumph of the saints: the separate churches of London, 1616–1649* (Cambridge, 1977), chs 7–8.

103 Leveller organisation deserves a full study. For the moment, see N. Carlin, 'Leveller organisation in London', *HJ*, 27, 4 (1984), 955–60.

104 *The Moderate*, no. 42, April 24–May 1 1649, BL TT E.552 (20). See also *The humble petition of the inhabitants of Buckingham-shire and Hartfordshire*, May 1646, BL, TT. E.669, f.10/115.

105 J. Diethe, '*The Moderate*: politics and allegiances of a revolutionary newspaper'. *History of Political Thought*, 4, 2 (1983), 247–80; R. Howell and D. E. Brewster, 'Reconsidering the Levellers: the evidence of *The Moderate*', *P&P*, 46 (1970), 68–86.

106 Manning, *English people*, chs 9–10.

107 C. Hill, *The world turned upside down: radical ideas during the English Revolution* (London, 1972), 114.

108 J. Lilburne, *An impeachment of high treason against Oliver Cromwell* (London, 1649), BL, TT, E.568 (20); see William Haller (ed.), *Tracts on liberty in the Puritan revolution, 1638–1647*, 3 vols (New York, 1934), III, 213.

109 Woodhouse (ed.), *Puritanism and liberty*, 55–7, 61–2, 69–71. On Leveller attitudes to the franchise, see K. Thomas, 'The Levellers and the franchise' in G. E. Aylmer (ed.), *The Interregnum: the quest for settlement, 1646–1660* (London, 1972), 57–78; J. C. Davis, 'The Levellers and democracy', *P&P*, 40 (1968); C. B. Macpherson, *The political theory of possessive individualism* (London, 1962), ch. 3.

110 Wolfe, *Leveller manifestoes*, 297.

111 J. Wildman, *A call to all the souldiers of the Army by the free people of England* (London, 1647); *The Moderate*, no. 36, 13–20 March 1649, BL, TT. E.548 (2).

112 Wolfe, *Leveller manifestoes*, 206; *To the supreme authority of England, the humble petition of divers well-affected women . . . affecters and approvers of the Petition of Sep. 11th 1648*, May 5 1649, BL, TT. E.669, f.14/27; Hughes, 'Gender and politics',

174–82; I. Gentles, 'London Levellers in the English Revolution: the Chidleys and their circle', *Journal of Ecclesiastical History*, 29 (1978), 281–309.

113 Wolfe, *Leveller manifestoes*, 288; M. Goldsmith 'Levelling by sword, spade and word: radical egalitarianism in the English revolution', in C. Jones *et al.* (eds) *Politics and people in revolutionary England: essays in honour of Ivan Roots* (Oxford, 1986), 65–80.

114 *The Moderate*, no. 37, 22–7 March 1649, BL, TT E.548 (21); *The Moderate*, no. 36, March 13–20 1649, BL, TT E.548 (2); *The humble petition of divers well-affected of the county of Leicester*, 19 March 1648, BL, TT. E.669, f.14/6; *The Moderate*, no. 14, 10–17 October 1648, BL, TT E.468(2).

115 W. Haller and G. Davies (eds), *The Leveller tracts, 1647–53* (New York, 1944), 159; *The Moderate*, no. 18, 7–14 November 1648, BL, TT E.472 (4).

116 *The Moderate*, no. 24, 19–26 December 1648, BL, TT E.536(2). *The Moderate*, no. 29, 23–30 January 1649, BL, TT E.540 (20); Haller (ed.), *Tracts on liberty*, II, 303.

117 Wildman, *A call to all the souldiers of the Army*; Haller and Davies (eds), *Leveller tracts*, 159.

118 L. Clarkson, *A general charge or impeachment of high treason*, 10–14, 17–18, 27.

119 J. Habermas, *The structural transformation of the public sphere: an inquiry into a category of bourgeois society* (Eng. trans., Cambridge, 1989), 14–27, 56–67; C. Calhoun (ed.), *Habermas and the public sphere* (Cambridge, Massachusetts, 1992); S. Pincus, '"Coffee politicians does create": coffee houses and Restoration political culture', *Journal of Modern History*, 67, 4 (1995), 807–34.

120 For important recent discussions of the Restoration, see P. Seaward, *The Cavalier Parliament and the reconstruction of the old regime, 1661–1667* (Cambridge, 1989); R. Hutton, *The Restoration: a political and religious history of England and Wales, 1658–1667* (Oxford, 1985). On the local history of urban politics in later Stuart England, see especially P. D. Halliday, *Dismembering the body politic: partisan politics in England's towns, 1650–1730* (Cambridge, 1999).

121 Siebert, *Freedom of the press*, chs 11–14; J. Walker, 'The censorship of the press during the reign of Charles II', *History*, 35 (1950), 219–38.

122 J. Raine (ed.), *Depositions from the castle of York, relating to offences committed in the northern counties in the seventeenth century* (Durham, 1861), 94, 116, 86, 134–5; for the timing of food riots in Elizabethan Kent, see Clark, 'Popular protest', 377–8.

123 Harris, *London crowds*, 74–5.

124 This is a fundamental flaw in Richard Greaves' two books: *Deliver us from evil: the radical underground in Britain, 1660–1663* (Oxford, 1986); *Enemies under his feet: radicals and nonconformists in Britain, 1664–1677* (Stanford, California, 1990).

125 Derbyshire RO, Quarter Sessions Records, Q/SB2/630.

126 See for instance Kleber Monod, *Jacobitism*, ch. 8.

127 Raine (ed.), *Depositions*, 239, 268–9.

128 Harris, *London crowds*, 28–9; Pincus, '"Coffee politicians does create"'; C. J. Sommerville, *The news revolution in England: cultural dynamics of daily information* (Oxford, 1996), 75–84.

129 Knights, *Politics and opinion*; Harris, *London crowds*; Harris, *Politics under the later Stuarts*, ch. 3; T. Harris, P. Seaward and M. Goldie (eds), *The politics of religion in Restoration England* (Oxford, 1990). See also J. Miller, *Popery and politics in England, 1660–1688* (Cambridge, 1973).

130 P. McDowell, *The women of Grub Street: press, politics and gender in the London literary marketplace, 1678–1730* (Oxford, 1998); Knights, *Politics and opinion*, 156, 159, 207–10, 224, 242–50; Harris, *Politics under the later Stuarts*, 95–6; Sommerville, *News revolution*, 60–1.
131 Knights, *Politics and opinion*, 190, 223, 228, 239, 245, 262, 320–3, 349; Harris, *London crowds*, chs 6–7.
132 Knights, *Politics and opinion*, 223, 169, 149, 171; A. Bellany, '"Raylinge rymes and vaunting verse": libellous politics in early Stuart England', in K. Sharpe and P. Lake (eds), *Culture and politics in early Stuart England* (Basingstoke, 1994), 285–310.
133 L. G. Schwoerer, 'Liberty of the press and public opinion: 1660–1695', in J. R. Jones (ed.), *Liberty secured? Britain before and after 1688* (Stanford, California, 1992), 199–230; Harris, *Politics under the later Stuarts*, 186–7; P. B. J. Hyland, 'Liberty and libel: government and the press during the Succession Crisis in Britain, 1712–1716', *English Historical Review*, 101 (1986), 863–88.
134 Pincus, '"Coffee politicians does create"', 831, 807, 811, 832–3, 813–14, 815; L. E. Klein, 'Gender, conversation and the public sphere in early eighteenth-century England', in J. Still and M. Worton (eds), *Textuality and sexuality: reading theories and practices* (Manchester, 1993), 100–15.
135 Harris, *Politics under the later Stuarts*, ch. 7.
136 Griffiths, 'Secrecy and authority'; Hindle, *State and social change*, 211–12; Knights, *Politics and opinion*, 178–80.

Coda   Beyond the Public Sphere: the Politics of the Poorer Sort in Early Eighteenth-Century England

1 H. T. Dickinson, *The politics of the people in eighteenth-century Britain* (Basingstoke, 1995), 177.
2 Cressy, *Literacy*, ch.6, 176–7.
3 P. Borsay, *The English urban renaissance: culture and society in the provincial town, 1660–1770* (Oxford, 1989), esp. chs 9–11.
4 See P. Springborg (ed.), *Mary Astell: political writings* (Cambridge, 1996).
5 Knights, *Politics and opinion*, 300–1, 309, 232–4, 335–6, 343; Harris, *Politics under the later Stuarts*, 89–90, 101–2, 167–8, 181, 199–202.
6 Harris, *Politics under the later Stuarts*, 201–2; N. Rogers, 'Popular protest in early Hanoverian London', *P&P*, 79 (1978), 91–2.
7 Harris, *Politics under the later Stuarts*, 217.
8 Kleber Monod, *Jacobitism*, chs 1, 6–8; N. Rogers, *Crowds, culture and politics in Georgian Britain* (Oxford, 1998), ch. 1.
9 Rogers, *Crowds, culture and politics*, 56–7, 50–1; Thompson, *Customs in common*, ch. 2.
10 S. Hindle, 'The growth of social stability in Restoration England', *The European Legacy*, 5, 4 (2000), 572.
11 W. O. Hassall (ed.), *Wheatley records, 956–1956* Oxfordshire Rec. Soc., 37 (Banbury, 1956), 71–5.

INDEX

Printed and bound by CPI Group (UK) Ltd, Croydon, CR0 4YY